SERVANT LEADERSHIP MODELS FOR YOUR PARISH

Dan R. Ebener

Paulist Press
New York/Mahwah, NJ

Cover design by Sharyn Banks
Book design by Lynn Else

Library of Congress Cataloging-in-Publication Data

Ebener, Dan R.
    Servant leadership models for your parish / Dan R. Ebener.
        p. cm.
    Includes bibliographical references and index.
    ISBN 978-0-8091-4653-6 (alk. paper)
    1. Servant leadership—Religious aspects—Catholic Church. 2. Christian leadership—Catholic Church. 3. Pastoral theology—Catholic Church. I. Title.
    BX1913.E24 2010
    253.088′282—dc22

                                                                    2009046434

Published by Paulist Press
997 Macarthur Boulevard
Mahwah, New Jersey 07430

www.paulistpress.com

Printed and bound in the
United States of America

CONTENTS

To John Kiley (1950–2009),
Jim Weller (1952–2009), and
Jeff Cottingham (1951–1993)
for teaching me about servant leadership

FOREWORD

Servant leadership is more than a passing fad or a recent phenomenon. It offers the wisdom of the ages to a world that desperately needs new approaches to leadership. It should be (and in many cases already is) a source of great interest in the church. Already the subject of many books, articles, seminars and workshops, and even scholarly journals, servant leadership has been adopted by many businesses as their corporate leadership philosophy. It needs to be endorsed by church leaders as our corporate approach to leadership as well. For those searching for how Jesus himself would lead, servant leadership is awaiting your discovery.[1]

This book reflects on the use of servant leadership and explains how it works in a church context. It explores the practice of servant leadership by describing seven behaviors that have been found in highly successful parishes. Three are recommended as leadership practices, and four are membership behaviors in servant-oriented parishes. This book is based on two studies. First is the *parish life study*, a series of objective measures of eighty-four parishes conducted by the Diocese of Davenport, Iowa, in 2005–06. Second is a *parish case study*, a field study conducted by the author in 2006–07 in three parishes. Using rigorous methods required for his doctoral dissertation in business administration, and connecting business theories, church teaching, and scriptural references, Dan Ebener provides real-life examples of what servant leadership looks like and how it works in a parish.[2]

The two parish studies upon which this book is based originated out of diocesan planning meetings about the closing, consolidation, and clustering of parishes. Trends such as the aging of the clergy, fewer ordinations, and fewer priests lead me to believe that the restructuring of parishes will be a persistent and difficult issue for the Catholic Church (and many other Christian denominations). The dwindling number of priests available for parish ministry is "producing widespread parish structural and leadership change."[3] Shifting populations, such as the decline in the number of people in certain rural areas and the growth in suburban communities, are also driving decisions about parish locations.

The restructuring that occurs is most traumatic when it involves the closing of a parish. The closing of a parish is a heartbreaking event for a community, for a neighborhood, and for a diocese. While every bishop would rather be growing the church than closing parishes, internal and external forces are pushing diocesan leaders into making plans for parish reorganization or restructuring. These plans often include parish consolidations. For some local people, this means their churches are eventually closed as the newly merged parish deals with maintaining too many parish buildings.

Many of the issues of Catholic parish structure and staffing were the topics of discussion for a series of regional meetings across the United States and a national conference sponsored by a coalition called **Emerging Models of Pastoral Leadership**.[4] Their purpose is "to identify and promote models of pastoral leadership that nurture and sustain vibrant and empowered Catholic parish communities." Their goals include "to promote vibrant parishes and leadership; to stimulate national conversation on pastoral imagination; and to provide solid research about models of pastoral leadership."

Their report raises several critical questions facing parishes, including:

- How are we providing quality pastoral care in our parishes?
- How are we dealing with the declining numbers of priest-pastors?
- How are ordained and lay ministers collaborating in providing parish leadership?
- What is the role of the parish council in providing pastoral leadership?
- How is the next generation of leaders being developed?
- What are the most effective models for staffing clustered or mega parishes?

The studies we conducted at the Diocese of Davenport, through Dan's leadership, addressed many of these same questions. However, we looked at strategic, operational, and behavioral measures of a parish in addition to the more programmatic and structural approach taken by Emerging Models of Pastoral Leadership.

The Need for Church Leadership

Given the sharpening pace of change in the church and the world, the growing shortage of clergy, the opportunities presented by the gifts and talents of our laypeople, and the increasing demands upon those of us who are in positions of leadership in the church, we have a real challenge to develop leaders in the church. Complacency on leadership development can be a slippery slope toward mediocrity or decline in our parish life. In the worst-case scenario, it can lead to the loss of viability. If parishes are to remain viable and become vibrant, we have much to learn from the great parishes, such as the lessons in this book. As we move toward an uncertain future, our church needs to address the sorts of questions addressed in Dan's book:

- How can we lead like Jesus?
- What should Christian leadership look like in a parish?
- How can parish leaders energize the laity and enhance more active behaviors of their laypeople?
- What leadership behaviors will increase parish performance?
- How can the people in the pews step up to these challenges?

Dan Ebener likes to say that *the best test of leadership is not how many followers you lead but how many leaders you develop.* He has been practicing that philosophy for us in the Diocese of Davenport for the past twenty-three years. His belief in the power of servant leadership has driven him to initiate many leadership training projects for us. He is training clergy and lay leaders for our parishes, in many different areas of ministry. This book is the compilation of many of the lessons Dan has learned and the stories he has accumulated over his thirty-three years of ministry. I highly recommend this book to you.

+ Most Rev. Martin Amos, DD
Bishop of Davenport

PREFACE:
Who Are We?

In this book, when referring to my personal experiences, I use singular pronouns like *I*, *me*, and *my*. Otherwise, the use of first person is usually indicated by the plural words *we*, *us*, and *our*. The research project that provides the basis for this book was conducted by a cast of many people. To refer to this work under a single pronoun would seem inaccurate and selfish.

We includes colleagues such as the bishops, diocesan staff, pastors, parish staff, and many leaders of the Diocese of Davenport; students and faculty at St. Ambrose University with whom I have debated these leadership issues; and most of all, David O'Connell, my dissertation chair, who provided extraordinary support over the five-year period of research and writing for this book.

I would still be writing if it were not for the ongoing support of these people over the past five years. Because it was such a team effort, the plural words *we* and *our* are used throughout many parts of this book—especially when discussing the parish life study and the parish case study that provided the groundwork for applying my thoughts and generating ideas about church life and servant leadership.

ACKNOWLEDGMENTS

A book like this is not possible without support from many people and places. It has been a labor of love that started in 2005 as a parish life study. By 2007, the study had turned into a doctoral dissertation, and by 2010, it became this book. The text took at least six major rewrites to transform it from a dissertation into a book. Those six rewrites occurred over a three-year period of reflection, discussion, planning, and writing. Each new draft was based on new insights and feedback from family, friends, students, and colleagues, many of whom read and reread alternative versions of parts of this text. A debt of gratitude is owed to the many people who made this book possible.

As this book made its way through those six drafts, parts of it were reworked and submitted in various forms to be published in various places. A variation of chapter 3 was published in *Church* magazine, a publication of the National Pastoral Life Center. Chapters 4, 5, and 6 were published as a series of eight articles in the *Catholic Messenger*, the newspaper of the Diocese of Davenport. An earlier version of chapter 8 was written with David O'Connell for *Nonprofit Management and Leadership*.

Special thanks to Laurie Hoefling and Suzanne Wiese, for being the servant leaders of this project; to David O'Connell, for his resounding belief in the connections between faith and business; to Jude West and Bill Ditewig, for wisdom to see the book in this topic; to Barb Arland-Fye, for being the consummate team player; and to Mark Ridolfi, Chuck Quilty, Frank Agnoli, and Glenn Leach, for donating considerable editing talents.

Countless thanks to the parishes, priests, religious, deacons, lay leaders, and people of the Diocese of Davenport: to Bishop William Franklin, for inspiring this book with your question; to Bishop Martin Amos, for your encouragement and support; to Msgr. John Hyland, for showing great interest throughout the five years of this project; to

Fr. Marv Mottet, Kent Corson, Richard Deats, and Jim Wallis, for your servant mentorship; to Char Maaske, Lynnette Sowells, Marj Gonzalez, Sr. Laura Goedken, Loxi Hopkins, Nora Dvorak, Mary Frick, Rob Butterworth, David Montgomery, Mary Wieser, IlaMae Hanisch, Pat Finan, Bob McCoy, and all the staff and volunteers at the Diocese of Davenport for your ongoing participation in this project; to my fellow parishioners at Sacred Heart Cathedral and to the leaders and members of the parishes who cooperated with such enthusiasm for this project.

To my colleagues and students at St. Ambrose University for providing rigorous, challenging, and authentic dialogue about leadership, including Randy Richards, Ron Wastyn, Shelly McCallum, Monica Forret, Joe McCaffrey, Arun Pillutla, Judy Schreiber, Karl Hickerson, Megan Gisi, Bill Parsons, Rick Dienisch, Regina Stephens, John Byrne, Brenda Dubois, and many, many others; to Clyde Mayfield, John Kiley, and Todd Graff, for modeling servant leadership; to my Bridges of Faith friends, for keeping me grounded through our interfaith dialogue; to James Douglass and Don Mosley, for getting me back into books; to my walking partner Mike, for listening to me talk about this for five years; and to my racquetball buddies, for giving me an excuse to take a break once in a while.

Most of all, thanks to my wonderfully supportive and loving wife De and our two awesome boys, Josh and Zach, for always believing in me; and to the rest of my close-knit family, including my mom, dad, four brothers, five sisters, five brothers-in-law, three sisters-in-law, six nieces, sixteen nephews, three grandnieces, six grand-nephews, as well as countless cousins, uncles, aunts, and other relatives who have taught me about servant leadership.

INTRODUCTION:
Who Are the Servant Leaders?

The Practice of Our Faith

Every leadership situation offers an opportunity to put our faith into practice. This book is about the practice of **servant leadership**. When we exercise leadership, whether it is in the context of a business, a church, or any organization, we can practice our faith. The practice of our faith cannot be separated from our daily lives and work. The challenge of our faith is to incorporate it into every situation we face. It is from this perspective that we approach servant leadership, which offers daily opportunities for leaders to practice their faith.

In a church context, servant leadership often comes from that quiet person who serves in unexpected ways and from unexpected places. In this book you will read about a woman who cleans pews on Monday mornings, a man who grabs tools from his pick-up truck to fix the front door of his church, and a volunteer teacher who calls the children in her parish by name. They are servant leaders in their own right. They are leaders and members of a parish that is a servant organization, one that embraces and encourages service as critical to leadership and membership.

You will also read about people who hold positional power in the church and the ways that they practice servant leadership. This includes stories about a pastor who is willing to admit his mistakes, a pastoral associate who turns to her parishioners for consultation in decision making, and parish staff who give credit to others when the parish succeeds and take the blame when things don't work out. The leaders we interviewed for this book know the true measure of leadership is not how many followers you lead but how many leaders you develop. They develop one-on-one **relationships** with members of

1

their parish as they coach, mentor, and support the development of new leaders.

A Sociology of Religion

Dozens of books have been written about the leadership wisdom of Jesus. Students, authors, and practitioners of these texts ask the question, "How would Jesus lead?" In response to this question, this book offers these three features:

1. A solid research base for our findings
2. A behavioral approach to servant leadership
3. A focus on parish life and leadership

This book takes a sociological approach to church leadership rather than the more theological approach found elsewhere. Our intent is to focus on the *human* dynamics of a parish. Issues of ecclesiology, theology, and liturgical practices are addressed, but only as they relate to the behaviors of the leaders and the people in our congregations.

The purpose of this book is to articulate the practice of servant leadership, considered as the leadership style of Jesus, and to demonstrate how and why it works in the context of a parish. We present behavioral evidence of how *love* is expressed among the people in a church, including the parish leaders and members. This book is intended for anyone interested in church leadership, especially the interaction between leaders and the people. It is written especially for those who want to enhance the liveliness of parishes and improve leadership in the church.

Religion and Business

Sociologists suggest that the five most powerful institutions in society are the family, religion, government, education, and business.[1] I like to ask my students, "Which of these five institutions is most powerful in our society? And how has that changed over the past several hundred years?" At the time of Jesus and for many centuries afterward, family and religion were certainly the most powerful forces in society. But in the past two hundred years, perhaps since the Industrial Revolution (1760–1850), it seems clear that *business* has become the most influential institution in our society. As the strength of business has grown, the role of religion in society has weakened. In today's world, it appears that business as an institution is calling the shots and influencing many choices that used to be controlled by religion, family, government, and education. In fact, it seems that the values of religion and business are often in competition with each other.

Business values such as efficiency, productivity, and effectiveness stand in contrast to many of our religious values, including service to others. Business emphasizes the bottom line of *profitability*, whereas religion emphasizes the bottom line of *faithfulness*. As the institution of business has grown in power, and the influence of religion in society has decreased, there has been more emphasis on consumerism, materialism, and secularism.[2] Religious institutions no longer can dictate certain matters such as how many hours, and which hours, people should work, and when stores should be open, what activities are held on Sundays, and what is most important in society.

On the other hand, those of us who are dedicated to religious values and priorities do not have to shun the lessons that can be learned from business. While searching for a doctoral program several years ago, I was surprised to learn that a doctorate in business administration (DBA) was focused not on finance, economics, and accounting, but on *organizational life*, which covers how to relate to people and get things done in teams and organizations. In fact, the faculty at St. Ambrose University suggested that DBA studies are 60 percent sociology, 30 percent psychology, and 10 percent political science.

Behavioral Signs: Love in Action

At many points during this research project, we heard from priests, parish leaders, and faculty members that neither parish life nor servant leadership can be measured. Indeed, neither has been the topic of many measurable studies. Very few empirical studies focus on how to measure parish life. While many of the best-known authors on leadership have endorsed the concept of servant leadership,[3] few empirical studies have been conducted to describe, measure, or explore servant leadership.[4]

This book presents three ways to measure the life of a parish: strategic, operational, and behavioral. Our focus is on the *behavioral* signs of success, as explored in a parish case study. Although the work we do in a parish can never be fully quantified, we think it is important to identify some measures that can indicate whether we are moving in the direction we want to go.[5] The strategic and operational measures described here, including demographic and financial statistics, are based on a rigorous planning process taken by the Diocese of Davenport in 2004–06. The behavioral measures we selected for our study are based on interviews with parish leaders and a rigorous review of the literature on parish life and organizational behavior.

One could argue that the most important measures of parish life should be based on faithfulness, not effectiveness. However, if we are being faithful by genuinely living the gospel and by meeting the needs of others, we should see some visible signs that we are being effective in our efforts. One way of framing this discussion about signs of success—or measures of success—in a parish is to think of *love as the ultimate measure.* Jesus suggested that love would be the visible sign of his kingdom. As John 15:12 reminds us, our mission in this world is to "love one another as I have loved you."

In the Lord's Prayer, we pray that God's kingdom will be built "on earth as it is in heaven." When people are practicing the love that Jesus preached, we should see some tangible signs of that love, including in the life and community of our parishes. However, the visible fruits of our labor may not appear for years to come. They might be the fruits of the Holy Spirit. The final results might include personal conversions, one-on-one relationships, attitude changes, community life, team cohesion, and cultural shifts, such as a change in values, practices, or beliefs. From a sociological point of view, we should see some behavioral evidence of the kingdom of God as it is being built.

Servant Leader Behaviors

The twenty-five essays on servant leadership published in the Spears and Lawrence collection, *Focus on Leadership,*[6] provide multiple lists of **leadership traits**, behaviors, or pathways to servant leadership that incorporate many divergent ideas about its essence. These lists often identify leader traits, behaviors, or practices that may be signs of effective leadership but are not unique to servant leadership. Much of what has been written on servant leadership is based on normative advice instead of empirical study.

By providing an extensive list of real-life examples of servant leader behaviors and by sharing inspiring stories about the practice of servant leadership, we hope to clarify what servant leadership is and how it is distinct from other forms of leadership, such as charismatic, transactional, or transformational leadership. We offer relevant examples of leadership traits, behaviors, and practices that we hope will help clarify the concept of servant leadership and pave the way for more empirical explorations of servant leadership.

An Anecdote

At the time that I was beginning my research into parish life, I visited with a British church leader at an international stewardship conference in San Francisco. He was concerned about a new British law requiring churches to measure their impact on society in order to maintain their nonprofit status. He explained that they had been studying this for months and had come to the conclusion that there was no way to measure effectiveness in a parish. He said flatly that no one could measure success in a parish. I asked him to give me two minutes to explain my model of measuring parish life. I explained how behaviors are observable, measurable, and therefore changeable. After my two minutes, he paused and responded, "You nailed it!" He simply had not considered a *behavioral* approach to measuring effectiveness.

The parish life study presented in this book includes a variety of measures that are indicative of success. However, we focus on the behaviors that are associated with high performance in a parish. Our study shows that while financial and demographic numbers were used to help locate the **high-performing parishes**,[7] it was the behaviors that we explored in their community life that explained how they reached that level of success. Those behaviors included leaders as well as the people in the pews, and they were examined from the dual context of the religious teachings of Jesus and the social psychology of leadership theory.

Leadership Theory

Leadership has been studied for thousands of years. The very best leadership philosophies can be traced back many centuries to religious leaders like Lao Tsu, Confucius, Moses, and Jesus.[8] After the Industrial Revolution, leadership studies became more formalized. However, the early focus was on *positional leadership*, and leaders were considered the "person in charge" or the "man at the top."[9] When a positional leader uses positional power for his or her own personal honor and glory, instead of the service of the group, I call this *pedestal leadership*. In this case, the position becomes a pedestal for the leader to sit and treat others as if they are royal subjects. Much attention has been paid to the personal traits of those who held positional power and led political and military campaigns.[10] Business leaders were assumed to be people hired into management positions, just as for centuries, leaders were assumed to be people who were born into positions of wealth or royalty.

That idea is now being challenged by many.[11] The focus of leadership studies is shifting. Today, the study of business leadership has moved to an *organizational* context. The assumption that leadership is positional is giving way to new thinking that leadership can emerge from anyone and anywhere in an organization. Interestingly, this new way of thinking about leadership is consistent with the way that Robert K. Greenleaf describes servant leadership as servants becoming leaders and vice versa.[12]

Thinking outside the positional leadership paradigm helped Greenleaf frame his new philosophy about servant leadership, an idea that sounded new in 1970 when he coined the term. However, servant leadership was not really a new idea as much as a new way of thinking about a very old idea.

Organizational Citizenship Behaviors

This book focuses on measurable behaviors of servant leadership and organizational citizenship. Once we decided upon servant leadership as the behavioral model for parish leaders, our next question was what model we should explore among the members in a parish. If leaders are acting with servant leader behaviors, what kind of behaviors would we see within the community of the parish? Our answer came in the form of *organizational citizenship behaviors* (OCBs).

Extensive research shows that organizational performance is enhanced when the workers or members of an organization demonstrate high levels of organizational citizenship behaviors.[13] Research shows that OCBs enhance team spirit, group cohesiveness, organizational commitment, worker productivity, managerial efficiency, and the ability to recruit and retain the best people to a team or organization.[14] These are behaviors that occur when members go above and beyond expectations to serve others and their organizations. They include such things as helping, initiating, cheerleading, housekeeping, participating, and self-developing. The research shows that leadership can make a difference in increasing OCBs.[15] The research also shows that supportive leader behaviors are particularly useful in increasing OCBs.[16] One of the fundamental beliefs of our parish case study is that servant leadership fits the definition of supportive leader behavior and therefore enhances organizational citizenship. Together, all of this enhances organizational performance.

The Emergence of Servant Leadership

Chances are that if you are reading this, you may have some positional authority in the church. While it may sound at odds with our belief that servant leadership can emerge from anywhere, we do believe that servant leadership can be practiced by those with positional power in the church. In fact, servant leadership that flows out of positions of authority in the church surprises, excites, and inspires church members. It empowers them to lead projects and take the initiative instead of waiting for the pastoral leader to tell them what to do. They feel a sense of ownership of the church instead of seeing their church experience as another business transaction. They serve the church and each other because they see their leaders modeling service themselves. The church becomes a family, a community, or a team that serves as Jesus intended (Mark 9:33–35).[17]

This book is intended for church leaders such as bishops and pastors, deacons and lay volunteers, pastoral associates and parish staff, diocesan directors and committee chairpersons. If you are reading this while holding positional power in the church, we ask these reflective questions:

- To what extent do you rely on positional power in getting things done?
- Is it in your nature to dictate rather than to consult and involve others?
- Do you persuade others to follow your lead or do you coerce them?
- Are you motivated by a desire to serve God and others or do you find yourself wanting to control things?
- Do people follow you with enthusiasm for ministry or does it feel like you are dragging them along?

It *is* possible to create a servant organization in which the members act willingly, give lovingly, and serve unselfishly to create a high-performing parish, a community of people serving God and each other. Unfortunately, many church leaders have yet to discover the leadership style that Jesus offered. Some are still *ruling* their parishes rather than leading them. Servant leaders realize that they can *lead* without ruling. The coercive power of dictatorial leadership stands in contrast to the persuasive power of Jesus, who is convincing when he simply tells his disciples, "Follow me" (Matt 4:18–22).

Servant leaders can be bishops and pastors, religious education coordinators and deacons, committee members and pastoral associates, parish secretaries and liturgists, parish council presidents and bookkeepers, ushers and altar servers. As stated previously, servant leadership can emerge from the top, the middle, or the bottom of an organization. It begins, as Robert Greenleaf advises, "with a natural feeling that one wants to serve, to serve *first*."[18]

Teachings of Jesus

Our servant leadership model is consistent with church teachings about parish life and with the message and example of Jesus. We draw heavily from the stories from the ninth and tenth chapters of Mark's Gospel, where Jesus stated, "Whoever wants to be first must be last of all and servant of all" (Mark 9:35). We also draw from his teachings about discipleship, particularly from the Great Commandment to love God and neighbor (Matt 22:36–40) and the Great Commission to make disciples of all nations (Matt 28:16–20). This theme continues in the writings of St. Paul when he implores the early church that love of neighbor is the fulfillment of the law (Rom 13:8–10).

Love of neighbor was not just a teaching of the early church. It was a practice. Records show that the early Christian believers practiced what they preached. The Acts of the Apostles describe a Christian community that acted with love for one another, that shared with one another, and that served those in need beyond the Christian community. Tertullian recorded that the very early Christian believers were known for their expressions of love.[19] Based on these Christian teachings and traditions, we find *integrity* between what was practiced and what was preached.

How and Why
Servant Leadership Works

This book addresses *how* and *why* servant leadership works in the context of parish life. We look at what servant leaders do, what servant leadership looks like, what results it drives, and how and why it works particularly well in a parish. The servant parish model proposed here is based on firsthand research conducted in three high-performing parishes. It is also supported by secondary research into organizational life as conducted by others.

The case study approach that we used as part of our research project was conducive to obtaining qualitative evidence answering questions of *how* and *why* something works. However, a limitation to case research is that is does not provide quantitative proof to your results. Actually, the purpose of our case research on parish behaviors was not to *prove* a theory, but to *create* one. As a result, we have discovered empirical evidence that (1) demonstrates that servant leadership works in high-performing parishes, and (2) explains how and why servant leadership works. The beauty of case research is that it describes and explains a theory *and* demonstrates how it might work. What you will find in this book is empirical evidence that describes how and explains why servant leadership works.

1

SERVANT LEADERSHIP:
Leading Like Jesus

The leadership style modeled by Jesus is often referred to as "servant leadership." The term **servant leadership** was coined by Robert K. Greenleaf in 1970.[1] Servant leadership is now embraced by many authors, theorists, and practitioners of leadership and adopted by hundreds of corporations as their official leadership philosophy.[2] As the concept becomes more popular, it has become important to clarify what exactly servant leadership is and how it is different from other approaches to leadership.

Greenleaf and Servant Leadership

In his original essay on servant leadership, Greenleaf suggests that a leader should first act as a servant, who "by acting with integrity and spirit, builds trust and lifts people and helps them grow"[3] and second as a leader "who is trusted and who shapes others' destinies by going out ahead to show the way."[4] Greenleaf stated that the best test of servant leadership is to ask, "Do those being served grow as persons? Do they, while being served, become healthier, wiser, freer, more autonomous, more likely themselves to become servants?"[5] For example, to assess one's communication skills, the servant leader should ask, "Am I really listening?"[6]

Servant leadership is an approach that centers on the needs and interests of other people. The servant leader serves the followers instead of the other way around. Servant leaders transcend their own personal needs and interests and serve others by helping them grow professionally and personally. Greenleaf suggested that a servant leader begins by acting with integrity, creating trusting relationships, and helping others to learn, grow, and develop into leaders themselves.[7] When leaders are truly committed to the development of their followers, they allow the freedom to experiment, to take risks, and even to make mistakes without the fear of punishment.

Servant leadership has been described as the way to "**lead like Jesus**."[8] In studying the leadership style of Jesus, scholars and theologians have examined the human interaction among Jesus, his disciples, and others in the gospel stories. The focus of this book is on the servant nature of Jesus as a leader and how he can be a model for leadership in the church and in society.

When Jesus lived in Palestine, his leadership approach would have been quite a contrast to the command-and-control methods of the Roman Empire. His style would also stand in sharp contrast to the leadership that is being practiced in most places today. Like many of the ways of Jesus, servant leadership is countercultural. Like Jesus, servant leaders do not strive for personal honor or glory. Like Jesus, servant leaders place themselves humbly at the service of other people. Like Jesus, servant leaders place themselves at the service of a mission or a cause that is greater than themselves.

Leadership Defined

The lexicon of leadership includes many definitions. Among them, the most common elements include a leader, a group of followers, an influence process, and the attainment of a common vision or goal.[9] **Leadership** is defined here as an influence process through which a leader inspires or motivates followers toward a common goal or a shared vision (see Figure 1). The leader creates a sense of shared vision about the future, articulates that shared vision, inspires commitment to that vision, and provides support and encouragement to the group in pursuit of that vision.

If leadership is influencing people toward a common goal, then servant leadership involves putting that common goal ahead of one's own personal goals and ambitions. The servant leader pursues common goals that are of mutual benefit to everyone in the group or organization. That means putting the needs, interests, and benefits of others ahead of your own and directing your ambition toward the mission of the team or organization. The servant leader is a serving

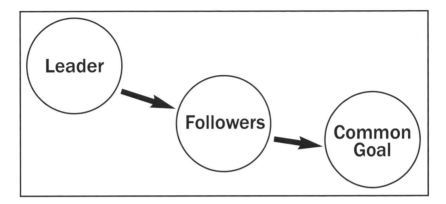

Figure 1. Definition of Leadership

leader, not a *self*-serving leader. Servant leadership is about influencing people toward common goals that benefit the collective interests of the group, the organization, or the community.

In the story by Hermann Hesse, *Journey to the East*, leadership emerges from the servant Leo.[10] He is the quiet man in the background of the story. As the servant of the group, everyone comes to depend upon him. When he is present, the group functions well together. He provides a sense of purpose and direction to others. When he is absent, everything falls apart. The group gets lost. He is recognized first as their *servant* and only later as their *leader*. Robert Greenleaf was inspired by the story of Leo to develop the idea of servant leadership and to illustrate these principles of leadership:

- Leadership can emerge from any place in any organization.
- The best leaders are servants first, then emerge as leaders.
- Most team members know intuitively who the real leaders are.

Leadership: Power and Service

Leadership and Power

If *leadership* is defined as the process of influencing a group of followers in the direction of a common goal, then how does servant leadership fit into that definition? As Greenleaf points out, the influence process involves **power**, whether that power is positional or personal.[11] Power is to the science of leadership what energy is to the science of physics. It makes things happen. *Power* is defined here simply as the ability to act. The power of the leader, as shared or combined with the power of others in the group, enables the group to reach its common goal. The source of power can be the legitimate authority that comes with a position of power. Authority is power that can be used to gain compliance. Power can also emerge from other personal, social, and spiritual sources.

Leaders with **referent power** are those to whom people naturally refer when leadership is needed.[12] Referent leaders do not rely on the authority that comes with a position of leadership. Instead, their power emerges out of a voluntary relationship between leader and follower. People look to referent leaders because of something innately appealing or inspiring about this leader. They sense that the referent leader has wisdom, expertise, or personal traits that draw others to them. The qualities of referent leaders inspire people to seek them out when leadership is needed.

Power has a mystical quality. When it is used to advance the capacity of others, it multiplies. Power is not limited to a *zero-sum game*.[13] In fact, many human sources of power are unlimited. Power can multiply through the process of **empowerment**.[14] Sharing power enhances the willingness, the ability, the skills, and the resources of the followers to get the job done, thus increasing **effectiveness** of those who are being led. This in turn increases the effectiveness of the leader and of the organization. By sharing power with others throughout the organization, the leader can maximize the efforts of people at all levels, such as targeting those who are closest to the day-to-day action, where the ability to make quick decisions can make a huge difference. This means that the front-row members of the organization, whether they are the salespeople in a store, the faculty in a school, the nurses in a hospital, or the ushers at the front door of a parish—all of whom may be far away from the centralized powers-that-be in the organizational flow chart—are enabled to make certain decisions without checking all the way up the chain of command. As James Kouzes and Barry Posner point out, empowerment develops in others "the **competence** and confidence to act and to excel."[15]

Leadership and Service

Like all forms of leadership, servant leadership involves power, but it is also about *service*. In this context, service means caring for the needs and interests of others and for the organization. Scripture suggests that Christians are servants who put the needs of others ahead of their own (Phil 2:3–4). A good and faithful servant in the time of Jesus would be a person who finds joy and delight in the success of the people he or she serves.[16] Servants would devote their entire lives being responsive to the needs of others.

Like power, service has a mystical quality. It can be used to advance the capacity of others. Like power, service is not limited to a zero-sum game. Service multiplies when those who are being served are inspired to serve others. Service enhances the willingness, the ability, and the skills of the followers to get the job done, thus increasing the effectiveness of both the leader and those who are led. When the leaders serve the people in an organization, the people reciprocate by serving others, by serving the organization, and by serving the community. As Greenleaf points out, one of the outcomes of servant leadership is that the followers are "more likely themselves to become servants."[17]

Like power, service grows in the face of yet even more service. In fact, power and service can propel each other in a servant-led organization. Servant leadership requires both power and service. Power is implied in the two arrows in our graphic definition of leadership (Figure 1). The first arrow focuses on the leader's *relationship* with the people. It signifies the power to influence people in some way. That might be facilitation, persuasion, inspiration, or other non-coercive forms of influence. Leadership does not include **coercion** because that involves forcing people, not leading them.[18] The second arrow focuses on the *task* of the group. It signifies the power of the vision, which means the direction that the group is taking. A shared sense of vision has the power to inspire people.

For servant leaders, the first arrow indicates that the leader places the needs and interests of the *followers* ahead of his or her own. The second arrow indicates that the servant leader places the needs and interests of the *organization* ahead of his or her own.

Two Dimensions of Leadership: Task and Relationship

Many leadership theories deal with the intersection of the two dimensions, task and relationship.[19] These are two principal elements of leadership.[20] Initially, leadership studies conceived of leadership as measured along a one-dimensional line between task and relationship.[21] (See Figure 2.) The weakness of this approach is that it implies that progress on the task takes away from progress on the relationship, and vice versa. This means that as the leader becomes more task oriented, the relationship automatically suffers. And as the leader becomes more relationship oriented, the task does not get done. Of course, this does not make sense.

Figure 2. Task and Relationship as One-Dimensional Model

Later studies suggested a two-dimensional model.[22] (See Figure 3.) In this model, the leader is able to do both: work on the task and the relationship. Leaders build trust, increase commitment, and develop a sense of cohesion among the relationships of the group and also get the job done. Task and relationship work enhance each other. The leader is able to increase the quantity of task completion by improving the quality of relationships—and vice versa.

Generally speaking, success in building relationships enhances the ability to get the job done. Similarly, success in getting the job done builds stronger relationships. A job well done increases the sense of trust, commitment, and camaraderie in the group, which is called **social capital**.[23] The social capital that is developed through strong relationships enhances the ability of the group to get the next job done, and the momentum gained by finishing one job in turn enhances relationships further.

In the two-dimensional model of leadership, the leader's behavior on the task is measured in terms of assertiveness versus passivity.[24] Movement up and down the vertical axis of Figure 3 is measured by

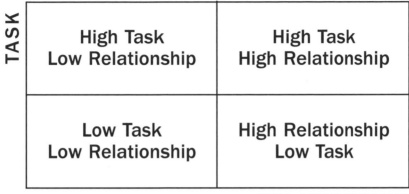

Figure 3. Task and Relationship as Two-Dimensional Model

how assertive versus how passive the leader is about the task.[25] The leader's behavior on the relationship is measured in terms of warmth versus hostility.[26] Movement to the left and right along the horizontal axis is measured by the leader's treatment of others. The suggestion here is that leaders can be assertive about the task (vertical movement) and yet warm in their relationship with others (horizontal movement).[27] To explain this, we need a two-dimensional model of leadership to demonstrate that the leader can focus on both the task and the relationship.

The servant leader works to become more cooperative on the relationship and more assertive on the task. The servant leader is cooperative about the interests of others and assertive about his or her own interests. However, it is difficult to be cooperative about the interests of others unless the others are assertive enough to inform you of their interests. In the same way, it is difficult for others to cooperate on your interests unless you are assertive enough to inform them of your interests. Otherwise, you take away the opportunity for the other person to be cooperative about your interests or to find collaborative opportunities around shared interests.

The difference between aggressiveness and assertiveness becomes an important issue here. Generally speaking, *aggressiveness* is competitive behavior that hurts the relationship, while *assertiveness* is collaborative behavior that enhances the relationship. As we become more dedicated to common interests and more concerned about the task, we will be more successful as we become more assertive, not aggressive, because aggressiveness jeopardizes the relationship.

Our Model of Servant Leadership

Power and Service

Like other leadership theories, servant leadership is a two-dimensional concept. It cannot be fully understood with traditional linear thinking. The leader is servant and the servant is leader. The servant leader is not a part-time servant and a part-time leader. We are not saying that the leader balances the occasional power of leadership with the occasional service of leadership. Both elements must be present for servant leadership to be in action. It is an *integration* of the two concepts, even though the two concepts seem to be opposites.

Power and service are the two elements held in the balance of servant leadership. They enhance each other. That is a paradox of servant leadership. It is a paradox that pushes us beyond the insufficiencies of linear thinking. The opposing viewpoints of the paradox are reconciled only by creating a sense of wholeness out of the apparent opposites.

Servant leadership is not about balancing the use of power and the use of service. It is not about serving lunch at a soup kitchen, or volunteering for Habitat for Humanity, and then going back to a command-and-control style of leadership. It is about *enhancing both service and power in a new relationship.*

As we serve others, we inspire, encourage, and allow for even more service among the followers. As we lead others, we inspire, encourage, and allow for even more leadership among the followers. The servant leader is not just someone who does the occasional service project. The servant leader is someone who *is* a servant and who *is* a leader. This is not about balancing your time between two opposing realities. It is about giving both realities a new meaning by integrating them into a new leadership reality.

In Figure 4, we see how the two-dimensional model we are proposing for servant leadership involves the intersection of power and service. The leader's behavior on the vertical axis is measured by lev-

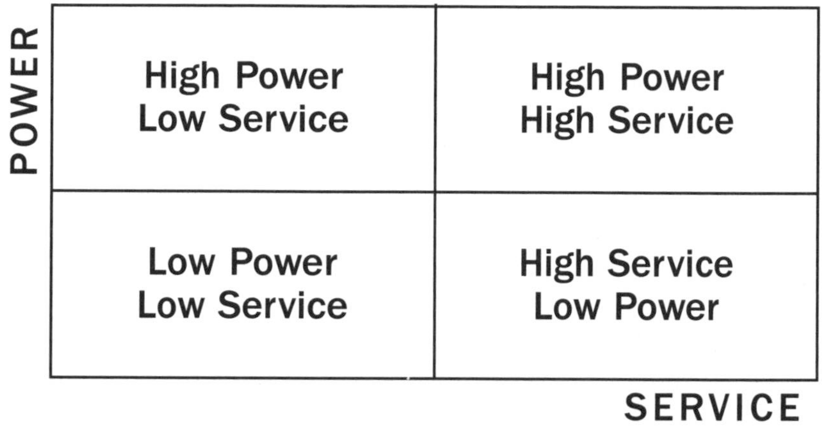
POWER
High Power
Low Service
High Power
High Service
Low Power
Low Service
High Service
Low Power
SERVICE

Figure 4. Power and Service

els of power and indicates whether the leader is active or passive in the use of power. Movement up and down the vertical axis of Figure 4 is measured by how weak or how powerful the leader is. The capable and powerful leader is contrasted with the weak and anemic leader.

On the horizontal axis, the leader's behavior is measured by levels of service and indicates whether the leader is oriented toward self or others. Movement to the left and right along the horizontal axis of Figure 4 is measured by how self-centered or service-oriented the leader is. The narcissistic and self-serving leader is contrasted with the caring and unselfish leader.

Servant leaders move to the upper right-hand corner of Figure 4 by integrating service and power. The servant leader is a servant with power. The servant leader is powerful and unselfish. The servant leader uses power and service for the sake of the team or organization. This contradicts two common notions about leadership in our culture: (1) that a person who serves others is not powerful and (2) that the person who uses power is self-serving. The servant leader model is counterintuitive because it defies the common sense of a culture that values either self-serving individualism or selfless collectivism without understanding the concept of servant-oriented power or embracing the concept of powerful service for the common good.

Power enhances service. Service enhances power. Service enhances the power of the servant leader and the members of the team or organization. Service can remove obstacles to group goals, provide resources to those in need, build capacity in people to act, and free them from their fears and weaknesses. Power enhances the amount of service that the servant leaders and members can perform. Service inspires people to act in powerful ways. The servant who cannot exercise the power of leadership is not yet a servant leader. Neither is the leader who does not practice service to others and the organization. The person who has power but does not serve the interests of others is more of a *ruler* than a *leader*. On the other hand, the person who serves without power is one who has no ability to change things or to influence people. The leader who tries to do everything and cannot delegate to others presents another case of service without power. The servant leader uses power and service in a way that integrates and expands the two into one reality.

Our model of servant leadership occurs along the intersection of service and power. To be fully understood and practiced, we need to understand this juxtaposition: The servant leader *develops power in the organization through service* and *develops service in the organization through power*.

Jesus as Servant Leader

In his role as leader of the apostles, Jesus acted in a similar capacity as Leo in *Journey to the East*. He was the servant leader who emerged out of ordinary circumstances. He was not born into positional power (at least not in this world). He was born in a stable. He was not a governor, a ruler, or a statesman. He was an itinerant preacher. He never wrote a book, although others remembered what he said and wrote his Gospels. He did not teach in a formal classroom but gave sermons on a mount and a plain. The leadership of Jesus emerged not out of earthly positional power but out of his character, his behaviors, his message, his sacrifice, and his treatment of others (Mark 1:22).

Like the leadership of Jesus, servant leadership can emerge from anywhere in any position in any organization. It is through the character, strength, and integrity of the person that servant leadership is formed. In the Gospels, we have many examples of servant leadership emerging from unexpected places. Mary and Martha, Peter and Paul, James and John. Each of them presents compelling stories and examples of servant leadership. They did not hold formal positions of power (at least not as we understand the current church hierarchy), yet they exercised leadership.

Servant leadership is a paradoxical concept that fits the teachings and example of Jesus. The integration of service and power into a model of leadership is typical of the paradox found in the gospel. Jesus taught in parables that were rich with the wisdom of paradox. His parables suggest that we should expect the unexpected. *He came to serve, not to be served.* He came to die so others might live. Jesus lived a paradoxical life, dying on a cross so others could gain eternal salvation. His example then leads his disciples now to pick up their own crosses and follow him by serving others.

Like Jesus, servant leaders serve their followers instead of the other way around. Instead of focusing on their own personal needs and interests, servant leaders are tuned into the needs and interests of both their followers *and* their organizations. They are willing to enter into the chaos of another person. Servant leaders guide the organization without dominating things and facilitate the growth of members of the organization without controlling them.[28]

Servant Leadership versus Pedestal Leadership

A Roman view of leadership, as experienced during the time of Jesus, was characterized by leaders who used positional power to command, control, dominate, and dictate; the followers responded with submission, passivity, compliance, and obedience, whether they wanted to follow or not. The political and religious leaders of that time approached power as hierarchical, as something that is formalized into the position of the leader who stands on a pedestal. Because **pedestal leadership** was the familiar model of leadership, the disciples expected the same style of leadership from Jesus (Mark 10:35–45).

The servant leader exercises power in a different way. The servant leader builds capacity in the team or organization by *sharing* power. The motivation for servant leadership is not the accumulation of power. Rather, it is the direction of power for the success of the group. The servant leader is not just a person who *does* service. The servant leader *is* a servant motivated out of a natural desire to serve.

Servant leadership can certainly be practiced by those who have **positional power** in the church or elsewhere. Leaders with positional power do not have to lead like Roman rulers (Figure 5). Leaders who are placed into a position to dictate can resist the temptation to be dictatorial. Just as important, they can resist the temptation to adopt a nature to dictate. Used constructively, positional power can enhance the service of the leader and the group.

In the ninth and tenth chapters of Mark's Gospel, some of the apostles are arguing about who is the greatest among them. Jesus responds by redefining what it means to be great. He suggests that the greatest is the one who serves. As Martin Luther King Jr. paraphrases Jesus, "Anyone can be great because anyone can serve."[29]

In Mark 10:35–45, when James and John ask Jesus if they can sit on his left and his right when he comes in glory, they conjure up images of Jesus on a throne. A few verses later, Jesus turns that notion around altogether, telling his disciples, "But it is not so among you; but whoever wishes to become great among you must be your servant. For the Son of Man came not to be served but to serve, and to give his life a ransom for many" (Mark 10:43, 45).

The Pedestal Leader	The Servant Leader
Commands others	Delegates responsibility to others
Controls others	Supports initiative by others
Makes solo decisions	Involves others in decisions
Relies on positional power	Emerges from anywhere
Uses power for personal interests	Accesses power for the team
Seeks personal glory and status	Gives glory to God and credit to others

Figure 5. The Servant Leader versus the Pedestal Leader

Some of the most powerful words of Jesus are recorded in this story from Mark when he describes the Roman style of leadership as "lord[ing] it over them" (Mark 10:42) and then says these four key words: "Not so among you" (Mark 10:43). This is a clear presentation of the contrast between these two models of leadership. Jesus is saying that Roman lording is the old way of thinking about leadership. He is presenting a new style of leadership. He is very clear about the fact that he does not want his followers to lead like Romans or like the Pharisees.

Throughout the Gospels, Jesus challenges his disciples to consider a new way of thinking. In the tenth chapter of Mark, Jesus creates a whole new paradigm of leadership, one that is based on service. Today's disciples still need to come to full terms with this. When it comes to leadership style, the choice is: *Do we lead like Romans? Do we lead like the Pharisees? Or do we lead like Jesus?*

Virtues, Values, and Traits

Leaders and followers should practice virtues and act on shared values. Practicing virtuous behavior—which means acting with wisdom, courage, justice, humility, and other virtues—builds *character* in leaders and followers. Practicing values—such as the **core values** and beliefs of the organization—builds *community* in the organization. We are not born with character. Rather, it takes an entire life to build character. Character is based on the integrity of the leader as a human being, whereas reputation is based on what other people think.[30] Building character is an inward journey that requires virtuous living, personal training, and self-discipline.

For many of us, leadership begins with faith: faith in God, faith in ourselves, faith in each other. Placing our faith in God is the starting point for being faithful as a leader. Having faith in God enhances our ability to have faith in ourselves and each other. When we have faith in ourselves, we call that **confidence**, an essential trait for leadership.[31] When we have faith in each other, we call that **trust**, a factor that is critical for the success of any team, office, or organization.[32] When we have faith in an organization, we call that *loyalty* or *commitment*.

We build trust by acting in a trustworthy fashion.[33] Simply put, people feel they can trust us when we act in a *trustworthy* manner. We become trustworthy when we act with **integrity**, which is the *integration* of our values and our behaviors. Integrity is practicing what we preach, walking the walk *and* the talk, following through on our promises. When we act on our beliefs, when we integrate what we say and what we do, we build integrity. This gives us believability, or **credibility**. The extensive research of Kouzes and Posner has concluded that acting with integrity is the most critical trait for effective leadership.[34]

Over the past one hundred years, two of the most effective ways to study leadership have involved studying traits and behaviors.[35] Traits describe the character, personality, or qualities of a leader, whereas behaviors describe the practices, actions, or performance of a leader. Another way to explain the distinction is that traits describe "how to be a leader,"[36] whereas behaviors describe "what leaders do."[37] The following list includes fifteen servant leader traits for leaders who practice virtues and live out their values in ways that are congruent with their beliefs. Because leadership traits and behaviors are often associated with each other, my suggested list of leadership traits includes a brief identification of a leadership behavior associated with each leadership trait. The list is organized into three categories, based on the three theological virtues articulated by St. Paul: faith, hope, and love.

Faith

The traits associated with faith come from the work of the Holy Spirit in our lives. Faithful servant leaders are

Reverent: Believing in God
Confident: Believing in yourself
Trustworthy: Acting in honest ways so others can believe in you
Humble: Acting in unselfish ways to show that you believe in others
Open-minded: Showing that you believe in new possibilities

Hope

This is not the same as *optimism*. Optimism is based on the evidence. Hope is based on imagination. The hopeful person struggles against the evidence to inspire change and create a better tomorrow, while the optimistic person looks at the evidence and determines whether tomorrow will be better. Hopeful servant leaders are

Passionate: Totally committed to the mission and values
Visionary: Looking at the future implications of today's issues
Creative: Thinking outside the box
Enthusiastic: Bringing energy to the whole team
Persistent: Being dedicated to the long haul

Love

The love that is described here is based on the Greek word *agape*, which is the unconditional love that Jesus preached in the Sermon on the Mount. Loving servant leaders are

Thoughtful: Paying attention to the needs of others
Helpful: Providing resources and support to others
Collaborative: Working hand in hand with others
Forgiving: Letting go of the mistakes of others
Patient: Taking the time to support the growth of others

Comparing Leadership Theories

Servant Leadership

The research shows that the practice of servant leadership has been associated with greater performance in the workforce and higher commitment among workers for their organizations.[38] Those led by servant leaders are more likely to respond in kind by serving others.[39] The research shows that servant leaders empower others to reach consensus decisions, create a sense of community, are sensitive to the needs of employees, and help others to reach their full potential.[40]

Unfortunately, servant leadership is sometimes viewed as overly simplistic, too soft, and limited in scope.[41] Servant leadership is *not* simple. It deals with complex human interaction. Servant leadership is *not* soft. It is much tougher to practice than command-and-control ruling. Servant leadership does *not* relinquish the leadership role. It enhances it through service to others.

As leadership theories go, servant leadership is relatively new. However, the philosophy and the practice of servant leadership have been around for thousands of years, especially in religious life and teachings. Servant leadership is perhaps best described as a *style* or an *approach* to leadership, although it is emerging as a leadership *theory*. Its focus is not entirely the same as other leadership theories, so it is difficult to compare and contrast.

Much of what has been written about servant leadership is normative advice instead of empirical findings. **Normative advice** is what we claim to be true, while **empirical findings** are what we demonstrate to be true. Much more research has been conducted on transformational leadership, another relatively new concept, yet one that seems to resonate with servant leadership.[42]

Servant leader behaviors identified in other studies include:

- Showing concern for the interests of others
- Encouraging others in their career goals
- Delegating important work responsibilities
- Emphasizing the importance of giving back to the community[43]

Transformational Leadership

James MacGregor Burns and Bernard Bass make an important distinction between **transformational** and **transactional leadership**.[44] *Transformational* leaders transform people and organizations by focusing on organizational change and a shared vision of the future. Transformational leaders want their followers to fulfill their potential. They listen and respond to people's needs. They stimulate and challenge followers to reach a higher level of motivation. They inspire others to achieve extraordinary outcomes. In the process, they transform followers into leaders by developing their own leadership capacities. The confidence of the followers increases and their concerns shift toward personal growth and achievement.

The four principles of transformational leadership, according to Bernard Bass,[45] are

1. *Idealized influence* (or *charisma*), through which followers identify with the leader and choose to follow her or him
2. *Inspirational motivation*, through which the leader creates a sense of shared vision among members of the organization
3. *Intellectual stimulation*, through which the leader encourages creativity among the followers to seek new ways to solve problems
4. *Individualized consideration*, through which the leader enhances the growth and development of each follower through individual attention

Both transformational leadership and transactional leadership deal with both task and relationship. Leaders build a relationship to motivate their followers to get the task done. Generally speaking, transactional leaders motivate their followers through a system of rewards and punishments, while transformational leaders inspire followers through appeal to a mission, vision, and core values of the organization. Inspiration is a more intrinsic form of motivation. Inspiration comes from *within the spirit*.

All leaders are trying to move their followers in the direction of a vision or common goal. The difference is that transformational leaders focus more on identifying, articulating, and explaining the vision, while transactional leaders focus more on implementing that vision. The successful transformational leaders create a *shared vision* of the future by involving people in a process of visioning or strategic planning that creates a sense of ownership in the vision.

Transactional Leadership

Research has clarified the distinction between day-to-day managerial issues, which are associated with transactional leadership, and the more strategic issues that demand the attention of the transformational leader. Managers, or *managerial leaders* as some would call them, are those who value stability, maintain order, and take control, while transformational leaders value creativity, take risks, and inspire people toward a vision.[46] Another way to view the distinction is that managers tend to focus on what is *urgent*, but not necessarily *important*, while leaders focus on what is important, but not necessarily urgent. *Effective leaders are the ones who create a sense of urgency about what is important.*

Transactional leadership focuses more on the day-to-day transactions between leader and follower, particularly the system of rewards and consequences needed to motivate others toward the common goal. Transactional leaders are more involved in the continuous operations based on the vision. Some suggest that transactional leadership can be viewed as *management* and transformational leadership as *leadership*.[47] (See Figure 6.) John Kotter enters the conversation about management and leadership by emphasizing (1) that successful organizations have a good mix of leaders and managers, and (2) that most organizations are "over-managed and under-led."[48]

The skills of transformational and transactional leadership offer opportunities to servant leaders in a parish. The church needs parishes that have proficiencies in both leadership and management. Charismatic leadership, on the other hand, is a mixed blessing.

Leadership and Management	
LEADERSHIP	MANAGEMENT
Transforming	Reforming
Visioning	Implementing
Inspiring	Motivating
Strategic planning	Operational planning
Initiating new projects	Operating current projects

Figure 6. Leadership and Management

Charismatic Leadership

The Greek word "charisma" means a special gift from God.[49] Charisma is described as the attraction between a leader and follower, and sometimes it rises to the level of a rare quality that attracts many followers to a certain leader.[50] Viewed this way, *all* leaders need to have at least a bit of charisma or they would have no followers at all. Those with lots of charisma are commonly referred to as **charismatic leaders**. Sociologists teach us that charismatic leaders often appear during a crisis.[51] They are able to articulate a solution to the crisis, one that resonates with the will of the people.

Charismatic effects on others can be spell binding. Followers are stirred to strongly identify with the leader, first with the message and later with the *persona* of the leader. Those who are recognized as charismatic leaders are gifted with extraordinary communication skills. At some point, the message and the leader become indistinguishable. That is a problem.

Charismatic leaders can be very charming. They charm people with their prolific communication skills. They draw followers by articulating a compelling vision of the future, often a solution to a crisis. They make a powerful presentation of themselves and their vision, creating a strong sense of loyalty among their followers. The problem occurs when people develop such a strong dependence upon their charismatic leader that the relationship becomes an unhealthy one.

All leaders begin with some charisma that draws followers to them. It can be very flattering to experience that reaction in people. If numbers of followers are considered a sign of a success, then when large numbers of people are attracted to a charismatic leader, it seems to be a sign of a successful leader. Unless that leader maintains some sense of humility about that success, charismatic leaders can become narcissistic.[52] When many people identify totally with the leader and believe that the leader can do no wrong, charismatic leadership has reached a danger point.

When the people identify personally with the leader, the *persona* of the leader becomes the focal point of the influence process. The followers become loyal, obedient, and compliant, sometimes to the point of blind obedience. Generally speaking, the charismatic leader is not interested in developing the skills, abilities, or leadership capacity of his or her followers. This is contrary to transformational leaders, who transform their followers into leaders. The followers of the charismatic leader tend to become so closely identified with the leader and committed to his or her success that it becomes hard to determine whether people are working toward the achievement of a common vision or for the glorification of the leader.

Once charismatic leadership has reached that point, then the leader has gained power and control *over* the followers instead of power *with* them. Instead of distributing power, as a servant leader does, charismatic leaders tend to consolidate power. This can look more like ruling than leading. It takes the focus off the attainment of shared goals and places the focus on the glorification of the leader. It reduces the follower into a permanent state of following, discouraging true initiative and denying voluntary participation.

Not all charismatic leaders become narcissistic and claim all the honor and glory that comes with success. Mohandas Gandhi, Martin Luther King Jr., John F. Kennedy, Robert F. Kennedy, and Pope John Paul II are identified as charismatic leaders who worked toward the common good of society.[53] However, the charismatic leader must be continually conscious of the effects that he or she is having on his or her followers. Charismatic leaders tend to bask in the glow of fame and fortune when instead they need to examine their conscience and their conduct for signs of narcissism versus signs of humility. This is true not only for the internationally famous charismatic leaders but also for those who are leading parishes.

Some leadership positions can be considered charismatic offices, ones that hold such an attraction that some people will be drawn to whatever person is sitting in that office. This can be the case of elected offices such as mayors, governors, and presidents. It can also be true of religious positions such as pastor, bishop, or pope. When someone is named to sit in a *charismatic office*, some people will place that person on a pedestal, whether the leader wants to be there or not. It is up to that leader to decide whether he or she wants to stay on that pedestal or to move off that position and become a servant leader.

Transformational Servant Leadership

People today are looking to those standing out in front. They are seeking inspiration about how to make the world a better place. Bernard Bass states that in the past "leadership was mainly a matter of how and when to give directions and orders to obedient subordinates."[54] Certainly, leadership studies today have advanced beyond that point, in theory if not in practice.[55]

Today, the study of leadership has featured new approaches such as transformational leadership, which is very compatible with servant leadership. The essence of transformational leadership is the transforming of people and organizations; these are critical elements of servant leadership as well. Together, these two theories—transformational leadership and servant leadership—create a foundation to a whole new approach to leadership that is explored in this book.

The transformational servant leader seeks power *with* others, for the sake of others. They try to lift ordinary people to extraordinary outcomes. They do not seek control *over* their followers; instead, they want to *transform* the followers into leaders. The focus is centered on the followers instead of the leader. The motivation to lead is based on a desire to serve, not to be served. Serving others brings out the best in people. It excites people and encourages those who are led. They learn, grow, and develop into their full potential as human beings.

In addition, the vision of the transformational leader or the servant leader is based on the needs of the people and is not personally identified with the leader. In charismatic leadership, the vision is conceived, developed, and articulated by the leader in a way that stirs the hearts and minds of people to follow the directives of the leader. In transformational leadership, as with servant leadership, the leader facilitates an interactive process whereby the leaders and followers develop together a sense of shared vision.[56]

All leaders need followers, but to what end? Is the leader drawing people for selfish goals or for the common good of the group or organization? Is the leader concentrating power for personal honor and status or spreading it around to enhance service to others and the organization? Is the leader advancing personal goals or pursuing collective goals for the entire group? In servant leadership, the purpose for leading is to meet the needs of the followers, not those of the leader. Greenleaf's test of leadership asks if the followers are becoming healthier, freer, wiser, and more likely to become servant leaders themselves.

Commitment to servant leadership can be integrated with other practices of leadership and management. Greenleaf suggested in 1970 that we were experiencing a *leadership crisis* that called for a new way of thinking about leadership.[57] That crisis does not appear to have been resolved, either in the church or in society. This demands a new approach to leadership, perhaps one that integrates servant leadership with transformational leadership.

The integration of transformational leadership and servant leadership has potential for creating synergy. The transformation of followers into leaders is a point of emphasis in both approaches. Individual consideration, a factor that Bass includes in his description of transformational leadership, dovetails well with servant leadership.[58] Meanwhile, Greenleaf places an emphasis on visioning as an important element of servant leadership when he says that "foresight is the 'lead' that the leader has."[59] Both transformational and servant leadership place a similar emphasis on envisioning the future and transforming followers into leaders.

When approaching similarities and differences among leadership theories, it is helpful to use Venn diagrams to show the overlapping of the theories, such as in Figure 7. For comparison purposes, one needs to know what is unique about each theory. These are the areas of one circle in Figure 7 that do *not* overlap with another circle. That is the issue that has driven the study of leadership in this book. While it is helpful to think that servant leaders must have excellent people skills, know their business, or manage their time well, these are required of *all* leaders. These are common areas represented by the areas of overlap within all three of the circles of Figure 7. The question we are trying to answer here is, *What is unique to servant leadership?*

Servant leaders can learn from the study of other leadership theories. Servant leadership is not contradictory or mutually exclusive of transformational or transactional leadership. Generally speaking, servant leaders need to develop skills in both transactional and transformational leadership. The question is, *How does transactional or transformational leadership look different when it is practiced by a servant leader?* Both the day-to-day demands of transactional leadership and the strategic

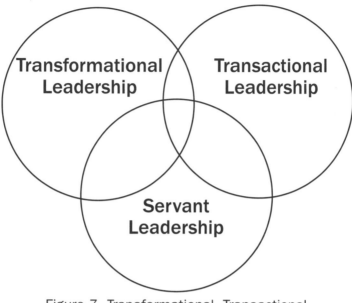

Figure 7. Transformational, Transactional,
and Servant Leadership

issues that require transformational leadership can be approached with servant leadership. We show evidence of that in our upcoming chapters.

Conclusion

The next chapter moves our focus from leader to follower. Leadership involves an active and reciprocal relationship between leader and follower. When leaders demonstrate care and concern for the team, the members are more likely to cooperate and to do so voluntarily. When the leader empowers the team, the members are more likely to take initiative and to do so with passion and creativity. In the best of all worlds, the leader empowers the follower to take initiative, and the follower in turn empowers the leader by taking initiative. This is what we mean by a **collaborative** relationship, one in which people are literally working together, building upon each other's strengths and gifts. **Initiating** is leading from within the ranks, or in a church context, leading from the pews.

The parish leader can have great plans, goals, and ideas, but unless that leader can build some consensus among the members of the congregation, rather than railroading everything by the people, the idea will fail. No one can go it alone, not even the pastor. The people might comply, but the influence is not voluntary. *Coercion is not leadership.*[60] No leader can succeed without followers.[61] Leadership and followership are reciprocal roles. Sometimes these roles can change from hour to hour, day to day or even from task to task. *Followership* is about the interaction, the connection, the relationship between leader and follower. The two are joined by the mission of the organization.

2

PARISH BEHAVIORS:
Leadership and Discipleship

When Jesus is asked to define who is our neighbor, he tells his disciples the parable of the Good Samaritan (Luke 10:30–37). His response could be described as a story about a person acting above and beyond the call of duty.[1] The Samaritan was attentive to the needs and interests of someone else. He was ready, willing, and available to care for the total needs of a person left for dead along a dangerous road. One of the paradoxes of the story is that the Samaritans were immigrants and were supposed to be the *enemy* of those hearing this parable. If the Good Samaritan could treat his enemy with kindness, then he could treat anyone with kindness.

This is altruistic behavior because it is centered on others. It is an expression of unconditional love, or "**agape**," that Jesus intends for his disciples. If we want our parishioners to act with *agape*, or to act with above-and-beyond behaviors, such as the Good Samaritan did, then the leaders begin this cycle of love by treating their parishioners with kindness and love. The Golden Rule suggests that we should treat each other as we wish to be treated (Luke 6:31). When we treat each other with kindness, we create a culture of kindness that is repeated by others. Sometimes the kindness returns back to us. Sometimes it is returned to others. Sometimes it is returned to a perfect stranger, perhaps an immigrant, an enemy, or a new member walking into your parish.

This chapter is about the behaviors of leaders and how they have an impact on the behaviors of followers. This book is about creating a culture of service in a parish in which people are serving people. If we want parishioners to devote their lives in service to God, service to each other, and service to the church, what can leaders do to promote service behaviors among their members? If we were dis-

35

cussing a business, and the goal was to promote customer service, the best way to engender better customer service would be to treat one's employees with kindness and respect. It is the employees who have the direct contact with the customers. If the employees are treated with kindness and served by their leaders, they are more likely to respond by serving the customers and treating them with kindness.

The same is true in a parish. If the leaders serve the members, the members will respond with above-and-beyond behaviors, such as taking initiative, helping each other out, and welcoming new members into the church. Those who are treated with kindness are more likely to treat others with kindness. Those who are served in a congregation are more likely to serve.

According to Tertullian, a prolific author and philosopher writing in the third century, the early Christian church was recognized for "the deeds of a love so noble that lead many to put a brand upon us. See, they say, how they love one another...and are ready even to die for one another."[2] A popular hymn suggests the same sentiment: "They will know we are Christians by our love." If today's Christians wish to live out the example of the early Christians and be known for their love, leaders need to create the conditions in which love can grow. When leaders become servants and empower followers to become leaders, we can expect that the people will reciprocate with love, kindness, and service to the church. In other words, if the leaders are serving others, then others will be moved to serve.

When Tertullian observed the early Christian communities, he was an outsider. He was drawn to these communities because he saw that they loved one another. The fascinating question about Tertullian's observation is, *What did he see that led him to conclude that this was a community based in love?* What were the observable behaviors that convinced him that what he saw was a loving community? In the same way, as we look today at Christian communities, we can ask ourselves, *What evidence of love would be found if someone were to view the inside of our parishes today?* What behaviors would be found in a parish community that is centered in love and practices love with each other and toward the world? What evidence would outsiders find today that the people in a parish loved one other? If God is love, and if love is the measure of God's presence, then how is that love manifested?

Our Model of Behaviors

If we are searching for observable behaviors that are associated with love, servant leadership is a likely starting point, because it has been associated with the life and teachings of Jesus. It fits the paradoxical nature of the message of Jesus. When looking for indications that love is being practiced, and for **leadership behaviors** that encourage the practice of love, it makes sense to look for behaviors associated with servant leadership.

In summarizing the behaviors, skills, and traits of a servant leader, Larry Spears suggests in *Focus on Leadership* this list: listening, empathy, healing, awareness, persuasion, conceptualization, foresight, **stewardship**, commitment to the growth of people, and building community.[3] While this list is certainly not exhaustive, it is a beginning point in looking at the behaviors, skills, and traits that are consistent with the philosophy of Robert Greenleaf.

The empirical study by Mark Ehrhart identified the following servant leader behaviors: developing quality relationships with employees; building a sense of community among employees; seeking input from employees before making decisions; reaching consensus among employees on major decisions; making the personal development of employees a priority; demonstrating an egalitarian relationship with employees; finding ways to help others; getting involved in community service projects; and giving back to the community.[4]

Greenleaf taught that in everything the servant leader thinks, speaks, and does, the goal is to be accountable for all others who are affected by those thoughts, words, and actions.[5] The servant leader, first and foremost, places the needs and interests of others and the organization ahead of his or her own. Based on these lists from Larry Spears, Mark Ehrhart, and Robert Greenleaf, observable servant leader behaviors in a parish might include:

- Personally inviting others in the parish to participate
- Listening intently to what others have to say
- Consulting with others before making decisions that affect them
- Delegating responsibilities to others who can perform certain tasks

- Placing oneself in humble service to the parish
- Encouraging others to take initiative
- Facilitating the growth of parishioners
- Removing obstacles hindering progress toward parish goals
- Maximizing the capacity of others in the parish to act
- Building a sense of community in the parish
- Reaching out to those who are hurting in some way
- Performing modest tasks with grace and humility
- Thanking others for their service to the parish
- Acting in concrete ways that help parishioners to perform their duties

Three Servant Leader Behavioral Categories

Our study focused on three general categories of leadership behaviors that we call *recognizing, serving,* and *empowering*. We think that these are consistent with the descriptions of supportive leadership behaviors that have been tied to the successful organizations.[6] They are also consistent with those prescribed by Greenleaf in his work on servant leadership. Elements of recognizing, serving, and empowering behaviors, as they are described and defined following, were gleaned from the study by Ehrhart, the philosophy of Greenleaf, and the teachings of Jesus. These three categories of leader behaviors were explored in the parish case study that became the basis for this book. (More details about the research process are explained in chapter 3.)

Recognizing

Recognizing involves acknowledging, affirming, and calling forth the gifts, talents, and efforts of parishioners. Such affirmation and calling forth is critical to Ehrhart's notion of developing quality relationships with members and building a sense of community.[7] It also intersects with Greenleaf's notion of community building, empathy, and commitment to the growth of people.[8]

Servant leaders call forth the gifts and talents of their parishioners in the same way that Jesus called forth the gifts and talents of his disciples. In the process, servant leaders develop quality relationships with members of the parish and build a sense of community. Recognizing is centered on the needs and interests of parishioners to be appreciated and to utilize their gifts and talents.

The idea suggested here is that if parish leaders acknowledge, affirm, and recognize their parishioners, then the people in the pews will reciprocate by helping, initiating, participating, and self-developing. People whose gifts and talents are appreciated are more likely to help others in the parish, take the initiative, participate in the life of the parish, and develop themselves as parishioners. In other words, servant leaders invite the members of the congregation to come forth and contribute their gifts and talents to the congregation, and they recognize and affirm these efforts when people come forward.

Serving

Serving behaviors are at the core of Greenleaf's idea of leadership. Greenleaf states that the difference between the servant-first leader and the leader-first leader "manifests itself in the care taken by the servant-first to make sure that the other person's highest priority needs are being served."[9] Greenleaf suggests that servant leadership begins with the natural inclination to serve. This stands in direct contrast with pedestal leadership, which seeks to *be* served.

Service by leaders can be seen as service to God, service to others, and service to the church. It is the service that Jesus prescribed when James and John were lobbying for a leadership role among the disciples: "Whoever wishes to become great among you must be your servant" (Mark 10:43). Ehrhart built on this idea of service, explaining that servant leaders consider the needs and interests of others ahead of their own, lead with a sense of humility, create an egalitarian relationship with members, and model servanthood by helping with menial **tasks** such as cleaning, making coffee, or setting up for meetings.[10]

Servant leaders work side by side while serving with others in and around the parish. Servant leaders influence others but do so with a sense of humility and create an egalitarian relationship with members. They help out with housekeeping tasks. Servant leaders act with a sense of equality toward others. If their position places them in hierarchical authority, they consider themselves not on pedestals looking over people, but instead as *primus inter pares*, or "first among equals," as Greenleaf suggested.[11]

Empowering

Empowering behaviors are those that develop or enhance the capacity for others to act on behalf of themselves and the organization. Empowerment is the sharing of power that enhances the power and the services of others.[12] Empowering involves collaborating with others in decision making, particularly with those who are most affected by the decisions being made by the leader.[13] This builds a sense of ownership and motivates others to get behind decisions about organizational roles, goals, and responsibilities.

The past fifty years of research in social psychology suggest that empowerment strategies can offer real benefits to organizational effectiveness.[14] The potential benefits of empowering behaviors include greater levels of commitment among the members of an organization, better decision making within the organization, improved quality of the task completed, more innovative behaviors of the followers, and increased satisfaction among followers. However, these benefits are only gained when the leaders are willing and able to give their followers significantly more control and access to resources and information.

Empowering is a **follower-centric leader behavior** that signifies the essence of transformational leadership[15] that changes people and organizations in ways that develop the capacity for members to act in pursuit of the organization's mission and vision. Servant leaders empower parishioners by delegating tasks and decision-making authority, by seeking their advice and consultation before making major decisions, by building consensus[16] around major concerns, and by making the **leadership development** of the members a priority so that leadership is shared among many parishioners.

Organizational Citizenship Behaviors

Once we identified servant leader behaviors as those describing the leaders in a high-performing parish, the next question was, *If the leaders are acting with servant leadership, what are the members of the parish doing?* What would Tertullian see the parishioners doing in a parish that might be described as "See how they love one another"? The search for an answer to that question led us to the research conducted on organizational citizenship.[17]

In a Christian context, the followers are those we call *disciples.* Discipleship literally means learning and following. Christian disciples are learning and following the way of Christ. Discipleship behaviors are ones that are consistent with the teachings of Jesus, such as the Sermon on the Mount (Matt 5–7). We propose that if the leaders in a parish act as servants, then their followers will respond in kind with their own service. Just as the servant leaders of the parish are serving God, serving each other, and serving the parish, the parishioners are doing the same.

The servant behaviors of the parishioners, referred to here as **organizational citizenship behaviors** (OCBs),[18] are viewed as voluntary, **prosocial behaviors** of the people in the pews. Our study applies OCB, as a theory of organizational behavior, to the context of parish life and to the high performance in a parish. Like **servant leader behaviors** (SLBs), OCBs are consistent with the message of Jesus to love and to serve. Both leaders and disciples devote themselves to a life of service. The parishioner who is acting with OCB is placing the needs and interests of the parish, or those of other members of the parish, ahead of his or her own, just as the servant leader is doing. The *servant parish* is one in which the leaders and the people live and act in service to God, service to each other, and service to the parish. In our study, this meant that the servant parish would exhibit high levels of both SLBs and OCBs.

Because leaders influence followers, it makes sense that certain leader behaviors will have an impact on certain member behaviors.[19] In this case, we propose that servant behaviors of the parish leaders will increase organizational citizenship behaviors of the parishioners (see chapter 8 for a full discussion of how this dynamic occurs). This was suggested in the very earliest articles on OCB.[20] It was also concluded in Ehrhart's study that servant leader behaviors increased certain OCBs.[21] The research shows that **supportive leadership** behaviors were the strongest predictor of OCB.[22] In other words, when leaders offer support to their followers by acting with SLBs, they invoke loyalty, trust, and reciprocal support, all of which are conducive to organizational citizenship.[23]

Criteria for OCB

Organizational citizenship behaviors are defined as altruistic behaviors that put the needs and interests of others ahead of one's own.[24] This definition of OCB includes behaviors that

1. Go above and beyond the call of duty
2. Have no extrinsic reward assigned to that behavior
3. Improve the performance of the organization

In the past twenty years of research on OCB, more than forty measures have been identified.[25] These forty measures have been distilled into seven dimensions: helping, compliance, sportsmanship, civic virtue, organizational loyalty, self-development, and individual initiative.[26] We decided to focus our study on four that appear to be most directly tied to scripture and to the teachings of the church.[27] The four OCBs were helping, initiating, participating, and self-developing. We suggested that we would find high levels of these four behaviors among the members of a high-performing parish:

1. They are helpers.
2. They are not afraid to take the initiative.
3. They show up for parish meetings and activities.
4. They are dedicated to continuous learning and growth.

Viewed here, OCB can be seen as discipleship, fellowship, and community building. OCB is commonly viewed as altruistic behavior, like that of the Good Samaritan. Altruism means the giving of oneself freely with nothing expected in return. This is very similar to the concept of *agape*, the word that Jesus used to describe love of neighbor. *Agape* roughly translates from Greek as "unconditional love," the kind of love that expects nothing in return but is given freely. In fact, this sort of love is the central message of the first encyclical of Pope Benedict XVI, entitled *God Is Love*.[28]

In his only reference to the behaviors that distinguish those who will gain eternal salvation, Jesus identifies servant behaviors in Matthew 25. Jesus urges us to practice the corporal works of mercy, such as feeding the hungry, welcoming the stranger, and visiting the sick.[29] These servant behaviors are like OCBs for Christians. We might refer to them as *discipleship behaviors*. They are prescribed by Jesus, and they are associated with the ultimate measure of success, that of eternal salvation.

Four Organizational Citizenship Behavioral Categories

Helping

Helping behaviors cover a wide array of religious behaviors encouraged by church documents, illustrated in parables of Jesus, and supported by Judeo-Christian and other religious literature.[30] Helping behaviors are informal ways that members reach out to assist each other. Just as the concept of servant leadership has a spiritual heritage, so does helping. The Good Samaritan story is a study of helping behaviors. Helping is evident in the Golden Rule, a core teaching in virtually every major religion.

Helping occurs when one person sees that someone else has fallen behind or has an extraordinary amount of work to do or a big project coming up. The helper offers to help that person with their heavy load. It occurs when someone in a parish offers to help someone who was perhaps sick for a while. People enhance the life of their parish when they live out the ancient wisdom of the Golden Rule: "Do to others as you would have them do to you" (Luke 6:31). Doing to others is a helping behavior that fits the definition of OCBs.[31] Helping captures the essence of altruism evident in the early studies on organizational citizenship[32] and is significantly associated with many measures of organizational performance including **efficiency**, customer satisfaction, and quality.[33]

Initiating

Initiating behaviors are voluntary steps to accomplish projects, to generate new ideas, or to start activities in the interest of the organization. Just as many businesses advertise for "self-starters" when they are looking for new employees, initiative is what many church organizations are looking for as well. Initiative by the laity plays a critical role in building a healthy parish. Several of the traits identified in the parishes described by Paul Wilkes in *Excellent Catholic Parishes* require the initiative of laypeople in parishes.[34] In his study of excellent parishes, Wilkes finds that important work is spread among the laity.[35]

Initiating behaviors occur when the members of the organization take action without waiting for specific directions from the leader. In a parish, initiative often goes hand in hand with helping. It happens when a person does not wait to be asked to help, but just steps in, takes the initiative, and offers to help. Laypeople can also take the initiative when they are involved in collaborative decision making,[36] express new ideas, start new projects, and reach out to build relationships among each other.

Initiative is much less likely to happen if the leader is micromanaging every move of the parishioners or is punitive when a new initiative fails. Initiative by the members of a parish is very dependent upon the temperament of the leader and whether the leader encourages that initiative. *Lumen Gentium* emphasized that pastors should encourage laypeople to take action on their own initiative.[37]

Participating

Participating means that members are engaged in the formal activities of the organization, whereas the helping and initiating behaviors are more informal.[38] Participating behaviors involve people showing up for activities, events, meetings, and programs sponsored by the parish. Just as social psychologists have emphasized the importance of participation in business organizations, its value was also emphasized in the Catholic church.[39] It is interesting that the emphasis on participation in business circles, called the "human relations movement,"[40] occurred at about the same time as Vatican II opened the doors for greater participation and involvement of laypeople in parish life.

In both cases, the emphasis was placed on engaging people more in the discussions, plans, and decisions that were directly affecting their lives. In both cases, those in power saw participation as a means toward greater ownership in decision making and ultimately more effectiveness in their organizations. The teachings of Vatican II opened the doors for greater participation by laypeople into the life of the church. The Vatican II document *Lumen Gentium* had a revolutionary effect on the role of laity in the Catholic church, as it urged the involvement of the laity in their parishes.[41] The human relations movement had the same kind of impact on workers.

Self-Developing

Self-developing begins with a belief in the inherent dignity of the human person. All people are destined to grow into their full potential. Self-developing happens when people take personal responsibility for reaching that potential. They are actively seeking to grow, to learn, and to develop themselves into their roles and responsibilities. Self-development also involves increasing familiarity with policies, procedures, and processes of the parish, so that they can be more effective as they emerge into parish leadership roles, such as chairing a commission or coordinating a parish event.

Self-developing includes reaching one's own potential as a leader and helping others reach their own potential. The willingness to grow, to change, and to innovate is a characteristic of members in the excellent parishes studied by Paul Wilkes.[42] Research shows that those who take responsibility for their own continuous learning will be most successful in their jobs. In volunteer settings, personal growth and development allows people to serve more effectively as their repertoire of knowledge, skills, and abilities grows.

Self-developing enhances a person's ability to help, to take initiative, and to fully participate. In order to help others in a parish or take the initiative on new ideas or become more fully involved in leadership positions in the church, laypeople need to develop themselves as potential leaders in the church. This includes enrolling in lay ministry training, attending leadership seminars, studying church teaching, and becoming more familiar with church policies in order to prepare themselves for parish ministry. It also involves prayer, reflection, and spiritual preparation for leadership roles in the church.

Self-developing is the fourth and final member behavior included in this model for parish success. Unless laypeople are learning, growing, and developing themselves, they will be unable to take leadership or fully participate in parish councils or commissions. Clergy and laity are in need of continuing education and training. However, as the number of Catholic priests and Protestant ministers continues to decline, and the roles and responsibilities of laypeople continue to increase, self-developing behaviors of parishioners are becoming even more critical to the success of a parish.

Conclusion

We propose that servant leaders who recognize, serve, and empower their parishioners will encourage the people to help out, take the initiative, participate in the parish, and take responsibility for their own personal growth and development (see Figure 8).

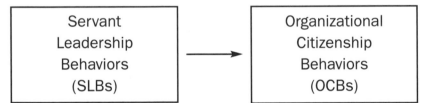

Figure 8. Servant Leadership Behaviors Enhance
Organizational Citizenship Behaviors

We propose that four OCB behaviors of the parishioners will enhance the effectiveness of the parish (see Figure 9).

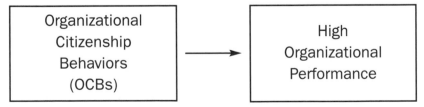

Figure 9. Organizational Citizenship Behaviors Enhance
Organizational Performance

We propose that servant leadership and organizational citizenship will lead to higher performance in parishes (see Figure 10).

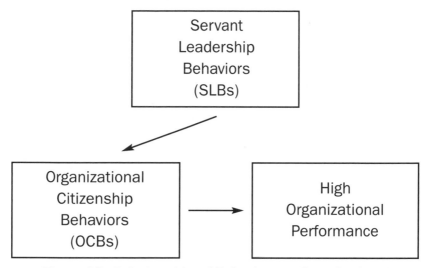

Figure 10. Relationship of Behaviors to Organizational Performance

We believe that in high-performing parishes, church leaders act with servant leadership. Their behaviors fall into the general categories of recognizing, serving, and empowering their people. The parishioners in these parishes are moved by servant leadership and respond by helping each other, taking the initiative on various projects, participating in the life of the parish, and taking responsibility for their own personal growth and development. In the next chapter, we describe how we went about testing these ideas about servant leadership and organizational citizenship.

3

MEASURES OF PARISH LIFE

The question that drove the research that led to this book was, "How do you measure the life of a parish?" Bishop William Franklin of the Diocese of Davenport posed this question to me in 2004 in the context of a diocesan staff meeting. It became the inspiration for an extensive parish study that became the research base for this book. The bishop had assigned me to staff a diocesan task force that was looking at the future structuring of parishes around the diocese. Like many dioceses, we were struggling with staffing issues created by the growing shortage of priests.[1] We were looking at many options for closing, consolidating, and clustering the eighty-four parishes in the diocese.[2]

The diocesan task force recommended a new policy that *no* parish should be closed due solely to the shortage of priests. Parishes should close *only* if they were no longer viable, that is, if they had no life in them. Upon my report of this recommendation at a meeting of the diocesan directors, Bishop Franklin agreed with the basic recommendation of the task force and asked how we would measure the life of a parish.

Performance Measures

The bishop's question is not easy to answer. In business, there is a saying that *What gets counted, gets done.* This suggests that if we cannot count something, it is not important and it does not get done. If we do count something, it must be important to get it done. The things that we can count in a religious community are limited. Generally we count dollars and people. We can also count programs, events, food, books, and units of services, but most of what we count can be connected back to dollars and people. How and what to count, or how to measure church performance, raises unique and challenging questions.

48

In some ways, the assessment of religious organizations using quantifiable measures misses the point of a faith community. The most important things in religious life can be difficult, if not impossible, to count. Unlike businesses, what counts most in a religious community is not countable. Much of what religion defines as success, such as the spirituality of the people and the salvation of souls, is mysterious to human beings and defies human measurement. The purpose of a parish is to enhance the faithfulness of its members. The essence of religious performance is *faithfulness* to God, not *effectiveness*.

The prime focus of church activity is centered on a relationship with God, and that relationship also extends to our relationships with each other. The purpose of a parish may have a supernatural quality, but the activities that people of faith engage in are social. Even in a church context, we should be able to observe and measure behaviors that are indicative of people who are focused on God.[3] Behaviors can be measured. Therefore, behavioral measures became the backbone of our examination of effectiveness in a parish. In our case study, we measured servant leader behaviors (as discussed in chapter 1) and organizational citizenship behaviors (as discussed in chapter 2) in three high-performing parishes. We also identified six other key characteristics in our model parishes (discussed in chapter 10).

Our Model of Seven Research Steps

The steps we took in measuring parish life, including the selection of our three model parishes, were part of a carefully crafted process. We explain next the seven research steps we took and how we selected our model parishes. Perhaps some of these steps can be helpful to other church leaders and inspire others to try new and creative ways to measure parish life. While the parish case study was a field study performed with the rigorous methods required of a doctoral dissertation in business, some of the other steps in this process were conducted in a way that is very doable for most parishes and dioceses.[4]

The first three steps in this research process, taken together, were referred to as the **parish life study** in the Diocese of Davenport. They included (1) the **parish self-assessment**, (2) the parish finance report, and (3) the parish demographics report. The next three steps were taken in the process of selecting our high-performing parishes. They included (4) the **parish life evaluation**, (5) the **parish life evaluator survey**, and (6) **the parish life evaluator interviews**. The final step in the process explored our behavioral measures of success in the selected parishes and became the inspiration for this book. We called it (7) the **parish case study**.

The Parish Life Study: The First Three Steps

The Parish Self-Assessment

All eighty-four parishes participated in the *parish self-assessment* by submitting a self-study that was designed by the Living the Faith Task Force of the diocese. The job of this task force was to convene parish leaders around the diocese, to conduct research on the future availability of priests, to assess the condition of church buildings, to evaluate the strength of our parishes, and to develop diocesan plans that could be useful for the future restructuring of all eighty-four parishes and the assignment of diocesan priests. The task force recommended that parish viability should be the basis for decision making about the closing, consolidating, and clustering of parishes. Bishop Franklin responded with his question about how to measure parish life.[5] His question galvanized the task force to develop the parish self-assessment (see appendix A).

This self-study was distributed by the diocese to all parishes, with a request from the bishop to evaluate themselves on nine areas of ministry: faith formation, family life, social action, liturgy, finance and administration, church life, evangelization, stewardship, and vocations. The questions explored whether the parish leaders considered themselves successful in meeting goals and objectives in these nine areas of ministry.

All parishes completed the self-assessment, and most sent volumes of supporting data such as bulletins, newsletters, minutes of meetings, flyers describing parish events, photograph albums of the parish, and much more. In all, the self-assessment included forty-three performance measures of parish life, many based on the nine areas of ministry. These self-reports were studied and scored by the members of the Living the Faith Task Force. Afterward, the task force decided that we needed to add data that was less subjective than a self-assessment. For this reason, we added operational measures of finance and demographics.

The Parish Finance Report

The diocese collected a parish finance report that included extensive financial data for all eighty-four parishes. We used the financial reports that parishes routinely send to the diocese to create ratios based on these financial numbers, compared them over a five-year period, and showed whether the numbers were moving up or down. Financial measures included average contribution per household, adjusted gross income of each parish, sustainability indices (the number of years the parish could operate on their current level of reserves), and the rate of growth of parish income (see appendix B).

The Parish Demographics Report

The diocese also compiled a parish demographic report that included extensive demographic measures for all eighty-four parishes. Most were gleaned from sacramental records and Mass counts. This included the number of individuals and families per parish, the rate of change in both of those measures, the percentage of members who attend Mass, and other data based on sacramental records, such as numbers of baptisms, confirmations, and professions of faith (see appendix C).

With forty-three points of data on the parish self-assessments, the ten measures in the financial report, and ten measures in the demographic reports, we had sixty-three points of data to report to all parishes.

Once the parish life study was completed, the Diocese of Davenport organized six deanery meetings to report the findings to parish leaders. About 450 people, representing every parish in the diocese, turned out to receive the reports. A diocesan staff member was assigned to each parish to help parish leaders discern what the numbers meant for that parish and to urge parish leaders to use this data as a beginning point for additional parish planning and action. We also suggested that the parish identify and gather other data that would be helpful for its parish planning, such as the number of youth in the parish and the percentage of those youth who are attending religious education, youth ministry, or sacramental preparation.

One of our surprises from the deanery meetings was the realization that most members of the parish council, finance council, lay trustees, and parish staff had never seen nor studied this data. In fact, most lay parish leaders did not even know this data existed. Statistics such as Mass counts are collected each November in parishes across the country. Those *should* be public records used during parish planning. Sacramental records are gathered by each parish each year and sent along with financial statements to every diocese in the country. In a business, this data would be used and studied by the owners of the business. Projections would be made as to whether the business was growing or not. Decisions would be made about the future of the business based on these calculations. The idea that planning future directions and strategies of an organization would occur *without* looking at the numbers simply would not make sense in a business context.

What the Diocese of Davenport did in collecting this data was simply to use the data that is already available in virtually every chancery across America. The added value on our part was developing the set of analytical ratios based on the data we already had. We also calculated whether certain numbers were going up or down in each parish, and we informed the parishes how they ranked on a scale of 1 to 84 with the other parishes in the diocese on each of these points of data, including the median score for each measure. As diocesan leaders are forced to make decisions about the future of parishes across the country, it makes sense to collect, explore, and use the data as part of strategic planning.

Because the parishes already had the raw data that were used to calculate these reports, the most unique contributions of the parish life study were the calculation of ratios and trend lines within each parish, the comparison of data from parish to parish, and perhaps most important: *the sharing of all this data with the lay leaders of the parish.*

Behavioral Measures

As important as it was to conduct the parish self-assessment and to collect, distribute, and study the financial and demographic data, we wondered whether we had really answered the question, "How do you measure the life of a parish?" Were full pews and parking lots on Sunday the best measure of parish life? Was there a correlation between the Sunday collection and the overall performance of a parish? Was high performance something that could be measured by numbers and data, or were these merely an indication that something was going right? Surely, parish life was about more than numbers.

While the numbers do indeed count for something in a parish, they are simply indicators. They do not answer the question of whether the parish is meeting its bottom line, which should be its mission. Like any not-for-profit organization, parishes are ultimately measured not by money and numbers, but by mission, vision, and values. While the numbers we gathered provided us with some indication of parish health or viability, we decided that it was insufficient. The accomplishment of the mission and the success of the vision depend on something else. Eventually, we decided to explore the behaviors of the people who are leaders, managers, and members of the parish, and whether they are acting upon their stated values, which is the essence of integrity.

Daily life reminds us of the importance of behaviors. We are told to set a good example, to practice consistency between what we say and what we do, and to live with integrity by integrating behaviors with values. We hear that actions speak louder than words and to practice what we preach. We need to walk the talk and live by example. I believe that people tend to act themselves into a new way of thinking rather than think themselves into a new way of acting. Over time, we can also think and act ourselves into a new way of being. Behaviors are critically important to understanding organizational life, especially when those behaviors are integrated with the values of the organization and when they resonate with the mission, vision, and message of the leader.

Because behaviors are so critically important, we asked:

- What would the behavioral signs of success look like in a parish?
- What would a visitor to a high-performing parish observe in terms of actual behaviors?
- What would a parish look like if Tertullian were to observe the parish and say, "See how they love one another"?
- If numbers are an indication of performance, then what would performance look like in a successful parish?
- What would the leaders be doing and what would the parishioners be doing?

These became the research questions that drove the next four steps of this research process: the parish life evaluation, the parish life evaluator survey, the parish life evaluator interviews, and the parish case study—looking for behavioral signs of success in three high-performing parishes.[6]

The Parish Selection Process

In order to perform behavioral research on high-performing parishes, we needed to devise a system for defining, describing, and identifying the high performers. Using the self-assessment, the financial data, and the demographic numbers to determine the highest performers seemed inadequate. Parish effectiveness includes qualitative factors such as the community life and spirituality of the people. To evaluate such phenomena, a measure of human judgment was needed. Thus the parish life evaluation was conceived as the fourth research step.

The Parish Life Evaluation

If parish effectiveness includes qualitative factors, we needed to add a measure of human judgment to the selection process. We asked twenty-four evaluators to examine the parish life study, including the parish self-assessments, financial records, and demographic data that had been collected, and then rate the parishes subjectively from number 1 to number 84. The twenty-four evaluators included the bishop, vicar general, chancellor, chief financial officer, and directors of all diocesan programs as well as the seven members of the diocesan personnel board that is responsible for advising the bishop on which priests will be assigned to which parishes.

Parish Size

To select three high-performing parishes for the case study, the eighty-four parishes of the Diocese of Davenport were divided into three categories based on size of parish. Three categories of parishes were included in order to account for the possible differences related to organizational size. We controlled for size of parish for three reasons.

First, the dynamics of parish life can vary according to size, because size of parish can affect the size of parish staff and therefore have an impact on parish behaviors. Large parishes tend to have larger budgets that allow for the hiring of more parish staff. Second, many of the smallest parishes in the Diocese of Davenport have been among those closed in recent years. The question that led to this study—"How do you measure the life of a parish?"—was asked in a discussion regarding criteria for closing parishes. By including three different-sized parishes, this study attempted to examine the quality of parish life in the smallest parishes that are sometimes considered most at risk of being closed. Third, the smaller parishes often express concern that they do not receive the same amount of attention as the larger parishes. Including them added a unique feature to this study.

The High Performers

Once we had divided the parishes into three categories based on size, we selected the highest-scoring parishes from the parish life evaluation for each of the three categories.[7] The three parishes selected were

1. St. Mary Magdalen's, Bloomfield, Iowa
2. St. Mary's, Solon, Iowa
3. St. Mary's, Iowa City, Iowa

These three parishes readily agreed to participate in our case study.

Parish Life Survey and Interviews

The Parish Life Evaluator Survey

We were almost ready to launch the parish case study to look for behavioral measures of organizational citizenship and servant leadership. But one additional question was still nagging us. We felt we needed to make sure the parish life evaluators were not using the same criteria in their evaluations as we were planning to use in the case study. The twenty-four evaluators had not been directed to use specific criteria upon which to base their subjective evaluations of the parishes. They were free to prioritize and interpret the data from the parish life study in making their evaluations.

If the criteria used by the evaluators were identical to the behaviors that we were looking for in the high-performing parishes, then the parish case study would be selecting on the *dependent variable*, which would make the case study redundant and unnecessary. Therefore, the parish life evaluator survey was designed to explore how parish life was measured by the evaluators (see appendix D). The results of the parish life evaluator survey were compiled, coded, and recoded following rigorous methods.[8]

Nineteen of the twenty-four evaluators responded to the parish life evaluator survey. The results showed that the evaluators were primarily interested in financial and demographic performance data, not the behavioral signs of parish life that we were considering for the parish case study. With these results, we decided to add one more step and interview the evaluators who responded to the survey.

Parish Life Evaluator Survey Interviews

Eight of the nineteen respondents agreed to be interviewed about their responses to the survey. The results of these interviews were compiled, coded, and recoded following the rigorous methods of case research.[9] The interviews were taped, coded, and analyzed.

The purpose of the interviews was to clarify the responses to the survey and to seek descriptive remarks from the evaluators. Interview items probed responses from the surveys, including:

- Tell me what you mean by "truly living the gospel."
- What do you mean by "discipleship"?
- Describe a parish where "the Spirit is alive and visible in all areas of parish life."
- Why do you think Mass attendance is a better indicator of performance than financial records?
- What behaviors would you observe when you witness "compassionate and collaborative leadership"?

The results of the parish life evaluator interviews also revealed that the evaluators were primarily interested in financial and demographic performance data. These results gave us the confidence we needed to move ahead with the case study, understanding that the evaluators had not already based their judgment about our model parishes on levels of organizational citizenship behaviors (OCBs) and servant leader behaviors (SLBs).

Definition of a High-Performing Parish

Another benefit of the parish life evaluator survey and interviews was the insight that the respondents gave into parish life. Based on their responses, we crafted the following definition for a high-performing parish:

> A high-performing parish is a vibrant faith community where people are growing in faith and in numbers. It is a place where all are welcome, where the Spirit is present, where people of all ages are involved, where leaders call forth the laity to participate, and where volunteers reach out to others in the parish and community. The high-performing parish is active in nine areas of ministry: liturgy, faith formation, social action, family life, vocations, stewardship, evangelization, church life, and finance.

The Parish Case Study

Upon the conclusion of the parish life evaluator survey and interviews, we began the case study. The purpose was to create a profile of behaviors and characteristics of a high-performance parish. We did this by evaluating the level of evidence for seven hypotheses based on three servant leader behaviors (recognizing, empowering, and serving) and four member behaviors (helping, initiating, participating, and self-developing) that we thought should be practiced in a high-performing parish.

Our parish case study employed multiple case research methods that were designed to address issues of reliability and validity. The behavioral measures of parish life were studied through four research methods: direct observation, focus groups with each parish council,[10] one-on-one interviews, and archival records.[11] These four methods helped us to *triangulate* the data, a critical aspect of case research.[12] **Triangulation** occurs when the study includes multiple research methods, multiple sources of data and multiple members of the research team.[13] Our study included all of these.

We involved multiple sources of data by including pastors, parish council members, parish staff, and other parish leaders. We kept rigorous field notes. We transcribed the one-on-one interviews and focus groups. We visited each parish to conduct one-on-one interviews, to hold focus groups, to attend Mass, and to observe other parish functions.

In addition to looking for evidence of the seven behaviors identified in advance, we kept an open mind to see what else might be happening in these three parishes. Our research questions for the parish case study were (1) What leader and member behaviors are associated with a high-performing parish? (2) What are other characteristics of a high-performing parish?

Data Collection

Focus Groups

We conducted focus group interviews with lay parishioners in each of the three parishes. The purpose of the focus groups was to explore and describe the occurrence of servant leader behaviors (SLBs) and organizational citizenship behaviors (OCBs). We searched for evidence of how the parish responded to critical incidents and how they evaluated themselves in nine areas of ministry (see appendix E). Participants included ten to twelve key laypeople representing members of the parish council, finance council, parish board of education, lay members of the parish staff, and lay trustees.

One-on-One Interviews

We interviewed the pastor and one lay leader in each of the three parishes. The purpose of the interviews was to explore the extent to which the three SLBs and four OCBs were being practiced by the leaders and members of the parish. The interview guide was designed to probe around critical incidents and the nine areas of ministry to determine the extent that these seven behaviors were in use in that parish (see appendix F).

Direct Observation

Our site visits to the three parishes included attendance at weekend liturgies, informal visits with parishioners, and the parish focus groups. We took advantage of these opportunities to observe what was happening in these parishes. Our observation guide included sixty questions that were answered "Yes" or "No" by all three members of the research team.[14] The guide also allowed for each of us to keep extensive notes and record what we were seeing and hearing (see appendix G).

Archival Research

In addition, we collected and studied extensive data about all three parishes. The parish life study was the most consistent and reliable source of archival records, especially for levels of participation for each of the three parishes. Its demographic and financial data helped to paint a picture of parish life in these three parishes. Church bulletins, program brochures, parish council agendas, newsletters, program flyers, and other printed materials were also gathered from each parish and searched for evidence of the seven behaviors.

Data Analysis

The transcripts of the focus groups and interviews were coded and recoded to determine the extent of evidence that was present for the seven hypothesized behaviors. The six one-on-one interviews and three focus groups were transcribed into 183 pages of data that, once coded, were analyzed to determine the extent to which the behaviors described in the interviews and focus groups were indicators of our seven behaviors (see appendix H).

In order to increase the reliability of the **coding** of the field data, check-coding was used in the coding of the data from the focus groups and interviews. Check-coding involves a second person coding the data in order to establish "an unequivocal, common vision of what the codes mean and which blocks of data best fit which code."[15] In the case study, the second coder was Laurie Hoefling, an administrative assistant with eighteen years of experience working at the Diocese of Davenport.[16]

The observation guides and accompanying field notes were completed by the three members of the research team. The observation guide was adapted from an evaluative tool developed for people interested in visiting area churches.[17] Each item in the observation guide was mapped to one of the seven behaviors in a process we called "categorizing the data"[18] (see appendix G).

The purpose of the archival data was to provide supporting documentation for the information that was provided through the other research methods, to confirm the story lines presented in the focus groups and the one-on-one interviews, and to help create a profile of life in the high-performing parishes.[19]

Conclusion

Reflecting back on the research process, we realized that our seven research steps provided three different ways to respond to the bishop's question, "How do you measure the life of a parish?" The parish measures include:

1. Strategic measures such as goals and objectives associated with the mission of the parish and its various areas of ministry. Our

strategic measures were developed around the parish life self-assessment that surveyed all eighty-four parishes on their performance in nine areas of ministry.[20]

2. Operational measures such as financial and demographic information from the parish. Our operational measures included twenty financial and demographic points of data that were collected for each parish and presented to parish leaders in a series of deanery meetings.[21]

3. Behavioral measures of the leaders and members of the parish. Behavioral measures centered around three servant leader behaviors (SLBs) and four organizational citizenship behaviors (OCBs) that were explored in the high-performing parishes.[22]

4

THE FAMILY APPROACH:
Life in Bloomfield

The town of Bloomfield rests amid the rolling hills of south central Iowa, near the Missouri border. It is the Davis County seat, one of the poorest counties in the state of Iowa. Bloomfield is a small town of 2,601 people in the middle of farm country. The town square brags a majestic county courthouse surrounded by dozens of small shops, restaurants, and small businesses.

The Exchange Bank in Bloomfield made national news when it went bankrupt in 1983 during the midst of the farm crisis. The bank building, located on the town square, has been converted into a coffee shop named Aunt Granny's. It draws local farmers, retirees, residents, and visitors who wish to pass time with small-town conversation. I have made several trips to that coffee shop and was always welcomed into those conversations.

Davis County is largely Baptist and Methodist, with a fair number of Amish. According to parish leaders, Catholics have always been a minority and have experienced some prejudice in the community. A small cemetery just south of town built many years ago to bury blacks and Catholics stands as a reminder of anti-Catholic bias; it is rarely used today. Driving around the county reveals signs of an Amish presence, including horse-drawn buggies on the roads, laundry on clotheslines, and houses with no antennas or electric power lines. Hitching posts for the horses that pull the Amish buggies are located just outside the town square in Bloomfield. Amish baked goods are easy to find in the small shops and restaurants on the town square.

Unique Characteristics

With forty-three families, St. Mary Magdalen's is the smallest parish in the Diocese of Davenport and the only Catholic parish in all of Davis County. Fr. John Spiegel, the pastor of St. Mary Magdalen's, lives twenty-five miles away in Ottumwa, Iowa, where he also pastors Saint Patrick's. He drives to Bloomfield about once a week. Mass is held at 5:30 p.m. on Sunday evenings, sometimes followed by a potluck supper.

In addition to the pastor, the parish employs one staff member, Sr. Ruth Ellen Doane, who is a part-time pastoral associate. She is described by Fr. John and by the people as "the glue that holds the parish together."' She lives in the rectory at St. Mary Magdalen's and drives to Ottumwa a few times a week because she is also the pastoral associate there. Sr. Ruth is paid 20 percent of her salary by St. Mary Magdalen's and the other 80 percent by St. Patrick's.

Davis County is one of only two counties in the diocese without a Catholic priest residing in the county. The church itself is a former supper club. From the outside, St. Mary Magdalen's of Bloomfield looks more like a ranch house than a church In recent years, the parish has made several improvements to the front yard, including a beautiful flower garden and church sign. The rectory is located across the gravel parking lot from the church. The basement of the rectory also serves as a parish hall for meetings and religious education classes.

The people, the pastor, and the pastoral associate describe the dynamics in Bloomfield as a family atmosphere. St. Mary Magdalen's has a simple structure that serves the parish well without the formalities of committees and task forces. The parish council acts as a *committee of the whole* and is the only parish committee that meets on a regular basis. It addresses all ministry areas and all parish concerns, including matters that might usually be handled by a finance council. There are few formal rules or regulations.

Stories from St. Mary Magdalen's

The Tulips

We heard stories suitable for a Hollywood script, but the most heart-rending was a story about Helen and Earl, a couple who have been stalwart members of St. Mary Magdalen's for many years. Once the parish renovation was completed a few years ago, Helen decided that the parish needed a new set of spring flowers to add some color to the gardens in front of the church.

After the Sunday evening Mass, Helen announced that she and Earl would be planting tulip bulbs in front of the church. She asked parishioners to donate tulip bulbs that she and Earl would plant. Everyone in the parish showed up the next week with tulip bulbs.

After Helen died that spring, a member of the parish built a flower bed around the tulips and the parish dedicated the flower garden to Helen. Another member built a new wooden sign in front of the church. Passers-by stop to admire the flower bed and sign. The pastoral associate notes that strangers come up to her on the street and say, "Wow, your tulips are really nice."

The Brownies

Another story that illustrates the helpful attitude of the parishioners of St. Mary Magdalen's involves Sr. Ruth needing brownies. The youth group was planning to rake leaves to raise money for a program that serves the poor, and Sister wanted to treat them afterward to brownies. Meanwhile, the Food Resources Bank was having a fundraising dinner and they needed desserts donated. To support these projects, Sr. Ruth announced after Mass that she needed brownies. As she tells the story, "I just said, 'People, please bring brownies,' and people put them on my back porch and in my car...." As they did with the tulip bulbs, everyone in the parish brought brownies. Sr. Ruth froze some brownies and donated others to another bake sale.

As one parish council member explains, "We're so small and we all take ownership, and if we don't give, then it will not happen." Another member adds, "There's no slack here. If we don't grab a hold of that yoke and pull, it isn't gonna get done."

The Church Bell

Another poignant story that demonstrates this family atmosphere involves Frank, an older gentleman who was responsible for going outside and ringing the church bell before Sunday Mass. Instead of doing it himself, Frank involved the young people in the parish by inviting them to join him. He made it lots of fun to ring the bell each Sunday. Frank would tap the shoulders of three or four children and they would go outside with him. Parents said this made a huge impression on their children, especially a third-grader named Clay.

When Frank died, Clay came up to the adults and said, "I'll take over ringing the bell before Mass." So he did. That's the kind of thing that happens at St. Mary Magdalen's. The young parishioner takes his bell-ringing job so seriously that he calls for substitutes when he is going out of town. Clay's father says the responsibility for ringing the bell gives his son a way to share in a sense of ownership that is so pervasive in this parish.

Other parish council members talked about the same sense of family their children develop in the life of this parish. One parish council member described her adult children as still feeling a part of the family of St. Mary Magdalen's. Another member explained that her children have experienced a sense of ownership by being altar servers or taking up the gifts at Mass. One parish council member says that when her daughter first decided to be an altar server, she was very nervous, "but everyone was so welcoming."

The Seven Behaviors

Here is how St. Mary Magdalen's modeled the seven behavioral categories—recognizing, serving, empowering, helping, initiating, participating, and self-developing—of servant leadership and organizational citizenship.

Recognizing

The parish council credited Sr. Ruth with taking great care in acknowledging the contributions of the parishioners at St. Mary

Magdalen's. She regularly uses the bulletin to thank people. She thanks people in her announcements after Mass. She explained how she sends cards, makes phone calls, or goes out of her way to personally thank people, even thanking visitors for coming to Mass. She seemed to institutionalize the behavior of recognizing by using the bulletin and the announcements after Mass in thanking people for their contributions to the parish.

Perhaps most notable as a sign of recognizing was the bulletin board just inside the entrance to the church. That area is used to acknowledge activities, accomplishments, or contributions of parishioners, including the art work of the children and stories from news articles about the older children being involved in various sports. It looked like a grandmother's refrigerator in the way it recognized the achievements, pictures, and stories of loved ones.

Serving

The parish council continuously described Fr. John and Sr. Ruth as humble servants who "are always doing menial tasks such as washing dishes and moving tables" and as caring persons who "are always there for us." A member of the focus group suggested that if someone in the parish needed a priest during an ice storm, that Fr. John would likely strap on his boots and drive twenty-five miles to get there. A member of the parish council also explained how Fr. John led a group of young people of the parish in making signs advertising the parish dinner and standing on the street corners in Bloomfield.

Sr. Ruth was described as a leader who is always giving credit to others, a behavior that was also observed during the focus group interaction. Both went back and forth giving credit to each other for successful projects in the parish. For example, Fr. John talked about how when the parish was holding a garage sale, Sr. Ruth was more than happy to move her car out of her garage to make room for donations. Sr. Ruth talked about how the parish would not be successful except that Fr. John allowed people to take initiative without commanding, controlling, or interfering with their initiatives.

Empowering

Many of the examples of empowerment in Bloomfield involved the simple ways that Sr. Ruth invited people to get involved in the parish or turned to ask for their help. She and Fr. John demonstrated time and again a willingness to reach out to the parish to involve the laypeople in many activities. For example, they asked the parish council to help plan and develop the Catholic evangelization program Why Catholic?[1] They regularly asked the parish council for their input, help, and assistance. When the people propose a new idea, they are open to those ideas and make every effort to get behind the people and provide support.

Helping

As the stories about the brownies and the tulip bulbs reflect, helping seems to be a hallmark of this parish. The pastor, the pastoral associate, and the parish council all described the parish as family members who help each other. With the sanctuary being just barely larger than some living rooms, the Mass felt like it was being conducted in someone's home. The people and the place felt very warm and friendly. As one long-time parishioner said, "This is a small parish...and everyone helps."

When parishioners need help, they do not hesitate to ask each other. And the parish responds. This dynamic of coming together to help is apparent in the following statement made by a parish council member in describing funerals in the parish: "Whenever there is a death, we come together, and we assist like a family."

Initiating

The small size of the parish seemed to have a direct relationship with the high levels of initiative by parishioners. The bureaucracy that sometimes stands in the way of people taking initiative does not exist at St. Mary Magdalen's. The people step up and take initiative because if they did not do it, no one else would. They said that when they see so many others getting actively involved, they are inspired to take initiative and get involved.

Sr. Ruth said the parishioners are always watching out for each other. She stated, "If they don't see somebody in church for a while, very often people will say to me, 'Do you know anything about So and So?'" and one of them will call that person and ask how he or she is doing. She added, "They tell me things they need. They will tell me in person, at church, before Mass or after Mass....It is really like a family....They just keep their eyes open, and they see a need, they just do it."

Frank showed initiative by inviting the youngsters to help. Clay did not wait for his father or anyone else to suggest that he should take over and ring the bell after Frank passed away. When a member of the parish read about Why Catholic?, the adult faith formation program for Catholic parishes, she decided to take it upon herself to start the program at St. Mary Magdalen's. She presented her case for starting this program to Sr. Ruth, who invited her to address the entire parish after Mass.

Participating

The Bloomfield parish has three Why Catholic? groups with thirty adults involved, which is astounding for a parish with forty-three families. According to the interviews and focus group, the high level of participation in the parish was directly related to the high sense of ownership of the parish. As one parish council member put it, "There is a sense in all of us, a sense of giving, a sense of ownership."

Parishioners of all ages were observed as participating in the liturgy. Several families with small children were in attendance, and one of them brought up the gifts at the Mass we attended. Children seemed to be very attentive and the pastor engaged them in several ways, including in his homily.

Self-Developing

The parish bulletin announced educational opportunities for the adults of the parish. A visitor from Africa was in attendance as she was there to talk about the Food Resources Bank project that the parish was supporting. The parish had high levels of subscriptions to the *Catholic Messenger*. The active participation in Why Catholic? and adult education opportunities noted in the parish bulletin offered ample evidence of self-developing.

Two members of St. Mary Magdalen's were involved in the lay ministry formation program, which is training future leaders for parishes in the Diocese of Davenport. Despite the fact that Bloomfield is geographically isolated from many of the training opportunities available in other parts of the diocese, self-developing seems to be a priority in this parish.

Conclusion

In sum, St. Mary Magdalen's, Bloomfield, is about family. The word *family* was used repeatedly by leaders and members in describing the parish dynamics in Bloomfield. The people at St. Mary Magdalen's treat each other as an extended family and care deeply about each other.

One story that exemplifies the family approach involved a parishioner who noticed that the front door of the church needed repair. In larger parishes, the parishioner might have talked to a member of the buildings and grounds committee who might write up a work request form that might end up on the agenda of a committee meeting. Or they might bring it to the attention of the pastor or the pastoral associate. At St. Mary Magdalen's, this parishioner just went out to his pick-up truck, pulled out his toolbox, and fixed the front door. This took about ten minutes, an efficient use of everyone's time.

This kind of initiative would not be possible in many larger parishes where formal rules and procedures outline how to respond to a need to make repairs on church buildings. But at St. Mary Magdalen's, they treat the parish buildings and church grounds as if it were their own home as well as God's. When a small repair needs to be made around the church, the parishioners just fix it. When flowers need to be planted, they plant them. When a new sign needs to be made, they make it. It sounds so simple. But this type of activity is made possible by the sense of family that we found in Bloomfield.

The dynamics of helping and initiating were illustrated in numerous stories. Families take the initiative when someone needs help. Family members don't wait for someone to tell them to help. They simply help each other.

The helping and initiating behaviors of the parishioners are not independent of those of the leaders. The recognizing, serving, and empowering behaviors of the pastor and the pastoral associate not only allowed the parishioners to take initiative, they encouraged and enhanced this family dynamic in Bloomfield. Imagine what impact the pastor would have if he scolded the parishioner who fixed the front door, or if he suggested that it was wrong to take that kind of initiative without getting approval from the pastor or pastoral associate. A new pastor coming into a small parish like Bloomfield would have to understand that *family* is a distinguishing factor that helps explain why St. Mary Magdalen's is a high-performing parish.

5

THE COMMUNITY APPROACH:
Life in Solon

The first impression you get driving into Solon, Iowa, is that the area is experiencing recent growth. New houses dot the rural landscape for several miles in each direction from Solon. With Cedar Rapids located twenty miles to the northwest and Iowa City ten miles to the south, Solon is seeing growth and development from both directions. New businesses are popping up around the outskirts of town, and downtown businesses appear to be thriving as well.

The church itself creates a stunning sense of welcome as it appears on a slight hill on the western edge of town, nestled beside a wooded area. From St. Mary's doorstep, you can see a rich panorama of life in Solon. You see several school buildings, a soccer complex, some baseball fields, and the entrance to a nature path that leads to a set of small lakes and picnic areas. The parish sanctuary was built about ten years ago. The parish hall was added a few years ago. These are signs of growth in the parish and particularly in its religious education programs.

Unique Characteristics

St. Mary's in Solon, with 516 families, is the medium-sized parish in this study. It is an interesting blend of small-town Iowa mixed with some large-city structures, systems, and expectations. The parish has a fair number of professionals, many of whom are new to town and are likely to work in Iowa City or Cedar Rapids. It also has a solid base of small-town Iowans and farmers. The varied groups in the parish seem to integrate very well. One of the first impressions you get upon entering the church is a sense of welcome. Said one member of the parish council:

This is an interesting area simply because this is an older community that has been around for more than 150 years. A lot of people have roots that go back a hundred years or more and yet we are right in the area next to Iowa City and Cedar Rapids where things are growing like crazy and we are blessed as a parish with a lot of people coming in. And the good part is that people seem to welcome the new people in. We are not a group of cliques, keeping other people out. It's a very open community.

The religious education program is a great example of the sense of welcoming and involvement at St. Mary's. For a parish of 516 families, having more than 300 elementary-aged children actively engaged in weekly religious education is remarkable. Every Thursday night, the new parish hall is filled with hundreds of children guided by about thirty-five volunteers who are teaching in the program. Meanwhile, about seventy-five high school youth are also gathering, and roughly forty adults are attending adult education classes on Thursdays.

St. Mary's utilizes the *commission model* of parish organization. Each area of ministry has a small group of people that is commissioned to that ministry. One member represents each commission on the parish council. Parish council members described a high level of collaboration between the commissions and a willingness to think outside the "silo" by collaborating on activities of the parish regardless of which commission is sponsoring the event.

Stories from St. Mary's, Solon

Parish Redesign

Several years ago, the parish council at St. Mary's was disbanded, reorganized, and eventually expanded. This parish redesign was initiated by the pastor at that time and facilitated by a diocesan leader, Deacon William T. Ditewig. It led to the creation of the commission model in the parish. Members of the parish council described this as a critical incident that enhanced the spirit of the Vatican II Council by providing the laity with more opportunities for participation. This resulted in a greater sense of ownership in the parish. Council members described the time as both a high and a low point in the life of the parish.

They said there was "lots of pain" when the parish council was first disbanded. However, they also said this redesign rekindled the life of the parish. The parish council agreed this was a turning point because it *forced* the laypeople to get more involved. St. Mary's is now actively engaged in all areas of ministry. But the most impressive ministry seems to be the faith formation programs that occur on Thursday nights.

Religious Education Night

A typical evening began with about three hundred children gathering in the main auditorium of the new parish hall. Sitting on the floor, the children watched a PowerPoint presentation leading a sing-along about Jesus. The children displayed hand signals for most of the verses. Within minutes, virtually every child was singing at the top of his or her lungs and displaying hand signals to the music. After a few songs, the music ended, and the adults led the children in reciting Catholic prayers such as the Hail Mary. Then the children went excitedly to their classrooms, where at least three adults were teaching in each classroom.

The Toddler Room

While these three hundred children were attending religious education, about twenty-five toddlers were being cared for in the Toddler Room, a corner room of the new parish hall. About eight volunteer teachers were caring for the toddlers while the parents of these children were teaching the other children or participating in the adult education classes in another section of the new parish hall.

Fr. David Wilkening, the pastor in Solon, originally did not agree with the parish lay leaders who suggested that one room in the new parish hall should be set aside for toddlers. Looking back, the pastor now considers that room one of the parish's greatest success stories. Not only does the room provide an opportunity for some parents of the toddlers to participate as adult learners or to volunteer as religious education teachers, it also is an excellent formation program for the toddlers themselves. It is well equipped and well staffed to care for these children.

Giving Credit

Fr. David, the parish council, and the volunteer teachers at Religious Education Night all gave credit to Julie Agne, the director of religious education, for the success of religious education night. Julie was described by parishioners as a young adult with massive amounts of energy, enthusiasm, and a spirit of service. The volunteers state that when she asks them to help, it is almost impossible to say "No" because she gives so much of herself to the parish and to its youngsters. Fr. David said, "We have a smart, articulate director of religious education who is totally committed to the faith. She is a real mover and a shaker. She gets things done. She gets all the credit for our faith formation program."

At the same time, Julie credited *everyone else* in the parish for the success of this program. She pointed to Fr. David for his servant-like leadership behaviors, the volunteer teachers for giving so freely of their time, and the parish council for their support. She also said that the success of the program was the work of the Holy Spirit.

Team Teaching

The teaching of religious education at St. Mary's was conducted in teams. Each classroom was staffed with a team of three to four volunteers. Some teachers said that the team approach enabled some people to participate when they might not have had the confidence, the time, or the energy to teach by themselves. According to one teacher, it is common for teachers in the religious education system to train their assistants to take their place when they are ready to retire.

The Seven Behaviors

Here is how St. Mary's in Solon modeled the seven behavioral categories—recognizing, serving, empowering, helping, initiating, participating, and self-developing—of servant leadership and organizational citizenship.

Recognizing

Fr. David was continually thanking his parishioners in his homily, in his announcements after Mass, and when visiting with people informally. Julie described her role in working with volunteers in the parish in this way: "You support them. You encourage them. You thank them, you thank them, and you thank them."

In his homily on the day of our field visit, Fr. David used a theme of "Thanks and keep it up" in talking about progress in the parish, including the annual diocesan appeal. He thanked the people for their past generosity and asked them to "keep it up." He used a similar style as he thanked the congregation for attending a recent event and asked them to "keep it up" by attending some upcoming events. The parish bulletin thanked members of the congregation for giving generously to the food collection for the local crisis center.

Serving

One member of the focus group said that Fr. David "is a servant from head to toe right through his entire system." Another described him as a humble man who "walks his talk." Someone else emphasized that Fr. David is one who always practices stewardship. Several people pointed out that he is readily willing to admit his own mistakes, as he had with the Toddler Room. Others said he is open to the ideas of others even when it doesn't fit his own personal needs and interests. Yet another parishioner noticed that Fr. David always waits for the others in the parish to go through the food line first at parish functions.

Julie noticed the same thing about the pastor. She said that at potlucks, "He's the last one to eat. It's a servant thing." In our interview with Fr. David, he deflected any credit for the success of the parish. He routinely *gave* credit for the parish success to laypeople such as Julie. He admitted his mistakes readily and talked about how he apologizes to members of the parish when he "needles them" too hard. He stated that he is "willing to do whatever needs to be done for the good of the community." Julie echoed that statement when she suggested that she is willing to help with all kinds of ministry projects, even when "you never know what you are going to end up doing."

Empowering

Fr. David described his approach to empowering his parishioners as "contact and consider." To him, this means that he personally contacts members of the parish and asks them to consider taking on a certain project or position of leadership for the parish. Then he contacts them again at a later time to follow up on the initial contact.

Julie demonstrated empowering behaviors when she said, "It's not only about thanking them, but teaching them to thank, to empower and to support." Fr. David illustrated empowerment with a story about telling his social action commission that he was willing to attend a workshop with them if they would go. He did this to increase lay participation. The parish council described Fr. David as someone who was continually inviting people to participate, to get involved, or to go to training sessions with him.

Several parish council members pointed to the parish council reorganization as a turning point because it empowered the laity to get more involved. The parish council went from a small group of four or five individuals to a much larger and more active team with intentional representation from each of the parish commissions, such as family life, social action, church life, faith formation, and liturgy. One of the most compelling statements about empowerment came from a parish council member who stated that Fr. David is "extremely adept at giving the people the power of feeling like they own things and they are involved."

During the field visit, Fr. David empowered the people by involving them directly in various ways during the liturgy. During the homily, he used a poll to ask the congregation questions about the readings. His presiding at the liturgy was warm, welcoming, and encouraging. He engaged the laypeople by enhancing the interaction between the priest and the people during the liturgy.

Fr. David and Julie have institutionalized their empowering behaviors by routinely asking the parish council and others for their input, by utilizing many volunteers in the faith formation program, and by offering to attend ministry trainings with parishioners in order to increase attendance at these events.

Helping

Fr. David described the people as "willing to help out," especially if it did not entail joining any sort of committee or require attendance at meetings. The former is an indication of *helping behaviors*, whereas the latter is more of an indication of *participating behaviors*. One member said that recognizing how hard the pastor works "makes you feel like if he needs a hand, you will help him out."

The team teaching style of the parish religious education program was another indication of helping. It was impressive that so many adults, including Julie and Fr. David, could call so many children by name. This was particularly true in the Toddler Room, where the adults knew each other's children and the small children were willing to go into the arms of adults other than their parents.

Initiating

The parish is described by the parish council as a place where "we have a lot of new things going on." Julie described many of the activities of the parish as "lay led," which is the essence of initiative. Parish council members explained how they take information that is presented at one meeting and share it at other meetings.

During the field visit, it became clear that Solon was a place where many new programs are being attempted, new ideas are being developed, and growth is occurring. The building of the new parish hall and sanctuary are wonderful examples of this growth and development. The new ideas being carried out in the various faith formation activities and the signs of life in the new parish hall are indications of initiative.

Participating

The commission model at St. Mary's, Solon, with its many manifestations in parish life, involves large numbers of people in the parish. More than two hundred adults were attending weekly sessions of Why Catholic? In addition, 375 children were attending either religious education classes or youth ministry on Thursday nights.

"Welcoming" is considered a participating behavior for the purpose of this study, and St. Mary's seemed to excel in this ministry. Several members of the parish council described the parish as an "open community" that is welcoming of new members. Upon our parish visit, the Sunday morning liturgy felt warm and inviting. The ushers smiled and greeted us warmly as we entered the church. All ages of people were singing and responding to prayer responses with a great sense of enthusiasm. The people went out of their way to greet us and each other with the sign of peace during the Mass and visit with us after Mass.

Self-Developing

Spiritual development is certainly an important part of self-developing for parish leaders. Fr. David and Julie both talked about prayer being an hourly part of their day. They are prayerful people who are very mindful of their spiritual development.

We heard many stories about Fr. David inviting parishioners to attend diocesan ministry trainings on social action, stewardship, and faith formation. Even more significantly, he offered to attend those events with his parishioners in order to encourage them to go. People in the parish responded more favorably to the invitation when he was willing to attend the trainings with them.

The self-development of the volunteer teachers was also an important factor in Solon. One teacher indicated that she was training another volunteer to take her place. This included formal training and mentoring. A parish council member expressed appreciation for the fact that the exceptional youth programs in Solon were not only helping the youth grow in their faith but were also helping them to "grow as parents."

Interesting Note

Solon (the medium-sized parish) ranked higher than Iowa City (the largest parish) but lower than Bloomfield (the smallest parish) in helping, initiating, and participating. Solon ranked in the middle on all of these behaviors (see appendix I).

Conclusion

In short, St. Mary's, Solon is about *community*. The most memorable part of the parish visit to Solon was the Thursday night faith formation program. The words used to describe this weekly event were a "deep sense of community." People greeted each other warmly, reached out to embrace each other, spoke joyfully about seeing each other, called each other by name, held each other's children, and seemed genuinely happy to be attending faith formation.

The parish staff walked around the parish hall greeting the arriving parents, children, and adults attending the faith formation programs held on Thursday night. The recognizing, serving, and empowering behaviors of the staff enhanced the participation among the laity. With about three hundred children and seventy-five youth in attendance, the leaders could easily have been running around taking care of the many details associated with such an event, but they clearly showed more concern about the relationships among the people. They were building a sense of community among the parishioners, and that was the most distinguishing factor for St. Mary's, Solon.

6

THE TEAMS APPROACH:
Life in Iowa City

St. Mary's, Iowa City, is located on the edge of the University of Iowa campus. The proximity of the parish to the campus is felt immediately when looking for a parking space near the church. St. Mary's is located on the corner of Linn and Jefferson Streets, a busy thoroughfare. One-way traffic heads along the south entrance to the church. With the campus right next door to the church, it is amazing that anyone finds a place to park, let alone the fifteen hundred or so individuals who attend Mass on an average weekend.

Iowa City is one of the wealthier areas of Iowa. The Big Ten Conference campus, a university hospital, and various research institutes provide an economic backbone that few areas of Iowa can enjoy. New housing for the city is sprawling in every direction, swallowing up the surrounding farmland. Commuters to Iowa City drive from surrounding towns and villages. The city has four Catholic parishes that were founded by various ethnic groups. While other areas of the diocese have been forced to consolidate and cluster their parishes, Iowa City is building two new churches, one to move and replace St. Patrick's, which was destroyed in a tornado a few years ago, and the other to move St. Thomas More from the central city out into the suburbs where the people are building new housing.

Unique Characteristics

With 1,690 families and 4,537 individuals registered in the parish, St. Mary's, Iowa City, is the largest parish in the diocese. A growing parish, St. Mary's accepted 473 new Catholics into the parish through baptisms from 2000 to 2005, which ranks as the second highest in the Diocese of Davenport during that period. Sharing a Catholic school system with three other parishes in the Iowa City area, St. Mary's devoted about 65 percent of its parish income to the Regina Catholic School in 2005, with that percentage growing in recent years.

Size was described as both a strength and a challenge for the parish. On one hand, the large size of St. Mary's offers lots of diversity and, with it, a myriad of gifts and talents among the parishioners. Fr. Ken Kuntz, the pastor, mentioned that he has a lawyer, a banker, an architect, and other professional people he can and does call upon. In fact, he points out that having such expertise in the parish frees him up to focus on pastoral ministry.

On the other hand, the large number of parishioners requires more formalization and standardization than witnessed in either Bloomfield or Solon. For example, the office manager described the record-keeping as demanding. The hired staff recruits, develops, and trains volunteers, organizes team activities, and keeps track of the varied events and activities, commissions and committees, councils and volunteers of the parish. Parishioners told us that it is easy to get lost in the crowd.

One of the ways that a large organization overcomes the challenges of its large size is by breaking into smaller groups, such as church commissions. Organizational theorists teach us that as organizations get bigger, they must get smaller. The proficient use of the commissions at St. Mary's is described by several parish council members as "teamwork." As one parish council member states, "It's just a team, and I really think that St. Mary's has that team together, through all these commissions."

One member of the parish council was quoted as stating in the focus group, "This is a community where everyone jumps in when called upon...but that's a spirit that is difficult to identify why. I think we all have a million other things that we have to do, but at the same time... seeing the people you know putting equal if not more amount of effort into making this church the way it is."

Stories from St. Mary's, Iowa City

Neighborhood Outreach

One of the biggest projects underway at St. Mary's is the neighborhood outreach and development project initiated in 2001. This project involves 190 parishioners who reach out to members of the parish in a neighborhood-by-neighborhood process. This is a massive effort to break down the large size of St. Mary's and to reduce it into manageable units of ten to twelve families per neighborhood group. According to one member of the parish council, each small group is led by a volunteer who makes sure that someone from the parish knocks on the door of very parishioner three to four times a year and says, "Hey, how's everything going?" Fr. Ken is hopeful that the neighborhood outreach groups will add "a social event each year and that eventually, maybe they could develop into small faith sharing communities."

The Second Graders

A focus group participant named Tom explained how he had decided to extend his commitment to be a second grade catechism teacher at St. Mary's when his wife passed away. He took a break from teaching his Sunday school class when he was grieving the loss of his wife and at one point, he decided to quit. At that time, Tom had a child in second grade. One day, he happened to be in the back of the classroom to pick up his child when the director of religious education was explaining to the rest of the second graders how Tom's wife had just passed away, using a butterfly to illustrate the cycle of life and death.

As Tom told the story, "Unbeknownst to anybody in the room, I was standing at the back of the room...and as soon as they recognized me, those second grade kids just filled my heart, ah, the love, the tears, the hugs, and that's why I am motivated to teach religious ed. I made a vow at that time that I was in it for the duration. I knew I was there for a reason." That was ten years ago, and he is still teaching second grade catechism at St. Mary's.

Social Action Ministry

For more than twenty-five years, St. Mary's, Iowa City, has tithed 5 percent of its parish income to address the needs of the poor overseas, in the United States, or in the local community. Local, national, and international projects to provide charity and work for justice are funded through a grantmaking process that is a lay-led activity of the peace and justice commission. This program has helped launch, support, and extend many services for the poor in Iowa and elsewhere. It has also increased the parish commitment to stewardship as a way of life.

The Seven Behaviors

The following seven sections track each of our seven behaviors—recognizing, serving, empowering, helping, initiating, participating, and self-developing—to the evidence of servant leadership and organizational citizenship that we found at St. Mary's in Iowa City.

Recognizing

Patti McTaggart, the youth minister at St. Mary's, is enthusiastic about sending thank-you notes, laminating stories about the youth in the parish, and finding creative ways to show appreciation for the many ways that parishioners are active. She often circulates thank-you notes around to the whole staff to sign them before she distributes them.

This parish has institutionalized the art of recognition. They have a systematic way of thanking people for their involvement. For example, the staff circulated greeting cards for birthdays, graduations, and any other special event they could think of, in order to thank people who were involved in the parish. The parish bulletin and newsletter showed appreciation for the efforts of parishioners and thanked specific people.

Parish leaders recognize the talents of the people and call them forth. They organize events to recruit volunteers for the commissions. They keep databases that track people's interests and involvement in certain commissions. They go out of their way to personally invite people to participate in some way. And they do it repeatedly. Once people sign up for a commission or step forward to volunteer in some capacity, the parish makes sure to keep track of that person's involvement, let them know when their term of commitment is up, and thank them for participating.

Fr. Ken was very articulate in describing his intent to recognize the gifts and talents of his parishioners. "I am very impressed with the shared wisdom of the people....I don't have to wake up in the middle of the night wondering how am I going to solve this problem. I have a lot of help from a lot of people," he said. This statement is supported by evidence from the focus group, where parish council members identified many ways that the gifts and talents of the parish are utilized because they were first recognized and called forth by the pastor and other leaders.

Serving

It was compelling to see the serving behaviors of St. Mary's leaders as they demonstrated humility in their approach with people. Parishioners regularly described the pastor and pastoral associate as willing to do anything to help the parish, which sometimes meant taking on menial or difficult tasks when it served the needs of others.

Fr. Ken and Sr. Agnes Giblin, the pastoral associate, demonstrated serving in an exceptional fashion as they gave credit to other members of the parish staff or parish council for the success of St. Mary's. They took turns in crediting each other for certain accomplishments. On ten separate occasions during my one-on-one interview with him, the pastor gave credit to someone else for a successful venture in the parish. He illustrated humility with this statement: "I find that many times, I don't have the best answer. I might not know what is the best way to go. And I find that by asking the people, by going back and forth with our ideas, it is just a co-mingling of ideas and wisdom of the whole group."

During the Mass we attended, we noted the self-deprecating humor used by the parochial vicar during his homily as a serving behavior because of the humility he demonstrated. The parish leaders demonstrated enthusiastic support for a homeless outreach program and other social service projects that the parish was promoting on the day of our visit. Before our focus group began, Sr. Agnes made sure that the coffee was on and that some refreshments were served. The exceptional hospitality shown by the leaders confirmed that they were practicing the service that they preached.

Empowering

The propensity to empower was illustrated with this quote from Fr. Ken: "We don't tell people what to do. We're inviting them to participate." The youth minister suggested that the high levels of participation at St. Mary's, Iowa City, are due to the leaders' willingness and ability to invite, empower, and prepare members for ministry. She stated, "We do everything in our power to make sure that (a) they are invited and (b) they are trained."

We witnessed empowerment in action with the organization of a multitude of activities on display at the parish on the day of our site visit. Virtually every commission in the parish was preparing, organizing, or holding some type of activity that Sunday. We also witnessed empowerment behaviors in the liturgy itself. For example, the enthusiasm of the music leaders as they elicited lay response, such as the encouraging manner in which they lifted their arms, was an invitation for the congregation to join them in singing.

One formal method of recruitment and empowerment is Invitation Sunday, an annual event when new members are recruited for all the parish commissions. Fr. Ken estimated that fifteen to twenty new laypeople emerge as new members of the commissions as a result of each Invitation Sunday. This is a way of institutionalizing the empowerment of laypeople into the ministry of the parish.

The system is designed to identify the gifts and interests of laypeople and to assign them to certain areas of ministry using the commission structure of the parish. The active nature of the parish council, finance council and lay trustees, and the commissions organized around all nine areas of ministry were indicative of empowerment.

Helping

As a large parish with many formal activities, it seemed that most of the activity at St. Mary's was more likely to be coded as participation than helping, because most ministry is usually done in the context of a commission or a formal program of the parish. However, despite our definitional differences between participation and helping, we found evidence of helping.

For example, Fr. Ken indicated that some members of the parish are called upon to provide legal or financial advice outside the formal avenues of the parish. The parish council praised two women named Rosemary who are always readily available "to show interest and help out." Patti told a moving story about a ninety-two-year-old woman who helps out every Monday morning by cleaning all of the pews in the church. This woman was described as a "quiet, unassuming woman…who never complains, just goes about her work."

Initiating

At St. Mary's in Iowa City, initiative takes place within the context of formal groups such as commissions. The participants in the focus group indicated that commissions are lay-led activities. According to the evidence heard in the focus groups and interview, the commissions are primarily led by the initiative of laypeople. Parish council members express confidence they can take initiative on certain ideas without worrying about interference from the pastor or other leaders in the parish. "They know what we are doing," one parish council stated, "but it's our thing."

Participating

Of the seven behaviors, empowerment and participation seemed to be the hallmarks of this parish. These two behaviors seem to run parallel to each other. Members of the parish council expressed a high sense of ownership of the parish, which was coded as a sign of participation. A number of parish council members indicated this with quotes such as, "I really take ownership of this." An extraordinary number of parishioners were participating in a broad array of formal activities at St. Mary's. As a parish council member stated, "There's a lot of options to be involved here."

The programs available to the parishioners form an impressive list, as evidenced by the packet of brochures, bulletins, and program materials provided by Sr. Agnes during our field visit. The packet was 6 inches thick! On the day we visited St. Mary's as a research team, activity in the parish was overflowing. Volunteers were performing a multitude of tasks in the parish hall. One group was conducting a flu shot outreach clinic. The peace and justice commission was recruiting parishioners to get involved at a homeless shelter. Other parishioners were attending one of several faith formation programs.

As Sr. Agnes said:

This morning, you could walk through and find five commissions with events. You've got the liturgy with the sacrament of the sick.... You've got the family life sponsoring the flu shot clinic in the parish hall, you've got the peace and justice asking for people for the homeless over-flow shelter, you've got fellowship serving coffee and donuts as well as sign-up for the altar and rosary bazaar, and you've got faith formation happening up at the Newman Center with the adults that are going to be professing their faith, being confirmed and making their first Communion.

Self-Developing

Opportunities for growth and development abound in Iowa City, a university town. Yet people in Iowa City are looking for some things that a *public* university cannot provide. Fr. Ken said that his parishioners were seeking opportunities for spiritual enrichment. "People really want to go deeper. It's really a mystery but we do have some people who really want to grow spiritually and develop themselves," he said.

The bulletin at St. Mary's was loaded with references to self-developing opportunities and activities. As one participant in the focus group stated, some type of ministry training is held every two to three months in this parish.

Interesting Note

The two highest scores in Iowa City were empowering and participating, respectively, which was the same as in Solon, where participating and empowering were the highest scores. These were the two larger parishes in this study. This suggests that as the size of parish increases, levels of participation and empowerment also increase (see appendix I).

Conclusion

In brief, St. Mary's, Iowa City, is about *teamwork*. The largest parish in the diocese bustled with a multitude of programs organized in many areas of ministry. It would be easy for a person to get lost in a parish this size, but St. Mary's seems to have mastered the art of organizing parish ministry through the use of teams and small groups that are sometimes referred to as commissions. These are teams united by a common sense of mission, as implied by the word *commission*.

The leaders of these commissions took their lay leadership very seriously, calling upon new parishioners to join in the ministry, organizing the fine details of upcoming programs, communicating that to the rest of the parish, recruiting new members to join the commission, and rotating leadership on the commissions so that leaders do not wear out. The degree of organization at St. Mary's was most impressive. It was clear that the leaders recognized, served, and empowered in ways that enhanced the high levels of participation. At the core of the organizational framework in this parish was the use of teams to pull all the areas of ministry together. For this reason, *teamwork* is identified as the distinguishing quality at St. Mary's, Iowa City.

7

PARISH RESULTS:
Love Is the Measure

The questions we explored in our model parishes include:

- What evidence of *love* would be found if outside observers were to view the inside of our parishes?
- What behaviors would be found in a parish community that is centered in *love* and practices *love* with each other and toward the world?
- What evidence would we find that the people in a parish *love* one other?

In other words:

- If God is love, and if love is the measure of God's presence, then how is that *love* manifested in a parish?

This chapter responds to these questions by describing the positive results we found for all seven measured behaviors. Our most significant results suggest that love is manifested through the behavioral signs of servant leadership and organizational citizenship. Our case study provides empirical support for our proposal that the practice of servant leadership nets strong positive results for parishes. It also adds support to the theory that organizational citizenship is a positive sign of organizational performance. In addition, we found evidence that explains how and why servant leadership enhances organizational citizenship (see chapter 8).

Certainly, there may be additional factors that explain why our three parishes are succeeding. Our study, of course, did not explore every possible explanation of parish success. It would be inadvisable to use the results of our study alone to argue that servant leadership is the primary cause of high performance in parish life. Yet it is significant that while the three parishes in our study were initially identified through financial and demographic data, each of these parishes showed the behavioral patterns that fit what proponents of servant leadership and organizational citizenship prescribe for high performance.

Our Results

We found positive and empirical support in each parish for each of the seven measured behaviors: recognizing, serving, empowering, helping, initiating, participating, and self-developing. These behaviors are emblematic of a community rooted in love. When leaders recognize, empower, and serve the people, they express their love for their congregation by placing the needs and interests of parishioners ahead of their own. When the people respond to the leaders by helping, initiating, participating, and self-developing, they express their love as well. The result in these high-performing parishes is a culture in which the leaders and the people put others first.

The evidence presented in this chapter posits that these seven behaviors typify high-performing parishes. This is especially true for empowering leadership behaviors and participating membership behaviors. In fact, empowerment and participation seemed to be associated with each other in the behavioral interaction that was identified among the leaders and members of these three parishes (as discussed in chapter 8).

Parish Life Measures

Our study began as an attempt to respond to Bishop Franklin's question, "How do you measure the life of a parish?" One important result of our study was the three-part model we created for measuring parish life.

First, parish life can be measured in terms of **strategic measures** such as mission, vision, and strategic goals. Strategic measures are reflective of nine areas of parish ministry: liturgy, faith formation, social action, finance, evangelization, stewardship, vocations, family life, and church life. Strategic measures were gathered in the

Diocese of Davenport when all eighty-four parishes submitted a self-assessment based on these nine areas of ministry.

Second, parish life can be measured by **operational measures** such as demographics and finance. Operational measures were the financial data and sacramental reports compiled in the parish life study. This data was identified by our parish life evaluators as the basis for selecting the three model parishes of this study. It included measures such as average number of people attending weekend liturgies and faith formation sessions, average monetary contribution per parishioner, and whether those numbers were moving up or down over a five-year period.

Third, parish life can be measured by **behavioral measures** that reflect the quality of community life and the interaction between leaders and members in the parish. Behavioral measures became the basis for the field study of three parishes. Behaviors are important because they can be observed, measured, changed, and taught. They can be measured because they can be observed. Once they are measured, they can be used to set benchmarks for behavioral change or to set goals that will target certain organizational results.

Behavioral Measures

One contribution of our study to the discussion about parish life and leadership is our focus on how and what organizational behaviors—including those of leaders and members—distinguish a high-performing parish. In our search for behavioral evidence, we tried to demystify some of the theological aspects of parish life by viewing the parish through the lenses of sociology, psychology, and political science. Parishes are organizations, and as such they can be explored as human behavior in a social environment. Our field study suggests that the behaviors of the leaders and members of a Christian parish can be viewed as successful, both in terms of organizational science and by the standards of religious principles, particularly the message of Jesus, who taught *leaders to be servants* (Mark 10:43) and *members to be disciples* (Matt 28:19).

Behavioral change through a conversion of heart was a recurring theme in the message and example of Jesus. He taught his disciples to turn away from self-serving ways and instead to love one another

(John 13:35). He challenged his disciples to change their approach to leadership when he stated, "Whoever wants to be first must be last of all and servant of all" (Mark 9:35). And in one of his most difficult lessons, he modeled service to others by taking up the towel and washing their feet (John 13:1–5).[1]

The Seven Behaviors

Our seven categories of behaviors—recognizing, serving, empowering, helping, initiating, participating, and self-developing— provide a description of what we found in our model parishes. Next we look at the behavioral results of our study and assess their significance for parish life and leadership (see appendix I for comparison of results across all three parishes).

Recognizing

Recognizing was an important factor for our model parishes, although not as high as the other two leader behaviors.[2] The leaders in our study rarely talked about recognizing behaviors but were observed as using them routinely in their interaction with parishioners. In his homily, the pastor in Solon followed the dual theme, "Thank you and keep it up." The parish bulletin in all three parishes was used to recognize parishioners for their special contributions to the life of the parish. Parishioners described how the "tap on the shoulder" from their parish leaders was an invitation to lay ministry.

Recognizing includes thanking people for a job well done, but it does not start or end there. In the model parishes we studied, recognizing began with the identification and calling forth of the gifts and talents of the parishioners. This is reflective of the advice of *Lumen Gentium*: "Each individual part contributes through its special gifts to the good of the other parts and of the whole Church."[3] After the gifts and talents of the parishioners are placed into service, their contributions were acknowledged as the leaders found various and creative ways to say "Thank you." Recognizing includes both the identification of the gifts and talents of the members as well as the affirmation of the contributions made.

Our findings suggest that if leaders recognize the gifts and talents of their parishioners and express appreciation for the contributions of members of a parish, parishioners will respond by helping, initiating, participating, and self-developing. Research on organizational citizenship has demonstrated that supportive leadership behaviors, such as recognizing, enhance OCBs such as the four we studied here.[4] The importance of recognition in a parish is also consistent with the research finding that the most important nonfinancial reward identified by employees in a workplace is "a simple Thank you."[5]

Serving

We found moderately high levels of evidence in each parish for serving behaviors. Defined here as putting the needs and interests of others ahead of those of the leader, serving is a core element of servant leadership. Robert Greenleaf's original essay on servant leadership stated that the servant leader is first and foremost a servant, someone who cares for others. "It begins with the natural feeling that one wants to serve, to serve first," Greenleaf wrote.[6] Leaders are to become servants and servants are to become leaders.

When James and John were lobbying for leadership roles among the disciples, Jesus stated, "You know that the rulers of the Gentiles lord it over them, and their great ones are tyrants over them. It will not be so among you; but whoever wishes to be great among you must be your servant" (Matt 20:25–27) .The key point here is "not so among you." Jesus is advising against the command-and-control leadership style of the Roman Empire or the scribes and Pharisees. Instead, he suggests a leadership style that serves others. This idea that leaders should practice *servanthood* later became the basis for the essays by Greenleaf on servant leadership.[7]

The leaders in these three parishes were not hierarchical leaders seated on pedestals, but were actively engaged with their people as servants. We found parish staff who approached their jobs as ministry instead of jobs. They viewed them as an opportunity to serve.

The service of the leaders in these congregations mirrored the bold words of Joshua, who stated, "As for me and my household, we will serve the Lord" (Josh 24:15). The service in these parishes began with a desire to serve God. Just as love of God is manifested through love of neighbor, these leaders' service to God was manifested in their service to their neighbors, those inside and outside of the parish. It also was evident in their devoted service to the parish itself.

Empowering

We found the highest level of behavioral evidence for the category of empowering behaviors. In fact, empowering was the highest scoring leadership behavior in each of the three parishes. Empowerment follows the "Iron Rule," which is inviting and allowing others to act on their own behalf. While the Golden Rule suggests that we "do unto others," the Iron Rule is a community organizing principle that suggests, "*Never do unto others what they can do for themselves.*" Empowerment is a sharing of power with others in such a way that builds the capacity of the people to do things for themselves.

Defined here as enabling members to fully participate, empowerment is clearly representative of what the OCB literature suggests is a supportive behavior.[8] Like recognizing and serving, the empowering behaviors found in our study were consistent with what the OCB research describes as *supportive* leadership behaviors associated with the enhancement of organizational citizenship and the ensuing increase in organizational performance.[9]

We found parish structures for lay involvement, the inclusion of parishioners in collaborative decision-making processes, and the teaching, modeling, and encouraging that builds capacity for others to act.[10] The benefits of empowerment were seen in the changes in the followers, in the reduced workload of the leader, and in the growth in parish activities. The pastors in our study said that empowerment led to a greater peace of mind as they awakened in the people a greater sense of responsibility for the parish. They also said it freed up their time and energy to devote themselves more fully to priestly ministry. The parishioners indicated a greater sense of ownership of the parish when they were empowered.

Empowerment fits the servant leadership model presented by Greenleaf, who suggests that the "best test" of the servant leader is whether those being served grow as persons and become healthier, wiser, freer, and more autonomous while being served.[11] According to Greenleaf, the role of the leader is not to dominate or to coerce but to serve others, to care for others "in ways that require dedication and skill and that help them grow and become healthier, stronger and more autonomous."[12] Servant leadership involves developing the followers in ways that prepare them for leadership.[13]

Self-confidence is a leadership trait that seems to be associated with empowerment. Ironically, it is the leaders who *lack* confidence who tend to be the most controlling. To allow parishioners to act on their own behalf requires self-confidence from the leader. While some may perceive empowerment as the transfer of power away from the leader, and therefore a loss for the leader, the empowering leader realizes that power can grow exponentially when the people are allowed the opportunity to take action. The parish leaders we interviewed were willing to delegate responsibility to others, even when they thought they could do it better themselves. A self-confident pastor who empowers parishioners can increase the participation of parishioners while benefiting from the opportunity to focus more clearly on the leadership responsibilities of being a pastor.

It seems logical to contend that if empowerment increases the capacity of members to act, participation should be enhanced when parish leaders empower their members. The evidence in our study supports that logic. Based on our findings, it seems clear that further research into the effectiveness of empowerment as an approach to parish leadership is warranted. Parishes need to pay particular attention to finding ways to increase empowerment of their members.

Helping

We found high levels of helping behaviors in all three parishes in our study. That helping behaviors would be associated with high performance in a Catholic parish is consistent with both the Christian norms of loving our neighbor as well as the organizational research that shows that helping behaviors enhance organizational performance in the workplace.[14] When Jesus is asked to clarify who was to be included in his definition of *neighbor*, he told the story of the Good Samaritan, who helps a stranger in distress. The research on organizational citizenship also uses the Christian story of the Good Samaritan (Luke 10:30–37) as an example of someone who practices helping behaviors because he showed altruistic behaviors without receiving a formal reward.

Helping is defined in the OCB literature as voluntary, altruistic, and prosocial behavior.[15] Empirical studies have consistently demonstrated that helping is significantly associated with nearly every measure of organizational performance, including efficiency, customer satisfaction, and quality indicators.[16]

The most interesting aspect of the findings about helping was the extensive levels of evidence discovered in Bloomfield, the smallest parish in our study—in fact, the smallest parish in the diocese. Size of parish seemed to provide some explanation of the differences in the results on helping. The only formal group at St. Mary Magdalen's is the parish council, which acts as a committee of the whole on business pertaining to any area of ministry. The parish has no other formal committees, commissions, or councils. Instead of formal participation, the OCBs exhibited in Bloomfield took the form of helping. The extensive helping that we observed in Bloomfield seemed to be congruent with the use of the word *family* that was used to describe the interpersonal dynamics at St. Mary Magdalen's.

Examples of helping behavior were exceptional in Bloomfield, where parishioners treated the church with the care and attention of a family home. The bulletin board placed inside the front door of the church reminded the research team of the pictures, photographs, news clippings, and children's art work that one might find on a grandparent's refrigerator. The parish council spoke of the church with a great sense of ownership.

Initiating

The discovery of evidence supporting the hypothesis on initiative in these three parishes was expected, but the difference based on size of parish was surprising. Like the findings on helping, what was interesting about this organizational citizenship behavior is that it scored much more highly in Bloomfield than in the other two parishes. In a small parish, it seems that having fewer formal groups means fewer formal rules, policies, and procedures. The leaders and parishioners said that when something needed to be done at St. Mary Magdalen's, someone would take the initiative. With fewer structural obstacles, the members of the parish seemed more willing to take steps to get things done.

The metaphor of family seems to fit a parish that takes initiative. When a family member perceives a need for someone else in a family, they do not wait for someone to tell them what needs to be done. An expression used several times by Sr. Ruth to describe the people in Bloomfield was "they just do it" or "it just gets done." It was not necessary to get permission to do things like welcome newcomers, organize hospitality for a church function, or fix the church door. When permission was necessary, they found a simple process to initiate a new project, such as the way they started Why Catholic?

Initiative was defined here as taking charge or volunteering to get a certain job done. Like the other member behaviors in our study, initiative was a behavior that meant going above and beyond the formal call of duty.[17] Initiative falls outside the parameters of one's job description or beyond the formal directions given by the leader. It takes a certain type of leadership by the follower to take initiative. It also requires a certain type of leadership by the leader to allow the person to take initiative. The leader needs to have the self-confidence to allow followers the freedom to take initiative.

Participating

All three model parishes scored very well in participating in our study. Size of parish seemed to affect the incidence of participation, with the larger parishes showing more participation instead of helping and initiating. At St. Mary's in Iowa City, the largest parish in the diocese, the parishioners are very actively involved in participating in many formal programs based in their highly efficient system of councils, commissions, and committees. The distinction between helping and participation, and the difference in size of parishes in this study, explains why a large parish like Iowa City scored more highly on participation while a small parish like Bloomfield scored higher on helping and initiating.

Participating involves a more formal activity. OCB studies refer to participation as "civic virtue" because it expresses the sense of being "citizens of an organization."[18] Participation was an indication that parishioners had a sense of ownership of the parish. People who own something are more likely to get formally involved. The essential behaviors of participation include:

- That parish members show up for programs and activities
- That parishioners are engaged in committee meetings
- That laypeople get involved in the governance of the parish
- That the laity is involved in various ministries of the parish
- That parish members speak openly about their opinions when decisions are being made

Several of those interviewed used the word *team* to describe the parish dynamics in Iowa City. Teams seems to be a fitting description for that parish given the size of the organization, the level of interdependence between the various commissions, the common sense of purpose, and the sense of group accountability that typify the work of teams.[19] With their efficient use of teams, parishioners in Iowa City who want to get involved have a broad array of formal opportunities for participation, whereas the size of the parish in Bloomfield left only one formal group for participation—the parish council that acted as a committee of the whole.

The team *dynamic* can also be explained by understanding what research has discovered about the effects of organizational size on the internal dynamics of any organization. As the size of an organization increases, it becomes more formalized, bureaucratized, and institutionalized.[20] A solution to the challenges of size, according to Larry Greiner, is the "decentralization of the entire organization."[21] In other words, as an organization gets larger, it has to figure out a way to become smaller. This helps explain why Iowa City needs to be so proficient in the use of teams.

Self-Developing

We found a moderate level of evidence on self-developing in each of the three parishes. *Self-development* is defined here as the discretionary activities that develop skills and knowledge for getting a job done.[22] Self-developing could include voluntary participation in training courses, educational programs, or informal activities that improve one's ability to contribute to the organization or daily activities that parish members practice to improve their preparation for ministry. Leaders and members in our high-performing parishes were sensitive to the need to learn and grow continuously, especially given the growing need for ministry in a fast-changing and secular world, the growing shortage of priests in the Catholic church, and the gap created between the supply of priests and the demand for services.

Self-developing has emerged as one of the seven primary dimensions of OCBs.[23] The argument is that self-developing behaviors of members in an organization should enhance the innovative and creative performance of an organization as members learn and grow through autonomous efforts to improve themselves. The encouragement of self-developing by servant leaders can be inferred from Greenleaf's "best test" that asks if those being served grow as persons, become healthier, wiser, freer, and more likely to be servants themselves.[24]

Greenleaf framed leadership effectiveness in terms of the growth and development of the followers because servant leadership is a follower-centric leadership approach. The success of the leader is defined in terms of the success of the follower. Servant leaders in our model parishes recognized the need to develop the ministry skills of their parishioners. They created opportunities for lay ministry training and made sure they were available, accessible, and effective for all in the parish. They also suggested that self-development among the laity will become even more important as we experience an increasing shortage of priests. High-performing parishes emphasize the importance of lifelong learning for everyone.

Conclusion

Our study found empirical evidence that suggests that high-performing parishes can indeed be described as actively engaged in servant leadership and organizational citizenship. We believe that the organizational citizenship is what drives the successful performance of the parish, and the servant leadership is what drives the organizational citizenship. This is consistent with the empirical findings that organizational citizenship behaviors are associated with high performance.[25] Research suggests five possible explanations for why OCBs generate high levels of organizational performance. OCBs

1. Enhance levels of trust, commitment, and other factors that add **social capital**[26]
2. Free up key organizational resources for more productive purposes[27]
3. Develop a greater level of team spirit and cohesiveness[28]
4. Lubricate the social machinery in an organization[29]
5. Help organizations to attract and retain the best people[30]

These five reasons might explain why we found high levels of OCBs in our three model parishes. Further research and study on OCBs in parish life would add more validity to our findings.[31] Nevertheless, the research in organizational citizenship has some of the most solid empirical findings in organizational science. The research shows that OCB in any organization adds a whole range of benefits. For a parish, this includes the efficient use of parish resources, the creation of team spirit, the attraction and retention of new members and leaders, the high levels of trust in the parish, and the development of social capital to bridge the space between people in a parish.[32]

The results summarized in this chapter are *descriptive* evidence of servant leadership and organizational citizenship.[33] In the next chapter, we provide *explanatory* evidence that links SLBs and OCBs in the life of a parish and explains how and why servant leadership works. To do this, we look at the relationship between the leader and member behaviors that we found.

8

SERVANT LEADERSHIP:
How and Why It Works

In chapter 7 we provided descriptive evidence for servant leadership and how it works in our three parishes. We now move toward explanatory evidence of why servant leadership works. We first provide a more thorough description of how servant leadership works. Then we offer a possible explanation of why servant leadership affects organizational citizenship by presenting seven possible behavioral mechanisms that we gleaned from our research. We think these mechanisms explain why the behavioral interaction between the parish leaders and members motivated the people to respond with organizational citizenship behaviors such as helping, initiating, participating, and self-developing.

Research cited earlier suggests that certain leader behaviors, such as supportive and follower-centric leadership, can enhance organizational citizenship.[1] Church teaching about parish life also supports servant leadership. The Vatican II document *Lumen Gentium* suggests that the full benefits of the diversity of religious congregations can be realized when church leaders provide every opportunity for lay participation and initiative "so that, according to their abilities and the needs of the times, they may zealously participate in the saving life of the church."[2]

The key to the human interaction between servant leaders and parish citizens is explained in this quote from *Lumen Gentium*:

> *Let sacred pastors recognize and promote the dignity as well as the responsibility of the layman in the church. Let them willingly make use of his prudent advice. Let them confidently assign duties to him in the service of the church, allowing him freedom and room for action. Further, let them encourage the layman so he may undertake tasks on his own initiative.*[3]

Our study provides many examples that reflect the truth of this statement, regardless of parish size.

How Servant Leadership Works

The most common example we found of behavioral interaction between leaders and followers was that empowerment enhanced participation in parish life. Empowerment, in the words of one parish council member, is "giving people the power of feeling like they own things and they are involved." What follows are some specific examples demonstrating how specific actions of parish leaders increased certain OCBs in these parishes.

Recognizing

Thanking the People

Patti, the youth minister in Iowa City, explained how her parish personally recognizes parishioners by sending regular thank-you notes, greeting cards, and gifts to people who volunteer in various ways in the parish. Of special note was a gift certificate the parish had just bought for a volunteer named Marie, a ninety-two-year-old woman who cleans the church pews every Monday. The whole parish staff routinely showed their appreciation for volunteers by circulating thank-you notes to parishioners.

Finding the Talent

When recruiting a new person to get involved with the youth in her parish in Iowa City, Patti said, "Bill, you are really good at woodworking and the kids are coming over to polish the pews. Could you be there to help show them how it is done?" Notice that in this case of recognizing, Patti is affirming someone else's talents and building his confidence to share that talent with the youth in the parish. This kind of recognition increases the likelihood that Bill would help the youth group.

A finance council member in Iowa City stated, "I had been involved with finances over the years, and he [the pastor] recognized that as a very valuable talent." In this example, a parishioner is pointing out that his participation in the parish was directly related to the recognition of his financial talents by Fr. Ken. Once the talent was identified and recognized as important to the parish, Fr. Ken called the person forth to use the financial talents for the benefit of the entire parish, thus enabling the parishioner to participate and to help out.

Fr. Ken told his parishioners that they need to discern "what gifts and talents" they have and "to take what God has given them and put it to good use." He said that when he sees a need in the parish and knows of someone with the gifts and talents to meet that need, he invites that person to help. In describing the large number of new volunteers who step up each year, the pastor said, "I am truly grateful. I am so grateful for what they bring to each commission that we have because they really do come up with great ideas." By recognizing these talents, Fr. Ken is creating opportunities for parishioners to more fully participate in the parish. He also is demonstrating how routinely he gives credit to others for the success of the parish instead of drawing attention to himself.

Serving

Listening to the People

A parish council member in Solon described Fr. David this way: "He's always visiting people and trying to get them involved....It makes you want to help." She described a series of focus groups held years ago that became a turning point in their parish, because at that time, these focus groups helped them "feel listened to and cared for" by the parish leadership. As a result of the act of listening by the leaders, parishioners said that when "you asked someone to help, they liked it and they wanted to help again. It seemed like before, everyone was kind of doing their own thing....Now it just seemed a lot easier to get something done." The "simple" act of listening demonstrates that the leaders care for the parish, which can turn around a difficult situation and enhance the ability of the people to participate in the parish.

Giving Credit

Giving credit to others was considered a leader behavior that enhances organizational citizenship among the parishioners. A parish council member in Bloomfield pointed out that whenever someone gives Sr. Ruth "a little recognition, she is quick to say, 'Well, So and So helped' and 'So and So did their part,' she just gives it right back…which makes us want to contribute." This is an example of servant leadership because it gives credit to others. It appears in this case that the giving of credit to others has a reciprocal effect, with people giving each other credit for the success of the parish. The resulting effect was encouraging parishioners to get more involved in the parish.

Julie told us that in Solon, "we are obviously blessed with people who are open to initiating new projects so God is already working in them. We provide the tools and the two can mesh." In this case, Julie is giving credit to others for the success of the parish and then notices that God is also at work here. As a parish leader, her responsibility is to "provide the tools," which is typical of supportive leadership, thus providing the means for the people to take the initiative and contribute to the parish.

An Iowa City parish council member stated that Sr. Agnes is the kind of leader who always gives credit to others, which inspires people to respond by helping the parish. "She just shines that light; she's like a mirror that just puts the light right back on the parishioners." Giving credit to others is a serving behavior that encourages the parishioners. Her kindness to others returned full circle as the parishioners gave further support back to Sr. Agnes by getting involved in the parish. Upon hearing these comments about her from the parishioners, Sr. Agnes responded by saying, "I always tell them it's they who support me and give me the courage and the strength."

Modeling the Way

A Bloomfield parishioner described the same kind of dynamic in her interactions with Sr. Ruth, their pastoral associate. When Sr. Ruth would ask the people to give of themselves in some way, they would look around and see how much she was already giving to the parish. "You figure you have to give too, to help the community." Sr. Ruth and Fr. John were described by a parish council member as "always ready to roll up their sleeves and help do whatever needs to be done." These comments describe leaders who are willing to get involved and work side by side with their parishioners. This approach inspired others to join in as well. Helping eventually became a part of the parish culture in Bloomfield. Sr. Ruth described how one day she woke up to see that the church was under a heavy blanket of snow. Before she could even make some calls for help, she said, "There were all these people who just showed up and helped clean the sidewalk."

A parish council member in Iowa City described her involvement in the parish by pointing to Fr. Ken and Sr. Agnes. She said, "When you see that all of their time, more than they even have to give, they are spent doing things for us, and if they ask us to do one small thing, how could that, you know, how could you say no to that?" Servant leaders model the hard work that they inspire in others. No job is beneath the servant leader. One parish council member explained that it is easy to get involved at St. Mary's in Iowa City because Fr. Ken and Sr. Agnes "are just as involved as we are." This kind of modeling was a source of great inspiration and it enhanced organizational citizenship.

Changing Your Mind

A number of people told us the story, recounted in chapter 5, about Fr. David's initial opposition to plans for a new Toddler Room. The persistence of the president of the parish council eventually persuaded Fr. David to change his mind. Now the Toddler Room is used on a regular basis. On the night of our parish visit, about twenty-five toddlers were being cared for during religious education classes. This also allowed some of the teachers to volunteer while their toddlers were cared for in the Toddler Room.

In this case, Fr. David showed servant leadership because he was willing to consider the needs and interests of others and was open to the ideas and concerns of others. More important, he demonstrated humility in changing his mind. In fact, during a tour of the new parish hall during the field visit in Solon, Fr. David went out of his way to tell this story and admit that he was initially wrong. Changing his mind and admitting his mistake was a great example of the confidence needed to engage in servant leadership. Fr. David mentioned how appreciative he is of the parish council president for persisting in her plans and that he is very proud of the success of the Toddler Room.

Involving Everyone

Patti tells the story of reaching out to a young teen with Down Syndrome and getting him involved in her Iowa City youth group. She gave this young teen all the credit for the success, saying he does "a fabulous job." Giving the credit to the young teen is a servant leader behavior. Recognizing that someone with Down Syndrome can contribute to the parish youth group demonstrates the heart of a servant leader. In this case, Patti reported that the participation of the teen with Down Syndrome not only provided this young person an opportunity to participate in the parish, it appears to have had a positive impact on the youth group by introducing them to the joy of welcoming this person into their group.

Being Present

Fr. David noticed that when a commission in his Solon parish is not performing well, his attendance at their meetings will increase the lay attendance as well. This act of servant leadership has a direct effect on increasing the participation of others.

Empowering

Delegating, with Support

Delegating responsibility to others was critical to the success of our parish leaders and to the successful participation and initiative of the people. Some leaders do not delegate responsibilities because they feel that it might be easier to do something by themselves. This can be deadly, especially when the staff in a large parish assumes all the responsibilities without involving the laity.

If parish leaders are going to delegate more project responsibility to their parishioners, and not just dump unwanted projects on them, some of those projects will require ministry preparation. This might involve sending parishioners to special conferences, ministry trainings, or leadership development programs. Fr. David encouraged his parishioners in Solon to attend lay ministry trainings by offering to go with them and to pay for their expenses. He stated, "To be a vibrant parish, you need to get good lay leaders who have a passion for ministry, who can really get in there and work hard. I am willing to spend money on commissions, give them real money and a budget they can really use. We need to train them. They come back inspired."

Consulting the People

Involving the parish council and consulting with them about major decisions was a frequent refrain in our study. Fr. Ken stated, "I find that by asking the people, by going back and forth with our ideas, it is just a co-mingling of ideas and wisdom of the whole group." This quote describes collaborative decision making at its best, the "co-mingling" of everyone's needs and interests to get to a win-win solution. The sense of ownership that results inspires others to get more involved themselves. Sr. Ruth stated that when she was uncertain where to turn for help with a project in Bloomfield, "I ask the parish council, 'Who in the parish can do this?'"

Encouraging New Ideas

Fr. John suggested that when his Bloomfield parishioners want to take initiative, "We encourage them that way.... We didn't say your idea has to fit this one modality and if it doesn't you have to get a new idea." This is a great example of empowerment because it demonstrates an attitude that welcomes and encourages others to get involved and take initiative. When the leader micromanages the work of others, it can stunt the growth and development of the people. Fr. John explained that when the laypeople are really motivated to start a new ministry in the parish, "We can't curtail it.... They'd be doing it out of their home or another venue. Those who are interested will carry on somewhere, some way, somehow."

Fr. Ken showed similar levels of confidence in his Iowa City parishioners. He was very willing and eager to encourage new initiatives and ideas from the people. He described the parish council as "very capable people who do the work with very little oversight on my part. They really are very supportive of one another, take care of each other, and get a lot of things done on their own." One might suggest that the people in Iowa City are supportive and caring and involved because Fr. Ken not only encourages that activity, he also models it in his words and actions.

Collaborating Based on Trust

Fr. John described the initiative of the laypeople in Bloomfield as *synergistic*, where the sum of activity is greater than all of the parts. He also described it as **collaboration**, where all parties view the result as a *win*. Once that level of trust, commitment, and involvement is reached, the role of the leader is to continue providing encouragement and support. Fr. John stated that many times people volunteer to get something done before he was even able to recognize that it needed to be done. His willingness to support those initiatives afterward is a key factor in the continuing success of the parish.

Inviting Parishioners

Sr. Ruth stated that in Bloomfield, "When I came, I said to them, 'Tell me what you want.' And they did. They look around. They see that something needs to be done, and they tell me it needs to be done. Or sometimes they tell me they will do it. Or they will just take care of it....If they see somebody in the parish needs something, they will help them out."

Members of the St. Mary's, Iowa City, parish council explained that sometimes Fr. Ken and Sr. Agnes "tap somebody on the shoulder, saying, 'We need a little help,'" and people get involved. Once a year, St. Mary's organizes Invitation Sunday to recruit volunteers for the various commissions and ministries of the parish. When a volunteer steps up in Iowa City, they get a personal contact, either a personal note or a personal call, from a parish staff member or a lay leader of that commission. As one parish council member in Iowa City explains, "We were asked and we stepped forward."

These invitations can be helpful when they are a good fit for the member of the parish and when they involve delegating instead of simply dumping boring tasks on someone else's desk. Invitations need to be perceived as *inviting* in the eyes of the person being invited. This begins with listening and learning about the parishioner, finding out what it would take to get him to a meeting and what he could contribute if he came to that meeting. Some contributions might not even involve meetings at all. Fr. Ken described an important nuance when he said, "We are not telling people what to do, we are inviting them to participate." This kind of invitation suggests a careful consideration of the gifts, talents, needs, and interests of the people being served.

Following Up with a Phone Call

Fr. Ken explained that the Iowa City parish keeps track of "which commission needs more participation" each year and they "make sure we ask people to get involved" in that commission. After the invitation is extended, and the parishioner has agreed to serve on a commission, it is essential that the chairperson "makes sure that everybody is called," as Fr. Ken tells it. This is particularly important in a large parish like Iowa City. As individuals register an interest in participating in one of the six commissions, the parish commission is responsible for the follow-up phone call.

The empowerment of the laity to move forward and provide leadership in the commissions has a snowball effect on parish activity. The people assuming lay leadership in the commissions know they have the full support of the pastor and parish staff. A Bloomfield parishioner said that Sr. Ruth may take the lead on certain parish activities, but does so in a way that "involves a lot of people in…what she does." Involving others gives them a sense of ownership and contribution to the parish. Once the layperson is trained, the parish staff is free to do other pastoral work and spreads out the responsibilities to more people. A parish council member in Solon said that Fr. David tries "to keep everyone involved in what is going on. It makes people want to help.…He is really a very effective catalyst." A parish council member said that whenever Sr. Ruth asks people to get involved, the people respond very positively.

Interaction among the Laypeople

We also found evidence that OCBs had a contagious effect on the people of a parish. When people saw others helping, initiating, participating, and self-developing, it had the effect of encouraging them to do more of the same. For example, a Bloomfield parishioner explained that when she looked around and saw how much people were doing for the parish, "I wanted to get involved." Another member told a similar story of being asked to serve on the parish council by a dedicated laywoman in the parish who was "a very good model, and whatever she asked, I wanted to be able to do." This kind of *leadership from the pews* occurs when the leaders are able to let go of some control and when members of a parish have specific roles and responsibilities delegated to them.

The welcoming attitude of a parish is another example of laypeople encouraging organizational citizenship. The positive attitude of the people can become the source of inspiration and involvement. A woman on the Bloomfield parish council talked about how excited her daughter was to serve as an altar server because "everyone was so welcoming to her." The warm and inviting style of a parish often begins with a warm and positive attitude of the leaders. Servant leadership nurtures a congregation and creates a positive culture that is supportive of the helping, participating, initiating, and self-developing behaviors of the parish.

Why Servant Leadership Works

The examples we have provided thus far in this chapter describe how servant leadership is linked to organizational citizenship. Now we explain *why* servant leadership works. In order to explain why the words and actions of servant leaders engaged the members of the parish to increase organizational citizenship, we went back and re-examined leader and member exchanges in each parish. Using an inductive search of the transcripts from our field study, we found seven behavioral mechanisms that seemed to unlock the organizational citizenship of the parishioners. Thus we call them the seven **keys to servant leadership**.

We think these seven behavioral mechanisms explain why servant leadership works. They are possible reasons why parishioners are motivated to perform with OCBs when the leader acts with SLBs. We believe that this is a significant contribution to our understanding of servant leadership. If parish leaders can encourage members to go above and beyond expectations, this could be a significant contribution to what we know about improving parish life. Our careful study of the interactions between leaders and members of these three parishes revealed four direct keys to servant leadership: (1) invitation, (2) inspiration, (3) modeling, and (4) affection. Three other keys to servant leadership that emerged from the data were indirect, or organizational: (5) cultural, (6) structural, and (7) strategic (see Figure 11).

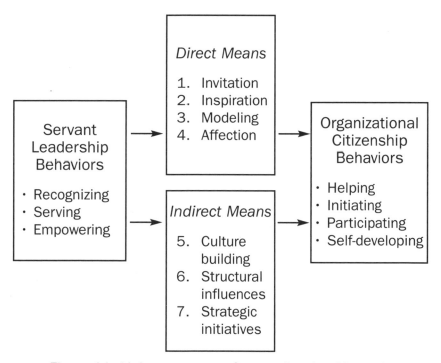

Figure 11. Linkages among Servant Leadership and Organizational Citizenship Behaviors

Four Direct Keys to Servant Leadership

Invitation: The Voice

Members of a parish are motivated when the servant leaders invite the people to act on behalf of the parish. Personal invitation by the leader increases the likelihood of member response. All three pastors in our study indicated that when they see a need in the parish and know of someone with the gifts and talents to meet that need, they *personally* and *directly* invite that person to participate or to help. How that invitation plays out is significant. Instead of coercing, controlling, or commanding, the leader invites in the nuanced way explained by Fr. Ken when he said, "We are not *telling* people what to do, we are *inviting* them to participate." In all three parishes, parishioners told us about being "tapped on the shoulder" by their pastors and other leaders.

When Patti, the youth minister in Iowa City, wanted to invite Bill to help with her youth ministry group, she first recognized the gift of the parishioner, and then she moved on to the invitation. Patti first pointed out to Bill that he was "really good at woodworking," which recognized his talent. Then she went on to identify the need for his talents by explaining that the youth ministry group was "coming over to polish the pews." She concluded her interchange with Bill by asking him to donate this talent when she said, "Could you be there to help show them how it is done?"

Sr. Ruth used a similar approach in Bloomfield. She considered the gifts and talents of her parishioners and called those forth by inviting that person. If she could not think of anyone to do a job, she turned for help by asking the parish council who would have the special gifts and talents that she needed. Then she would call that person and personally invite them to get involved. Sr. Ruth was using a shared leadership approach that involves the parish council in the recognizing phase of the invitation.

Servant leaders continuously invite members to acts of service. They asked them to serve the parish in some particular way, such as participating in an upcoming project or activity. Leaders were not shy about asking people to step up to participate in the life of the parish.

They encouraged them to share in the ministry of the parish. This finding amplifies the developmental role of servant leaders.

Remember that Robert Greenleaf suggests that the "best test" of servant leadership is whether the followers are learning, growing, and becoming servant leaders as well.[4] Serving does not merely mean doing things *for* others, but doing things *with* others. It requires a willingness to give and to receive service. Servant leadership directly encourages other people to join the leader in living a life of service as well. As Greenleaf pointed out, servant leaders engage the followers to become whole people.[5] As the people become more fully human, the organization becomes more effective. The followers become more actively involved in the mission of the church. When the servant leader enriches the life of the followers by recognizing their gifts and talents, they are inviting them into fuller, more active, and more conscious participation in the church.[6]

Inspiration: The Spirit

Servant leaders also fostered organizational citizenship by inspiring members to devote their efforts to the parish. **Inspiration** is seen here as an intrinsic form of motivation. Inspiration comes from *within the spirit*. Members in all three parishes noted that humble service by parish leaders was a source of inspiration for them. When the parish leaders humbly place themselves at the service of others in the parish, the members in the parish are inspired to reciprocate with service to the congregation.

One example found in all three parishes was that leaders gave credit to others for ministries that were succeeding and took the blame for ministries that were struggling. Jim Collins calls this the "window and the mirror,"[7] where leaders look out the window to give credit to others in times of success and look into the mirror and take the blame in times of failure. It was very significant that the pastor and pastoral associate in all three parishes were observed and described repeatedly as giving credit to each other, to God, and to others in the parish.

Servant leaders inspire their members to acts of parish citizenship. At first glance, it might be hard to distinguish between inspiration and invitation. In both cases, the servant leader is influencing the followers to move toward a common goal. In both cases, the servant leader allows the follower to freely choose to follow. The key difference is that invitation is a direct request for action, while inspiration is less direct. Inspiration raises the aspiration level and fuels the internal motivation of the follower. Invitation provides a direct call. Inspiration provokes an internal one.

Modeling: The Hands and Feet

A third key to servant leadership is modeling the way. Servant leaders motivate others into parish citizenship behavior by modeling service. A role model provides a template for action. Many kinds of learning can be facilitated by social modeling.[8] Prosocial behaviors can be modeled as well. This is in line with the modeling done by transformational leaders who show the way to effective action.[9] Modeling provides an example and demonstrates the behaviors that the leader is seeking from others.

Servant leaders model examples that can be emulated by others within the whole parish. Fr. David was modeling the way when he encouraged his parishioners in Solon to attend social action trainings by offering to go with them. Sr. Ruth modeled the way when she offered to attend a conference with a parishioner who was being trained to lead ministry in Bloomfield. Fr. Ken modeled the way when he attended the meetings of commissions that were not performing well. The result was that lay attendance at these meetings increased when the pastor began attending their meetings.

Parishioners in all three parishes said their leaders were just as involved as they were. In Bloomfield, a member expressed a similar sentiment by saying that when she looked around and saw how much Fr. John and Sr. Ruth were doing for the parish, she concluded, "You figure you have to give too, to help the community." Leaders were depicted in all three parishes as role models of service to the congregation.

Affection: The Heart

The fourth direct way that servant leaders promote parish citizenship is through personal *affection*, which is defined here as expressing care and concern for members of the parish. Servant leaders show that they care for others. In return, the parishioners show that they care too. Bloomfield parishioners told the story of how the parishioners would show up to shovel snow for Sr. Ruth after a snowfall. They described Fr. John as someone who would strap up his boots and drive through a blizzard if they needed him. Parishioners expressed love and concern for their leaders because, as one parish council member said, Sr. Ruth and Fr. John are "always ready to roll up their sleeves and help do whatever needs to be done."

A number of laypeople in our study explained that when their parish leaders listened carefully to the members of the congregation or ministered to their needs or demonstrated in some way that they cared for the parishioners, the members of the parish were more inclined to help or to participate. Parishioners described parish leaders in each parish as visiting people in their homes, listening to their stories, being there in times of need, and showing that they cared. One parish council member described Fr. David in this way: "He's always visiting people."

Servant leaders encourage congregation members to acts of citizenship by demonstrating that they care for them. When leaders show high levels of concern and genuine interest in the followers, the leader is also establishing trust and building a sense of commitment that can motivate people to spend extra effort on behalf of the leader and the organization. As the research indicates, high-quality social exchange relationships between leader and follower invoke loyalty, trust, and support on the follower side.[10] This means that followers are more likely to accept leadership from those who care for them. A number of studies specify that the quality of the relationship between leader and follower is what motivates people to engage in organizational citizenship because it increases "their sense of obligation, desire to reciprocate and trust, liking for and commitment to the leader."[11]

Three Organizational Keys to Servant Leadership

As mentioned previously, the four individual keys to servant leadership are *direct* ways that parish leaders influence their followers to increase OCBs. As we examined and reexamined the transcripts from our parishes, it became clear that parish leaders also had an impact on the behaviors of followers in three *indirect* ways. These occurred even when the leaders were not personally present or when they had no direct contact with the follower. We called these indirect mechanisms *cultural*, *structural*, and *strategic* ways that leaders evoked parish citizenship.

The Servant Culture

Servant leaders set norms for citizenship behavior. Through the organizational influence of parish leaders, a culture of service was established in our parishes. This had an impact on the beliefs, norms, values, assumptions, and behaviors of the followers. A culture of service was evident in the comment by Fr. Ken when he said that people volunteer to get some things done "before I was even able to recognize" that it needed to be done. One of his parishioners suggested that Fr. Ken created an environment of encouragement and support, stating that "your idea [does not have] to fit this one modality and if it doesn't you have to get a new idea." Fr. Ken described a culture of service when he said that he was able to sleep soundly knowing that people in the parish were responsible for certain tasks. He concluded, "I have a lot of help from a lot of good people." Through a network of help and support, service became a norm in our three parishes.

Organizational culture is seen simply as "the way we do things around here."[12] It is seen as a set of basic assumptions, beliefs, and values about an organization. Culture establishes norms that are taught to others as the right way to do things.[13] In our study, the parishes had cultures of service because they enhanced the service of the people. In business, this is akin to the way others have spoken of organizational cultures. For instance, developing a culture that emphasizes worker safety is an important part of making an organization a safer place to work, and creating a culture focused on quality is an important element of building high-quality products on a sustained basis.

The Servant Structure

Parish leaders also created systems and structures that enhanced the capacity for members of the congregation to serve. By building community and establishing networks, servant leaders structure their organizations in ways that foster organizational citizenship. The two largest parishes created various councils, commissions, or committees that were small enough to invite participation, nurture helping behaviors, encourage initiative, and enable members of the parish to develop their own knowledge, skills, and abilities. The smallest parish utilized a different structure, one that acted more like a family. Governance was structured through a parish council that acted as a committee of the whole, without an intricate system of committees.

Parish structures promoting citizenship provide laypeople an opportunity to take initiative and to actively participate in governance, planning, and activities of the parish. While doctrine and culture might be shaped through public proclamation from a pulpit, *structure* is shaped by creating systems to share power and decision making in an organization. In our study, the parish structures enhanced the service of the members. Clear and consistent structures enable parishes to attend to certain issues, select priorities, and continue to act in predictable ways, all of which provides members with an opportunity to make sense of the organization.[14]

Servant Strategies

Servant leaders also facilitate a process to articulate the mission, set common goals, establish priorities, and express the vision of the parish. It is critical that they involve parishioners in the planning process. In our study, parish leaders spoke about developing mission and vision statements, putting funds behind parish priorities such as lay ministry formation, and involving large numbers of parishioners in the planning and decision-making processes.

The willingness to involve people in the planning—even to let them take the lead—is illustrated in the following story from Bloomfield. Sr. Ruth reported that the parish council was meeting one night without Fr. John, who was out of town. When the pastor called during the meeting, he asked, "How's it going?" And Sr. Ruth said, "'Well, it's going fine; we're gonna add on to the church." After a moment of dead silence, Fr. John said, "Well, just make sure you make it big enough."

When the pastor involves the people in strategic decision making, the results motivate the people in a parish to respond with citizenship behaviors. Like culture and structure, strategy has a macro-level influence on the behaviors of the parish. Strategic planning methods, such as sessions in which the leaders facilitate a process of gaining input from the people about core values, strategic goals, or visioning of the future, can empower large numbers of people by giving them the opportunity to participate and to take initiative.

Transformational Servant Leadership

As explained earlier, transformational leaders transform people and organizations.[15] Research shows that transformational leaders enhance citizenship behaviors.[16] They encourage OCB when they support their followers. The servant leaders in our study had a transformational approach to parish life. They transformed parishioners by turning them into leaders. They transformed the parish by changing the culture, structure, and strategies of the parish. In this way, our servant leaders were also transformational leaders.

The seven keys to servant leadership explain possible ways that servant leaders were transforming in their leadership style. The four direct keys illustrate ways that leaders changed the members of the parish by using their voices to invite people, by moving the spirit to inspire people, by moving their feet and hands to model service, and by moving the heart by showing affection for their parishioners.

The three organizational mechanisms—culture, structure, and strategy—explain macro-level keys to servant leadership. These are ways that servant leaders transform the parish and therefore increase citizenship. The transformational servant leader behaviors we observed reinforced or created three things: a culture of service, structures of service, and strategies of service. Each of these enhanced parish citizenship.

Conclusion

Understanding the dynamics of leader–member relationships is a significant part of parish life and leadership. Our stories of behavioral interaction between parish leaders and members provided the evidence for our seven keys to servant leadership, which explain how servant leadership works and why servant leadership can create a vibrant and servant-oriented parish community by enhancing citizenship behaviors.

Our parish field study set out to explore whether we could find evidence of three servant leadership behaviors under the general categories of recognizing, serving, and empowering. These behaviors were identified in *advance* of our field visits. We went into these parishes looking for signs of these behaviors. On the other hand, our seven leadership keys were gleaned from the research findings *after* the field visits. While the three servant leader behaviors and four organizational citizenship behaviors are descriptive of life in these parishes, the seven leadership keys are explanatory of the effects of leadership on parishioners.

Our findings support the multiple teachings of the church advising that the diverse gifts and talents of our congregations can be fully realized when church leaders provide every opportunity for lay participation and initiative.[17] They also support the extensive research on organizations that suggests that supportive leadership enhances organizational citizenship and that OCB increases organizational performance.[18] Our findings also suggest that servant leadership fits the definition of supportive leadership, thereby enhancing OCB and increasing organizational performance.

Of course, in order to make these claims more boldly, more research is needed to generalize our study beyond the limitations of three Iowa parishes and to test this model of servant leadership more broadly, seeking to confirm the proposed linkages of servant leadership and organizational citizenship in a variety of congregations. Our hope is that more research can be conducted to help us all better understand these linkages so we can foster the growth and nurture the effectiveness of leaders and parishes.

The interest in servant leadership that is expanding today is due in no small part to its association with Jesus and Christianity. As various types of organizations turn to servant leadership, it will be increasingly important to clarify exactly what it is and how it works. We suggest that servant leadership is more than a leadership style that fits Greenleaf's advice about leadership: Servant leadership is an effective approach to leadership that is consistent with the message of Jesus and the teachings of the church.

Servant leadership is an approach that works in a parish.

9

SERVANT PARISHES:
Three Sizes

Parish dynamics can vary greatly depending on parish size. In a small parish, it is common for everyone to know each other and call each other by name. In a larger parish, it may be almost impossible to get to know everyone's name. The largest parish in our study holds an occasional "Get Acquainted" weekend, sometimes known as "Name Tag Sunday." Parishioners are invited to wear an adhesive name tag during liturgical services, adult education programs, and fellowship activities. The leaders encourage parishioners to connect with people they do not know. The people walk up to folks they do not know and introduce themselves. This is one example of how large parishes try to "get smaller."[1]

This chapter looks at how the dynamics of parish life vary according to parish size. We look at how leaders recognize, empower, and serve the people and how congregation members help one another, take initiative, actively participate in congregational life, and pursue personal growth.[2] We identified three servant parish models—family, community, and teams—and discovered commonalities and differences among the three.[3] We begin with one story that illustrates our case.

Planting Tulips

The recessional hymn came to a close at the Sunday evening Mass at St. Mary Magdalen's Church. Quiet whispers gave way to hearty conversation among the parishioners in the cozy former restaurant in Bloomfield, Iowa. Some chatted in the aisles of the small sanctuary while others headed for the front porch, where the walls were decorated with news clippings and artwork made by the children of the parish. A white-haired woman of eighty, Helen raised her voice to make an announcement, "It's kind of cold this evening. But Earl [her husband] and I are thinking ahead to how nice it would look to have a patch of colorful tulips in front of the church come spring. So next Saturday morning at 8:00, we'll be here. If you would like to come by and donate some tulip bulbs, Earl and I will be glad to plant them. Thank you."

Some asked Helen about what kind of tulips to bring. Others smiled and thanked her for volunteering to start the flower garden. A week passed. On Saturday morning, a line of cars and pickup trucks gathered around the church, carrying hundreds of tulip bulbs. As Earl tells it, "Everybody brought tulip bulbs. We planted every one of 'em....587 to be exact." As it turned out, Helen did not see the spring blossoms. She was hospitalized in Des Moines when they bloomed. So several parishioners drove two hours to visit her in the hospital and to decorate her room with large photos of the tulips. After Helen died, church members built a flower bed around the tulips and the parish dedicated the garden to Helen. They later built a new wooden sign in front of the church. The garden became the talk of the town in Bloomfield and a neighboring church built a new flower bed and sign modeled after St. Mary Magdalen's.

This snapshot of parish life in the rolling hills of southern Iowa shows a glimpse of a warm and loving servant organization. This is the kind of community that interests many churchgoers. Yet this story comes from a parish with only forty-three families.

Why Parish Size Is Important

In our study, size of parish was controlled for three reasons. First, size of parish can affect the size of parish staff and budget, and this can affect the dynamics of a parish. Staff members are hired to assume leadership roles that volunteers might fill in smaller parishes, such as an organist, a janitor, or a Sunday school teacher. The smaller parishes do not have the budget to hire people for these positions. Hiring staff can totally change the dynamics of parish life. Whether it is beneficial to the parish community depends on whether the staff members are encouraging laypeople to step into leadership roles or whether they are simply doing everything by themselves. Hiring staff for jobs traditionally performed by volunteers can discourage initiative and weaken the participation of the people in the pews, unless the staff members who are hired take a servant leadership approach to their jobs.

Second, many of the smallest parishes (throughout the United States, not just in Iowa) have been among those closed in recent years. The bishop's original question that inspired this book was asked in a discussion regarding criteria for closing parishes. The task force planning for the future of the diocese was particularly concerned about smaller parishes that are lively but sometimes are difficult to justify assigning a pastor, given the shortage of clergy. By including a large, a medium-sized, and a small parish in our study, we examined the quality of parish life in various sizes of parishes, including the smallest parishes that are sometimes considered most at risk of being closed.

Third, the smaller parishes often express concern that they do not receive the same amount of attention as the larger parishes. Including them added a unique feature to our field study. It was our assumption that parish life can be great and vibrant regardless of size of parish. We sometimes assume that some parishes are dead because they are small. We certainly found hearty signs of life in Bloomfield, which is the smallest parish in the Diocese of Davenport.

The Family Approach

"There's no slack here. If we don't grab a hold of that yoke and pull, it isn't gonna get done."
—Parish council member,
St. Mary Magdalen's, Bloomfield

Helen and Earl showed initiative in organizing the tulip-planting activity described earlier. Many members of the Bloomfield parish freely participated in the activity. The close personal connection between members was clearly demonstrated by their caring for Helen when she was hospitalized.

The close family feeling at St. Mary Magdalen's was also apparent in the way that the children posted their artwork and photos on the bulletin board in the entryway of the church. The word *family* was used repeatedly by leaders and members in describing the dynamics at St. Mary Magdalen's. Parishioners and staff treat each other as an extended family and treat the parish buildings and grounds as their own.

The recognizing, serving, and empowering behaviors are evident in Fr. John, the pastor, and Sr. Ruth, the pastoral associate. They foster the **family approach** in Bloomfield. They enhance the helping and initiating of the people. As in healthy families, the people take the initiative when someone needs help. Members expressed appreciation and respect for Sr. Ruth. With great affection, one parish council member described Sr. Ruth as "a mother to us." She humbly gave credit to others and inspired people to get involved in the parish.

Members also expressed affection for Fr. John. One parish council member said, "He knows each one of us....This is a small parish. It is very easy to know, acknowledge everybody, visit with them." Fr. John demonstrated the power of shared leadership by delegating many pastoral responsibilities to Sr. Ruth. She is available at the parish at times when he is not. Fr. John says that the parish is augmented by her presence in the Bloomfield community. He said there is a "sense of pastoral ministry that is going on," and he and Sr. Ruth are "exercising their own pastoral ministry with and for one another."

The size of parish dictates that they have only one weekend Mass, but this brings the advantage of getting the whole parish together once a week. Fr. John said, "The community gathers as a community, and we know who's there and we know who's not there." One parish council member stated, "In a parish this size, most people pretty much know the circumstances of other people."

The Community Approach

"They participate in whatever program or activity we are promoting as a parish."
—Parish council member, St. Mary's, Solon

It is Thursday night in Solon. Heads bobbing, arms swinging, three hundred elementary school children laugh and jump as their voices shake the rafters of the new parish hall. "Rise and shine and give God the glory, glory; Children of the Lord!" This song is followed by another, then one more. As the music ends the mood quiets for a few minutes as an adult leads them: "Hail Mary, full of grace..." and then, "Our Father, who art in heaven...." Moments later, the children bump and jostle, a flurry of T-shirts and sneakers as they hurry to their respective classes, where three adult volunteers are teaching in each classroom.

Off in the corner of the auditorium, the Toddler Room bustles with twenty-five bundles of energy, warmly cared for by eight adult volunteers. As adult classes begin, a few more parents stop at the doorway. They sign in their children, and volunteers reach out to hug them and call them by name. Then the parents head off to attend a Why Catholic? discussion or teach in one of the classrooms. At the center of the activities, guiding, directing, and encouraging is Julie, the director of religious education, a young energetic woman described by Fr. David, the pastor, as "smart and articulate, able to get things done."

St. Mary's in Solon is the **community approach** to parish life. People greet each other warmly, reach out to embrace each other, show joy in seeing each other, and seem genuinely happy to be involved in parish life. With hundreds in attendance, the leaders could easily have chosen to run around taking care of the many details associated with such an event, but they show more concern for relationships among people as they welcome the children and their parents.

The parish is too large to be led effectively by just one person. As one parish council member said, it's "too much...for one person to take charge of it. I think Father is extremely adept at giving people the power of feeling like they own things and they are involved." While this parish is in a growing area, the people are aware of how the declining number of priests will affect the future of the parish. As one participant stated, "If you want a church in Solon, it needs to be a larger church because there are going to be fewer priests and Masses."

While a newcomer will be readily recognized in the small family parish, he or she may slip by more easily in this larger community. As Fr. David said, "People want connections and we are not always so good at reaching out to the newcomers." When compared to the family parish model, St. Mary's in Solon seemed more like an extended family, a community, one that showed more evidence of some formal systems and structures. Ministry is organized into a set of about six commissions. "The commission system is really working in this parish," declared one parish council member, who added that commissions are represented at parish council meetings, where they "hear everything that's going on...and they take it back to their smaller groups."

The Teams Approach

"We have six very active commissions, one for each area of ministry, and each commission has a representative to the [parish] council."
—Sr. Agnes Giblin, St. Mary's, Iowa City

It is Sunday morning at St. Mary's, Iowa City. Masses are scheduled every hour and a half. Older adults, college students, and families with small children fill the church. The parish bulletin is loaded with nineteen pages of announcements about parish news and events. Downstairs, the parish hall is filled with activity, including a blood pressure check conducted by volunteer nurses, a sign-up table for those who wish to support a homeless shelter ministry, a planning meeting for one of the commissions, and an area for those who just want to socialize over coffee and donuts.

This parish is a system of teams. The largest parish in the diocese bustles with a multitude of programs. It would be easy for a person to get lost in a parish this size, but St. Mary's seems to have mastered the art of organizing through an intricate system of commissions. These are not the usual committees observed in many churches. Instead, the **teams approach** features people with a common sense of mission implied by the word used to describe them: a *commission*.

Like in Solon, people in Iowa City are actively called to serve on commissions. Their system has six commissions; they have about thirty committees or subcommittees, many of them organized as part of one of the six major commissions. New members are recruited on "Invitation Sunday," which happens every fall. This is a time for members to find out about and sign up for commissions. The commissions have formal processes and assigned roles. One member noted the route to involvement in a commission as "a simple invitation. You could sign up by the card...then somebody would call you and explain what the commission was."

These commissions not only serve to get work done, they become key points of identification with the parish. One parish council member said, "I've become extremely close to my team....It's my primary parish community." Another suggested, "St. Mary's has been a really great place to be because it really consists of multiple communities." When needed, the commissions work together in ministering to individual needs. For instance, one parish council member told about the care and concern he received when his wife passed away: "Through all these commissions, I am sure...it was all taken care of for me....I don't know how I would have done it without Sr. Agnes, Fr. Ken, all those people."

In the teams parish, the structure of the formal organization is stressed. As Sr. Agnes stated, "This parish is very organized. There are hundreds of things going on here every day." The parish seems to flow from the organizational skills of Fr. Ken, the pastor, as evidenced by one parishioner's comment, "If you ever see the checklist we follow...," and another who said, "He's got it organized." In fact, another parishioner mused, "He checks his e-mail every day."

The lay leaders of these commissions take their roles very seriously, calling upon new parishioners to join in ministry, organizing the fine details of upcoming programs, communicating that to the rest of the parish, recruiting new members to join the commission, and rotating leadership to avoid burnout. The degree of organization is greater than that of the community approach. The system of teams is impressive and it is clear that the leaders recognize, serve, and empower in ways that encourage participation.

Our Results Based on Parish Size

The member behaviors that seemed most affected by parish size in our study were, helping initiating, and participating.[4] Helping behaviors were most evident in the smallest parish, which we refer to as the family model, while participation was strongest in the largest parish, which we refer to as the teams approach. The medium-sized parish, which we refer to as the community approach, had medium levels of helping and participating. While each parish showed positive evidence of all of the proposed servant leadership and organizational citizenship behaviors, the variance was interesting.

Differences in Helping

Helping was viewed as members providing informal assistance to each other, to the leaders, or to the parish. This could mean working collaboratively with other members of the parish, going out of the way to help someone, or responding to informal requests for assistance. The look and feel of helping differed somewhat across the three parishes.

In the family parish, assistance is very concrete and personal, touching individuals and families. When someone needs a babysitter, they call on members of the parish. The people gather in all-church potlucks that the pastor described as having a family-like atmosphere. One parish council member suggested, "Whenever there is a death, we come together, and we assist like a family." Helping in Bloomfield has a highly personal touch.

In the community parish, helping can be more organized. For instance, about eight parishioners help staff the Toddler Room for parish events. The focus is different from Bloomfield, where individuals seek other parishioners to provide child care. In Bloomfield, the parishioners described this as assisting "like a family." Julie observed that parishioners in Solon serve as "extended family" to those who move into the parish. A parish council member commented, "People seem to welcome the new people in....[We are] a very open community." So while Bloomfield helps like a family, in Solon, the helping plays out as an extended family or a community.

In the teams parish, helping often takes the form of providing assistance to the church as an organization. Fr. Ken noted, "We have some rank-and-file business people who really help us with our finances." He also identified an attorney who volunteers if legal work becomes necessary in the parish. The commission structure is instrumental in the helping in the teams parish. As one parish council member stated, "It's not any individual....I really think that St. Mary's has that team together."

Differences in Initiating

Initiating is defined as members taking action on their own, without waiting for parish leaders to tell them what needs to be done. Initiating includes presenting new ideas, launching new parish activities, and stepping up to work on a new project, program, or commission. Initiating happens when members act without leaders telling them what needs to be done. As seen in the case of helping, initiative had the most personalized look in the family model, with more organizational emphasis in the parish models described as community or teams.

In the family parish, Sr. Ruth said, "They just kind of keep their eyes open and they see a need, and then they just do it. I don't think they think anything about it." The pastoral associate sees church potluck suppers as largely self-organizing with people taking initiative. "It just happens. I mean people bring in their food, and other people take care of it, and I don't have to do much at all." On occasion, a meal may even extend far beyond church borders. One parishioner took the initiative to organize a pork loin dinner for a statewide bicycle event that brought thousands of people passing through town.

In the community parish, individuals taking initiative are more likely to be involved with some structures in the church. For instance, when parish council members hear about parish activities they "take it back to their smaller groups." One parish council member agreed to chair a fundraising drive if someone else would cochair. The two of them organized a committee by making personal contact with parishioners. She said, "We started calling people we thought we would like to have on the fundraising committee. A large number came."

In the teams parish, examples of initiative relate even more to structures in the parish. For instance, Patti the youth minister stated, "If there is a new idea, it is usually brought forward through a commission, first and foremost." A parish council member noted that it was a simple invitation "from another member of the commission" that got her involved in parish life.

Differences in Participating

Participation is defined here as parish involvement in a formal sense. Participating is a means of engaging people in programs or activities of the formal organization. It includes such things as being active in the life of the parish by attending Mass or parish functions, joining parish programs, receiving the sacraments, contributing financially to the parish, or being actively involved in parish commissions.

In the family parish, participation means taking ownership in the parish. Parish council members said that in addition to it being God's church, "This is *my* church," or "This is *our* church." The personal ties in this small parish are intimate and cohesive. Periodically, the whole congregation comes together after the Sunday evening Mass for a potluck supper. Fr. John noted that the Sunday evening Mass "brings forth volunteer ministries" that involve parishioners as ushers, lectors, and musicians. Rather than attribute it to planning and structure, he noted that at St. Mary Magdalen the liturgy simply "gels." Additionally, this small parish of forty-three families is actively involved in Why Catholic? Thirty adults are involved in this faith formation course.

The community parish, Solon, is filled with formal and informal activities. Fr. David said that "something is always happening around here." As described earlier, on Thursday nights the parish has more than three hundred children in K through 9, about seventy-five high school-aged kids in youth ministry, and about twenty-five kids in the Toddler Room, while many of the parents are active in an adult education course. Overall, there are more than two hundred adults involved in faith formation programs. The Knights of Columbus is another formalized ministry in Solon. While some may look at it as service, and others as fellowship, one described it as a place where "men can find ways to participate in the life of our church."

In the teams parish, Iowa City, participation is more formalized. As Sr. Agnes stated, "This morning, you could walk through and find five commissions with events going on in the parish." This large parish launched a major effort to break the parish into neighborhoods and to plan regular outreach to all members. About 190 members are involved in this massive effort to reach out to the parish at the neighborhood level. Fr. Ken pointed out that the commissions were a key aspect of parish organization and that "each commission has a representative to the council." At Invitation Sunday, twenty new people stepped forward to volunteer for various commissions.

This distinction between helping and participation, and the difference in size of parishes in this study, help explain why Iowa City and Solon scored more highly on participation than Bloomfield. With the efficient use of teams, parishioners in Iowa City, and to a lesser extent, Solon, have a multitude of formal opportunities for participation. The smaller parish in Bloomfield has only one formal group—the parish council—with work accomplished as a committee of the whole.

Some larger parishes could just as well be labeled bureaucracies, since the **organizational structure** tends to be more formal and complex. However, the teams approach seems to be a more fitting description for St. Mary's, Iowa City, where parishioners are proficient in the use of the parish commission structure and show a high level of interdependence between the various commissions. They use the commission structure *to get smaller as they got bigger.* Their commissions serve a common purpose and promote the sense of group accountability that typifies the work of teams.[5]

The names we gave our three models—family, community, and teams—are based on the attention we paid to servant leadership and organizational citizenship in these parishes. The names reflect different dynamics typical of each parish. Together, they provide a broad overview of parish life. Prescriptions for parish life should take size nuances into consideration. While every parish expects to demonstrate competence in each area of ministry, the parish structures that enable the parish to be involved in these ministries might look a lot different.

Research on Church Size

The impact of church size on parish life is of particular interest in those denominations in which a shrinking clergy base has led to difficult choices about closure of parishes, clustering of congregations, and construction of larger churches so that the diminishing number of clergy can minister to larger numbers of people at one time.

A number of other typologies of parish size have been offered by others.[6] Generally speaking, research shows that as the size of parish gets larger, the pastor spends more time on administrative duties such as overseeing the budget, raising funds for capital campaigns, or supervising staff.[7] In the smaller congregations, with smaller budgets and fewer staff, the emphasis on the pastoral skills of the clergy is greater.[8] However, in all parish sizes, paperwork and financial accountability are growing concerns that require more time and energy of parish leaders and administrators.

The research shows that participation per member declines as parishes get bigger.[9] As organizations grow in size, specialized roles grow and member participation can decrease.[10] Formalization of certain offices and professionalization of some roles can exclude some lay members from certain kinds of congregational participation.[11] As churches grow, communication also becomes more formalized, making it difficult for a pastor to interact personally with all members. The research also shows that large parishes can compensate for this disadvantage of size in many ways, such as hiring business managers and accountants, updating technology, and working more in smaller work groups and teams.[12]

A number of studies demonstrate other potential negative impacts of church size.[13] Research shows that congregation size is negatively related to both commitment and conformity. This means that smaller parishes have higher levels of both.[14] Organizational scientists have also identified the "free-rider" problem that relates to larger parishes. As organizations grow in size, more members are more likely to take a free ride.[15] These members can hide from membership requirements of the organization while benefiting from certain programs, social activities, or specialized services. Parish examples can include members who use the parish for family weddings or funerals without attending weekly worship, donating time, giving money, or even supporting the beliefs of the church.[16]

Research shows that larger congregations have lower revenues per member and lower costs per member.[17] Larger parishes can also have lower accountability for parish participation, unless the parish organizes social networks or small, intimate groups that can hold parishioners more accountable for contributing to the parish with time, talent, and treasure.[18] This explains why many congregations, especially those following the "meta-church" organization design, use small groups as the main building block of the church.[19] This provides the large parish the opportunity to establish a sense of intimacy within the parish while increasing the commitment of parishioners.[20]

Conclusion

While our research discovered many of these differences in the patterns of behavior across our model parishes, we also found that high performance came in all three sizes. Perhaps the genius of the high-performing congregations lies in the creative ways that strong relationships and intimacy are fostered, regardless of church size. While the family congregation can govern itself with one committee of the whole and is small enough to place family pictures and children's artwork in the church entryway, more formalization is necessary in both the community and teams congregations to gain the same sense of intimacy that is felt in the small parish.[21]

Another explanation for these differences may go beyond size. When volunteers have a high level of identification with their organization, they tend to be more committed and satisfied with their experience. Likewise, they tend to show higher levels of prosocial behavior, which is associated with organizational citizenship.[22] When people identify personally with a parish, they see themselves "as integral to the collective and their fates intertwined."[23] Loyalty, commitment, and ownership may also increase prosocial behavior.[24] Other research shows that the larger the congregation, the more important leadership is in overcoming the negative impacts of large size.[25] In our study, it seems that both organizational structure and servant leadership played key roles in fostering a sense of identity, greater commitment, and prosocial behaviors among the members.

The nuances in our findings based on size have important ramifications for those who wish to measure and to improve the life of a parish. It appears that measuring parish behaviors might not be a simple formula. Theories of organizational structure help to explain these differences based on the formalization, bureaucratization, and standardization that occur when parishes grow in size. Church leaders should consider the differences based on parish size when planning for the future.

While each parish should be able to demonstrate competence and activity in several areas of ministry, the parish structures that enable the parish to be successful in these ministries might look a lot different. The larger parish might be better suited to follow the Iowa City example of teamwork with its emphasis on separate commissions for each area of ministry. The medium-sized parishes might develop the Solon model of community building, which includes some independent commissions for some areas of ministry but places more emphasis on personal relationship building. The smaller parishes might follow the family example of Bloomfield by utilizing the parish council as a committee of the whole for all areas of ministry. Although the parish structures varied from parish to parish in our case study, the bottom line was a high-performing parish in each parish size, functioning well in all areas of ministry.

10

SIX OTHER CHARACTERISTICS OF SERVANT PARISHES

As we explored our seven categories of behavior of the high-performing parish, we kept an open mind about what else we would find in the model parishes of our field study. This chapter presents the findings that were not expected but were discerned from studying the results. We found six common characteristics of model parishes:

1. Managerial proficiency of the parish staff
2. External focus of the parishes
3. Credibility of the pastor and the parish staff
4. Spiritual explanation of parish success
5. Centrality of prayer in the lives of the parish leaders
6. High performance in nine areas of ministry

Managerial Proficiency

A surprising yet consistent finding in our study was the level to which the pastors and pastoral associates demonstrated signs of **managerial proficiency**, including fiscal oversight, fundraising acumen, and operational **management**. This was especially true in Iowa City, the largest of our three parishes, where management responsibility was a key ingredient because of the size and complexity of the organizational systems. Fr. Ken (the pastor) was clearly knowledgeable about the budget, financial statements, and accounting of all funds in the parish. He also was keenly aware of his need to consult laypeople in financial and legal matters. He spoke highly of involving laypeople in the financial management in his parish.

Operational management skills also were apparent in each parish, especially in the larger two parishes at which leaders were proficient in operating their parish boards, commissions, and councils. As Fr. Ken pointed out, they recruit new members for their commissions every year and they rotate the chairpersons of the commissions every two years "so we don't wear people out." This requires continual monitoring of the leadership and membership of these councils and commissions and intentional recruitment and careful training of new lay leaders. The parish staff takes great care to personally know as many members as possible in order to take advantage of the various individual and professional competencies that parishioners bring.

Another example of operational proficiency in Iowa City was the massive undertaking of their neighborhood outreach program, which involves hundreds of parishioners. It took managerial sophistication to organize and operate that system. As the largest parish in the diocese, St. Mary's uses Excel spreadsheets to maintain lists of members and to keep track of how they are involved in the parish.

Both Solon and Bloomfield demonstrated fundraising skills by using local talent to complete recent capital fund drives. In both cases, the parish staff and key lay leaders were very involved in managing the fund drive. In Solon, the people raised $2.2 million in pledges, and according to Fr. David, "People are paying those pledges very well." In Bloomfield, where the parishioners organized their own successful capital campaign to raise more than $100,000, they referred to Sr. Ruth as "our fundraising consultant" because she became self-taught in the ways of raising funds. Sr. Ruth simply saw this as practicing good stewardship.

In chapter 1, we discussed the differences between leadership and management.[1] Adding managerial proficiency to the list of characteristics of high-performing parishes is a reminder that parish life needs *both* servant leadership *and* management proficiency to reach high levels of performance. In fact, management and leadership can have a reciprocal relationship; each enhances the other.

An example is the story presented by Fr. Ken involving a situation in which homeless people were sleeping on the porch of the Iowa City parish center. While he did not want to evict the homeless, the pastor was concerned about fire safety because of the cigarette butts found on the porch. He did not have the management ability to solve the problem, but he used his leadership abilities to delegate the problem to a parishioner who had the expertise needed. The parishioner who had expertise in property management issues suggested they lay down a new floor that included a fire retardant in the tiles. Fr. Ken's behavior is an example of empowerment, but it also shows how a servant leader delegates certain responsibilities to address management issues in an effective manner.

While management and leadership are two distinct concepts, they are complementary.[2] Both management and leadership are needed for organizational effectiveness. It may be difficult to find managerial proficiency and leadership capabilities within the same person, but the two must exist in the same organization and work hand in hand.[3] The pastors in these three parishes demonstrated managerial abilities, particularly in the area of financial and operational management, while also showing the willingness, the leadership abilities, and the self-confidence to call upon the managerial gifts and talents of their parishioners and to entrust managerial work to laypeople who knew how to get things done. One result of this approach was that it allowed the pastor to concentrate more fully on servant leadership and pastoral ministry.

Peter Drucker points out that leadership is about *effectiveness*, or doing the right thing, while management is about *efficiency*, or doing things right.[4] An organization that is totally focused on management and efficiency bears the risk of operating on all cylinders but moving in the wrong direction. The organization that is totally focused on leadership and effectiveness might be moving in the right direction but spinning its wheels getting its new ideas implemented. Transformational leaders facilitate a process of strategic planning and create a sense of shared vision. They clarify the core values, articulate a sense of purpose, and develop a sense of direction for a parish. Transactional leaders or managers implement the strategies, plans, and ideas that emerge out of the strategic planning in order to meet the goals, reach for the vision, and accomplish the mission of the parish.

Role of the Pastor

John Kotter states that most organizations are "over-managed and under-led."[5] He explains that organizations need both efficient managers and effective leaders. Our study found the convergence of both leadership excellence and management proficiency in the parishes was largely due to the pastors being willing and able to consult with parishioners about decisions, to invite others to take on leadership roles for parish life, and to delegate managerial responsibility to others in the parish.

In our study, the managerial participation of laypeople was enhanced by the recognizing, serving, and empowering behaviors of the pastors who called forth the gifts and talents of parishioners, accepted with humility the greater management experience of certain parishioners, enabled laypeople to utilize their gifts in volunteer service to their parish, delegated real work to others instead of trying to do everything themselves, and celebrated in the fact that they had more free time to devote to being a servant leader and a pastor.

Some believe that the church is in a "managerial crisis"[6] and have suggested that the management skills necessary to address this crisis "can be found among the ranks of lay professionals."[7] Evidence from our three parishes provided support for this assertion. The empowering behaviors of the pastors we interviewed enhanced the participation of accountants, bankers, lawyers, insurance agents, and other professionals who volunteered for their parishes. This type of leadership, as James Kouzes and Barry Posner describe it, is "liberating people to use the power and skills they already have. It's a matter of setting them free, of expanding their opportunities to use themselves in service of a common and meaningful purpose."[8] Our three pastors spoke confidently about the contributions made by these trained lay professionals and appreciated the freedom it gave the pastors to concentrate on pastoral ministry.

External Focus of the Parish

Another common characteristic of our model parishes is the extent that they demonstrated an **external focus of the parish** activities. In the words of one Bloomfield parish council member, this means "involvement in the community outside the church." In Iowa City, where the parish tithes 5 percent of its income to fight poverty and injustice, the pastor said, "We are a community that stands for something." The faithful actions of the leaders and parishioners in these parishes included a multitude of outreach ministries of social action and evangelization. Not only were people in our model parishes serving each other as servant leaders and members, they were also serving the outside community.

In Solon, the parish started "Moms in Touch," a mothers' group that prays for the teachers and students in the public schools. The Knights of Columbus were, naturally, involved as volunteers in the community. And the parish participated in local outreach to the poor, such as a food pantry. In Bloomfield, the parish collaborated with other congregations and community groups in social programs such as the Lord's Cupboard, a food pantry for the poor; Moms in Touch, which prays for public schools; the Food Resources Bank, which raises money for overseas relief; and "I Care," which raises money to buy gifts for needy children at Christmas. In Iowa City, the parish was involved in several ecumenical social action projects, including an ecumenical potluck supper and the local crisis center. The parish responded generously to emergency calls at the door while also collaborating with the crisis center and other agencies that aid the poor.

In all three parishes, social ministry relied heavily on ecumenical activity. These parishes were very inclined to collaborate with ecumenical or interfaith efforts such as food pantries, social justice workshops, peacemaking efforts, and Thanksgiving prayer services. This was especially true in Bloomfield, where the parish council members emphasized that, because they are such a small congregation, the most efficient and effective way for them to make a social impact on their local community was working ecumenically.

During the weekends of our parish visits, each of the parishes was actively engaged in some kind of effort to serve the external community. In Solon, the parish was thanking parishioners for a successful food collection for the hungry. In Iowa City, volunteers were organizing for a homeless shelter program. In Bloomfield, they were hosting a guest from Africa who was speaking about the Food Resources Bank.

The church has been described as a *hotel* for saints and a *hospital* for sinners. The hospital analogy helps to dispel the notion that a person must be perfect to join a church. However, both the hotel and hospital are inwardly focused metaphors. They focus on caring for members inside the congregation. The parishes we studied acted not only as hotels for saints and hospitals for sinners, but also as headquarters for outreach workers who served people beyond the parish. Our parishes were not only inwardly directed but also outwardly focused. While the direction came from within, the focus of parish activities did not stop inside but also went outside the walls of the church.

Organizations that interact regularly with their external environment are characterized as "open systems."[9] These organizations measure effectiveness not only by internal criteria such as growth in membership or profitability but also in terms of the effects they have on the outside world.[10] Church teachings in social action suggest that high-performing parishes should be highly engaged in external systems such as their local communities as well as the global stage.[11] Action on behalf of justice requires that parishes are involved in the social and political environment. Global solidarity relies on parish and personal involvement with sisters and brothers around the world.[12]

Our parishes demonstrated servanthood that served people inside the church. They also practiced servanthood that served others outside the church, in their local communities and beyond. The external focus of these servant parishes gave the people a greater sense of purpose and meaning to their faith. Based on that faith, the members of these parishes went out and became involved in the community by performing works of charity, justice, and evangelization.

Credibility of the Leaders

Another common element that appeared to be an important factor in each of our model parishes was the extent of trust that the members of the parish expressed in the character of their leaders. *Credibility* is defined here as the believability of the leaders. When the members of a church cannot believe in the leaders, they begin to question all of the other beliefs that are the very foundation of the church. Credibility is related to trust because the essence of trust is that people believe in each other. *Trust* in a parish is built when leaders act with integrity, which means acting in an honest, credible, and trustworthy manner. This finding is consistent with the advice of James Autry that "one of the basic foundations of servant leadership is trust."[13]

Parishioners in all three parishes spoke emphatically about the integrity of their pastor and the trust elicited by the credible actions of all the parish staff. In Bloomfield, Sr. Ruth was lovingly described as "just so soft spoken and very caring." In Iowa City, a parish council member said this about the entire parish staff: "It helps, too, that they are just involved as we are. I mean, they are not asking you to do something that they are not willing to help you with or get involved with." In Solon, a parish council member described Fr. David by saying, "He's a servant. Head to toe right through his whole system. He serves." Another added, "He just walks his talk. He is so humble.... People really appreciate the example he sets."

In their research involving tens of thousands of people on six continents, James Kouzes and Barry Posner conclude, "What we found in our investigation of admired leadership qualities is that more than anything, people want leaders who are credible. *Credibility* is the foundation of leadership. Above all else, we must believe in our leaders."[14] The clergy sexual abuse crisis that jolted the church illustrated the depths to which an institution can plunge when its integrity is challenged. Given the experiences of the past few years, it seems clear that the credibility of leaders and the trust between leaders and the people are critical elements for high performance. In our study, it was significant that parishioners not only addressed the credibility of their leaders, but also that because of that credibility they expressed confidence in them.

The credibility of the leaders in these three parishes was consolidated by a solid foundation of humility found in our pastors. Rather than leading in order to achieve power, fame, or glory for their own behalf, these pastors acted with a sense of humility, which was one of the key characteristics identified in Robert Greenleaf's essays on servant leadership.[15] As Charles Manz points out, "The seeds of greatness derive from humility and service."[16]

Humility is a virtue practiced and preached by Jesus, who washed the feet of his disciples, taught them to wash each other's feet (John 13:1–5), and stated, "For all who exalt themselves will be humbled and those who humble themselves will be exalted" (Luke 14:11). Those who practice humility will have a special place in the reign of Jesus, as suggested by this saying: "Whoever becomes humble like this child is the greatest in the kingdom of heaven" (Matt 18:4). Jesus taught that the key to success was service to others when he said, "Whoever wants to be first must be last of all and servant of all" (Mark 9:35).

High levels of humility illustrated in the leaders of our model parishes are reminiscent of the Level Five leader described by Jim Collins in his study of organizations that made the leap from "good to great."[17] In that study, the great leader was viewed as having the paradoxical combination of a personal sense of humility as well as a professional will to drive great results.

Spiritual Explanation of Success

Another form of humility was discovered in the way that members and leaders of these high-performing parishes gave credit to God for their success. In the same way that successful corporate leaders have been described by Collins as attributing their success to luck,[18] leaders in these parishes repeatedly attributed God as a causal factor in explaining the success of their parish activities. The parish spokespersons in our model parishes gave credit to God's grace, God's power, or God's spirit rather than their own efforts. This comment became so routine that it stood out as one of the common characteristics of these parishes. These leaders and members believed so firmly in the providence of God that they gave credit to God for their high performance.

Asked how she recruited two hundred parishioners to be involved in an adult education program in Solon, Julie the director of religious education stated, "God put those two hundred people here and opened their hearts." When asked to explain how more than three hundred children and seventy-five teens are involved in their religious education programs, Julie said, "It is Christ that invites them…and we welcome them in his name." Asked to explain why she initiated Why Catholic? in Solon, a lay volunteer stated that it was probably the movement of the Holy Spirit.

When asked to explain how his parish was able to get so many people involved, Fr. Ken responded, "It seems to be the work of the Holy Spirit. I'm not sure exactly. It truly seems to be a mystery. There are a lot of unanswered questions." When asked how to explain the quick and successful capital campaign in Bloomfield, Sr. Ruth responded, "It was a strange thing. Maybe, I think probably, it was God working." Asked what leaders do to enhance the behaviors of parishioners, a Solon parish council member stated, "I truly believe the Holy Spirit brings you what you need." Asked to explain the dynamic whereby laypeople get involved in the parish due to the behaviors of leaders, Fr. Ken said laypeople become involved "when they are committed to the person of Jesus." As one parish council member stated in the Iowa City focus group, "This is a community where everyone jumps in at the time they are called upon....But that's a spirit that is very difficult to identify why."

The instinct to explain success in a parish by giving credit and glory to God indicates an appreciation for God's providence and a sense of spiritual guidance and direction. It shows that the people in these parishes have a spirituality that places confidence that God is present in their lives of faith and active in their faith community (Matt 18:20). Indeed, people of faith recognize that their relationship with God has a direct impact on their relationships with each other and the success of their human endeavors.

When people of faith believe that God is at the center of human relationships, the search to describe and understand the behaviors of leaders and members in a parish explains not only how to run a more effective parish, but how to practice our Christian faith. The search for God in our lives is conducted by practicing our religious beliefs in the context of human relationships.

Focusing on organizational behavior, such as we are doing here, does not deny the theological foundation and religious beliefs of the parish as a religious institution. Actually, the teachings of Jesus should apply to the thoughts, actions, and plans of parish leaders and members. His life and example as a leader provides a role model of servant leadership. What we found in our successful parishes is that they were putting those religious beliefs into practice in the way they treat each other in the parish.

The parish leaders and members who were attributing parish success to the work of God are similar to the humility of exemplary business leaders who have been depicted as explaining their organizational success to luck.[19] The success of the parish should be linked to the work and the presence of God in the lives of faithful people.

When offered spiritual reasons as the basis for success in a parish, we probed further by asking our parish leaders to add sociological explanations for parish success. We asked, "So when God works through members of this parish, and when people here are inspired by the movement of the Holy Spirit and when they are committed to Christ, what leader and member behaviors would be observed in this parish?"

The leaders and members of these parishes came up with compelling responses to this question. Julie stated, "Just that serving and the compassion. Putting others first instead of putting self first." A parish council member in Bloomfield stated it this way: "What drives you, when you walk in Christ...is giving....He came to serve, not to rule." Patti, the youth minister in Iowa City, expressed a similar sentiment. When asked to explain how five young men from the parish have become candidates for the priesthood, Patti's first response was, "We have been praying for this, a monthly holy hour for vocations, for the past two to three years." When asked how her behavior may have affected these five men, Patti recalled how she asked one of these men to be a lector for his confirmation class, how she went out to lunch with others to talk to them about the priesthood, and how she told another of them when he was in junior high, "You would really make a nice priest some day."

Eventually, each of these exchanges evolved into a discussion about servant leadership and organizational citizenship behaviors that can be observed when people are devoted to God, committed to Christ, and open to the movement of the Holy Spirit. The essence of these conversations revealed the wisdom of the adage, "Work like everything is in your hands and pray like everything is in God's hands." Or as Julie put it, "I think God gives everyone, every place, what is needed and you've got to nurture those gifts to be used and to be served."

Daily Prayer

Giving credit to God for success was but one indication of the spirituality of the leaders and members of our model parishes. The centrality of prayer and spirituality was described as a key factor in the lives of the leaders and members of these parishes. All three pastors spoke highly of the role that daily prayer played in their lives and how prayer was incorporated into their schedules. The pastors specifically mentioned that each day began with Morning Prayer (Lauds), which set the tone for the rest of the ministry performed during the day. As the pastor in Iowa City stated, "My day always starts out with prayer. We also start each office day out with prayer for the whole staff."

The emphasis on prayer that we heard in these parishes was not just a matter of giving lip service to a behavior that is expected in religious organizations. Rather, it was stressed as *the* source of strength needed to provide servant-led ministry when it is countercultural to do so. The servant nature of these parishes *requires* prayer because a servant mentality is one that focuses on the needs and interests of others. Prayer moves us away from our own needs and motives and helps us see that others have concerns that might be different from our own. Prayer also can help us move away from the self-serving emphasis in our secular society and turn to the other-oriented nature that God wants for us.

When asked to describe their prayer life, our parish leaders discussed how they were mindful of the needs and interests of parishioners during their daily prayer. Fr. David explained that through his daily hour of prayer every morning, he often reflects on how he has treated his parishioners in Solon. He explained how his prayer life has sometimes enlightened him to realize a need for an apology. He added, "It seems like I'm always needling someone into doing something or another. If I am not gentle enough, then I try to be more diplomatic the next time, and I apologize if I've pushed them too hard."

The prayerful behaviors of the leaders in our three parishes became a model that was also reflected in the prayerful lives of the parishioners. A number of parishioners talked about the centrality of prayer in their lives. When asked what behaviors are most observable among his parishioners, Fr. David stated, "The parishioners respond by getting really involved. They pray, receive the sacraments, go to Mass and confession, they get involved in Eucharistic adoration. They are committed to the person of Jesus."

Prayer provides strength and inspiration. When prayer takes the focus away from the person who is praying and places it on the needs of others, it becomes the catalyst for servant behaviors.

Nine Areas of Ministry

The survey of the parish life evaluators described in chapter 3 provided insight into what many dioceses call "areas of ministry." While the structure, process, and methodology may vary according to size of parish, *all* parishes should be active in nine areas of ministry. While the original model in the Diocese of Davenport was focused on six areas of ministry, our parish life evaluators indicated that the evaluation of parish life can best be captured by considering these nine areas of ministry:

1. Liturgy
2. Faith formation
3. Social action
4. Finance and administration
5. Family life
6. Church life
7. Evangelization
8. Stewardship
9. Vocations

The last three of these were the ones added by the parish life evaluators. Previously, evangelization, stewardship, and vocations were considered a part of church life. Success in all these nine areas of ministry was another common characteristic in our model parishes.[20]

A topic of conversation that was brought up repeatedly during the parish life evaluator interviews, as well as the one-on-one interviews in our model parishes, concerned the areas of ministry that were most crucial for parish success and how many areas of ministry to include in the best model of parish life. In our study, we selected these nine areas as a result of our interviews with the parish life evaluators. We then proceeded to use those nine areas as the basis for our interviews with leaders in our model parishes and found that the parish leaders there agreed that evangelization, stewardship, and vocations should be considered as their own areas of ministry. In settling on the model of nine ministry areas, we were looking for a model that was both parsimonious and comprehensive in evaluating successful parish ministry.

Conclusion

While the three parishes we studied were selected because of their successful performance using strategic and operational measures, they had other common characteristics as well. In addition to being community to each other, acting as servant leaders and disciples, these parishes had six commonalities.

First, they were proficient in managerial responsibilities. This is significant because many people assume that transformational leaders cannot be transactional leaders, or vice versa. In these parishes, the management function was performed well. Often it was a case of leaders delegating management responsibilities so they could focus on pastoral roles and leadership responsibilities. But the pastors and parish staff in this study were intricately aware of the management issues in the parish, even if they were not fulfilling the role of manager themselves.

A second characteristic was the external focus of these parishes. While our study was focused on the internal dynamics of the parish, particularly the community relationships in the parish and how they treated each other, it was significant that these parishes also paid attention to the world outside the parish. The church should be a place where we are inspired, informed, and strengthened so we can go out and make changes in our lives and in the world. Our liturgies end with the message to go out to love and serve the world. Our faith formation programs inform and prepare us to live the Christian life in the outside world. In these parishes, where they treated each other as a community of faith, they also went out into the secular community and lived out their faith.

The third quality of these parishes was the integrity of the leaders, which gave them credibility with their people in the pews. The pastors and the parish staff lived out their faith in simple and genuine ways. They were not living with integrity so they could build their credibility. They built credibility because they lived with integrity. If the parish is a community of faith, the people can usually tell if the leaders practice what they teach and preach. Church leaders are held in high esteem by the members of their congregations. That makes it all the more important that they are consistently practicing their faith, not as perfect Christians, but as models of faith who are believable to the people inside and outside the parish.

The most unexpected of the six common characteristics of our parishes was what we called "spiritual explanation of parish success." The tendency of the pedestal leader would be to take credit for success in the parish and to find ways to deflect criticism. In fact, it is human nature to attribute something that we did as the reason for success of the team or organization. We build self-esteem by looking at the positive contributions we make. When others recognize those contributions, it can build our self-confidence. But the servant leader is one who can transcend those personal needs and realize that others have a need for recognition as well. Servant leaders try to acknowledge others when things go well and accept personal responsibility when things do not go well. They also accept and appreciate the fact that God has blessed them with the gifts and talents that make success possible in the first place.

Giving credit to God and taking the blame yourself is a practice that requires spiritual discipline. It was no surprise that one of the common features of our high-performing parishes was the active prayer lives of the leaders. They turned to God for help and strength in their leadership journeys. The more that others rely on the leader for support, the more important it is for the leader to find strength in their spirituality. Prayer restores our sense of purpose in life. It also gives direction for the future.

Purpose and direction are two critical elements of leadership. Without them, the leader is lost. It is through the centrality of prayer in their lives that our parish leaders were able to keep going. Visionary leaders have a strategic view of the whole organization. Decision making for one aspect of the organization is not made in isolation of the needs and interests of other aspects of the whole. *All* organizations have departments or divisions that tend to compartmentalize their work and to look inwardly and apart from the rest of the organization. Leaders need to see the big picture and encourage others to see it.

Generally, the departments of an organization will not collaborate unless someone responsible for more than one department gives them incentives for collaboration. That is a function of leadership. In a parish, the compartmentalization often occurs around areas of ministry. Parish leaders can encourage collaboration by inspiring a shared vision of parish life that includes all areas of ministry and generates interest for each person outside of their area of special interest.

11

FOUR MODELS
FROM OUR STUDY

This chapter presents four models that we created in the process of studying parish life. We also discuss the limitations of these four models and our suggestions for future study. The four models are

1. *Three Measures of Parish Life*. Parish life can be measured in multiple ways. Our model: Strategic, operational, and behavioral measures.
2. *Three Servant Leader Behavior Categories*. Servant leadership is an approach that can be distinguished from transformational, transactional, and charismatic leadership. Our model: Three behavioral categories—serving, recognizing, and empowering—that describe how servant leadership works and what servant leadership looks like in a parish.
3. *Seven Behavioral Mechanisms*. Servant leadership enhances organizational citizenship, which enhances organizational performance. Our model: Seven behavioral mechanisms that explain why servant leadership works in a parish.
4. *Three Models of Parish Size*. Servant leadership behaviors look different in a large parish that operates with teams than in a small parish that acts as a family. Our model: Three parish sizes that are named the *family, community,* and *teams* approaches.

Three Measures of Parish Life

Parish life can be judged by the quality of liturgies, the effectiveness of teaching methods, or the extent of outreach to neighborhoods and communities. In our study, we explored behaviors of leaders and members as well as the dynamics of people in relationship to each other. It may seem curious that parish life would be evaluated through the lens of organizational behavior rather than one of theology or religion. As mentioned earlier, we believe that in a religious community, faithfulness is more important than effectiveness. But in reality, the two are hard to separate, and both are critical for parish life.

Parish Effectiveness

The relationship between faithfulness and effectiveness applies not only to social justice and peacemaking but also to parish life. As a parish, if we are striving to be faithful, how can we not worry about whether we are being effective? Being faithful should translate eventually into being effective. Results may not be visible in the short run. They may take years to come to fruition. But if we are acting on faith, and if we are sharing our faith with others, it makes sense that at some point we will see signs that we are being effective in ways that express our faithfulness.

Effectiveness is an observable sign that people are acting out of faithfulness. Behaviors are outward signs of the love that we profess for God, for our neighbors, and for each other. Understanding that first we must be faithful, how can we not concern ourselves about effectiveness, especially when we are talking about our behaviors as Christian people? While faithfulness may be measurable only in God's eyes, we think that parish effectiveness can be measurable in behavioral ways.

An Anecdote: Thomas Merton's Letter to a Young Activist

In the 1980s and 1990s, I attended many retreats for peace and justice activists at Kirkridge, Pennsylvania. At one of these retreats, we were discussing Thomas Merton's "Letter to a Young Activist," in which Merton suggests to Jim Forest (who is now a veteran peace activist), that God calls us to be *faithful*, not *effective*.[1] The consensus that was beginning to emerge around our retreat circle was agreement with Merton.

Then a woman from Harlem stepped into the discussion. She spoke as a grandmother worried deeply about the future of this country. I remember her saying in essence:

> *It might be easy for you middle-class white folk to sit there and be satisfied with your faithfulness, but that is not enough to put bread on my table and a roof over my head. I know that God calls us to be faithful, but in my mind, that is the same thing as being effective, because God doesn't want me and my grandchildren living in poverty. If you are faithful to God's teachings, you will keep working until you are effective.*

That message made a lifelong impact on me. The passion in her voice and the power of her conviction woke up the rest of us activists who were about to congratulate ourselves for being faithful without worrying about whether we were being effective. What she said makes sense in this context as well. *If we are striving to be faithful, we will want to be effective.*

Another Anecdote: Grace or Works?

The debate about faithfulness versus effectiveness is similar to the debate about grace versus works. Fifteen years ago, my son Josh and his friends, about twelve years old at the time, were debating grace versus works in our living room. One of his young friends was arguing that he would rather believe that we are already saved by grace because then he would not have to work to get to heaven. Another of Josh's young friends was arguing that we should work to get to heaven because then we would make the world a better place. That is when my son Josh, wise beyond his twelve years, told his friends, "I believe that if we have grace, we will *want* to do good works."

In the same way that we now teach the duality of grace and works, we argue here for the duality of faithfulness and effectiveness. If we have grace, as Josh said, we will want to do good works. In the same way, if we are faithful, we will want to see signs of faithfulness through our effectiveness.

We created a three-part model of parish effectiveness that includes:

1. *Strategic* measures constructed as a parish self-assessment that we used to explore performance in nine areas of ministry
2. *Operational* measures such as financial and demographic information that we gathered from the eighty-four parishes of the Diocese of Davenport
3. *Behavioral* measures of parish life, such as servant leadership and organizational citizenship, upon which we based our parish field study

Strategic Measures

Data collected as operational measures can become the basis for goal setting and evaluation. It is difficult for people to know if they are succeeding unless they have some measures of success. When parishes set goals and measure their progress toward those goals, these are examples of **strategic measures**. The data collected as operational measures can be used in an interactive process in which parishioners study the data and use it to assess internal strengths and weaknesses and match them against external opportunities and threats. This creates the SWOT (Strengths, Weaknesses, Opportunities, and Threats) analysis. Based on that information, parish leaders identify their *strategic issues*, which are the major questions, challenges, or problems facing the parish.[2]

The parish identifies three to five strategic issues that can be written as questions such as, "How can we address the distractions of our culture to recruit more volunteers for parish ministry?" Once a strategic question like this has been formulated, the next step is brainstorming possible answers to the question. The best ideas become strategies, and the parish limits these strategies to a few strategies for each strategic issue. Finally, for each strategy, the parish sets measurable goals and action steps, designates who will be responsible for each item, determines timelines and deadlines for activities, and continues to evaluate progress toward their goals.[3]

Goals can and should energize and motivate people. They facilitate clear communication. They enhance constructive conflict. They maintain team focus on achieving results. They forge work groups into teams.[4] This is especially true when the goals are developed interactively and communicated widely, and when progress toward the goals is shared with the people involved with those goals.

Parish planning and goal setting is only effective if the parish follows up by monitoring, evaluating, and making changes to the plan as adjustments become necessary. Once strategic planning is done, the parish moves into **strategic thinking**.[5] This is the continuous process of studying and considering trends in church and society, identifying changes in the world around us, evaluating how those changes are affecting our strategic plan, and making the adjustments necessary as the world changes around us.[6] Strategic thinking occurs in the context of measuring progress in a strategic plan. But without measures of success, strategic planning and strategic thinking can become meaningless activities that lead to nowhere.

Operational Measures

Most of what we consider **operational measures** in our study involve measuring numbers of people and dollars. All parishes measure *something*. They measure expenses and income. They measure the average contribution per parishioner, the average percentage of parishioners attending Sunday Mass, and how many people are attending liturgies, religious education, and other events. These financial and demographic statistics are examples of operational measures in our study. (The full range of operational measures we used in our study is reported in appendices B and C.)

One surprise in our study was the realization that most parishes rarely release this sort of quantitative information to the entire parish. When we reported the results of our parish life study to hundreds of leaders of the eighty-four parishes in the Davenport diocese, through a series of six deanery meetings, we found that very few laypeople knew about Mass counts. Parish council presidents, finance council chairpersons, and lay trustees were unaware of the fact that Catholic parishes conduct Mass counts in November each year and report those numbers to their diocese.

The use of operational measures can be very helpful in a strategic planning process. The gathering of data, often conducted as a

SWOT analysis, is called an "environmental assessment."[7] Counting how many people are involved in various areas of ministry, such as weekly liturgy, religious education, and social action, can become the basis for goal-setting activities. Some parishes ask their ushers to take Mass counts every week. They report those numbers in the weekly bulletin and use the information to set goals for the parish.

Behavioral Measures

In addition to operational and strategic measures, we added a unique category of measures based on servant leadership behaviors and organizational citizenship behaviors. The main advantage of using **behavioral measures** in our model is that behaviors are *action oriented*. Behaviors of leaders and members are observable, measurable, changeable, and, therefore, trainable. Our behavioral model includes three servant leadership behaviors and four organizational citizenship behaviors. We suggest that servant leadership enhances organizational citizenship, which in turn enhances organizational performance.

Human resource activities in not-for-profit organizations (such as churches) are critically important because the accomplishment of the mission depends on the behaviors of the people who are leaders, managers, and members of the organization. While our model parishes were selected primarily on the basis of financial and demographic measures, our study found that high-performing parishes also demonstrated organizational citizenship and servant leadership behaviors.

Colloquial sayings and clichés remind us of the importance of setting a good example, practicing consistency between what is said and what is done, and living with integrity by integrating behaviors with values. We say, "Actions speak louder than words. Practice what you preach. Walk the talk. Live by example. Do what you say." And in the words of St. Francis of Assisi, "Preach the gospel at all times and, when necessary, use words."

These familiar sayings suggest that behaviors are more important than the message. Behaviors and the message need to resonate with each other. My experience has been that people are more likely to *act themselves into a new way of thinking* than to *think themselves into a new way of acting*. This suggests that more attention should be paid to actions and behaviors.

The Leadership Behaviors of Jesus

While servant leadership is the leadership style most associated with Jesus, Jesus stands in contrast to most of today's leaders. He never wrote a book, held a political office, led an army, or ever taught in a school. He was not the chief executive officer of a large company and did not make a lot of money. He was born into poverty and died without any worldly possessions. He lived the life of a vagabond, leading a ragtag group of uneducated fishermen and tax collectors, most of whom abandoned him at the hour of his death. He was not a positional leader in a formal group. Nor was he successful in most ways that today's society measures success.

Yet if we measure leadership by numbers of followers that he has led or by numbers of leaders that he has developed, Jesus must be counted among the most effective leaders of all time. After he was crucified, he left behind a few hundred followers.[8] A few years later, the number of disciples had grown into the thousands.[9] Within five generations, it swelled to the millions of Christians. Today, two thousand years later, Jesus has "almost as many Roman Catholic followers as *citizens* of China."[10] When taken together with the Protestant ecclesial community, Christians number nearly 1.5 billion more than any other religion in the world.

Jesus was both faithful and effective. He was faithful to God, to the people around him, and ultimately to his mission in the world. But he was also effective in ways that the world does measure success, including the sheer numbers of followers he led and still leads, and the number of leaders he developed and still develops. The leadership that Jesus demonstrated, developed, and practiced among his disciples was instrumental to the growth of the church.[11]

The leadership field is beginning to discover the power of the leadership methods practiced by Jesus. Dozens of books and hundreds of articles have been written on the leadership style, wisdom, lessons, secrets, and behaviors of Jesus. A consensus is emerging among the authors of these books and articles in naming the leadership style of Jesus as "servant leadership."[12] Servant leadership offers those who are "religious" an opportunity to practice their faith whenever they practice leadership. It also has great potential to show practical results in many organizations, including commercial ones.

Church Behaviors

Bob Briner and Ray Pritchard suggest that some churches have wonderful mission statements that declare an intention to develop leaders as "caring servants," but the churches do not reflect this in "the way they perform in the small everyday interactions with people."[13] Briner and Pritchard lament the fact that the leadership lessons of Jesus are not being practiced in churches, despite the fact that they consider servant leadership "the single surest formula for success ever enunciated."[14] They state, "There is almost no expectation for the rank and file of church members beyond the hope that they will show up and contribute funds."[15]

Our study found just the opposite in our high-performing parishes. We found that servant leadership was being practiced and that the rank-and-file members were reciprocating with organizational citizenship behaviors. The parishioners were performing behaviors above and beyond showing up and donating money. The people in the pews were practicing stewardship—exactly what one would expect of disciples of Christ.[16]

Three Servant Leader Behaviors

Our study clarifies what servant leader behaviors look like in a parish. This is particularly important because servant leadership is a relatively untested concept that is often confused with other forms of leadership. The specific examples of servant leader behaviors provided here help clarify and distinguish servant leadership from transformational, transactional, or charismatic leadership. In appendix G, we provide an extensive list of examples of specific leader behaviors to illustrate servant leadership in action.

We also found plenty of real-life examples of servant leader behaviors that fit into these three categories—recognizing, serving, empowering—and that could be helpful for creating behavioral scales like the one created by Mark Ehrhart.[17] These scales can identify and test the unique elements of servant leadership. Some of the very specific behaviors that we gleaned from our study are listed below. We suggest that the servant leader:

- Gives credit to others when things are going well
- Takes the blame when things are not going well
- Drops what he or she is doing when others are in need
- Visits with marginalized members of the group
- Helps set up and clean up for meetings
- Is not the focal point of organizational activities
- Attends to the needs of others before his or her own

We placed the specific behaviors and leadership activities we saw and heard about in our parishes into three categories of servant leadership:

1. Recognizing
2. Serving
3. Empowering

Seven Behavioral Mechanisms

Our study found that servant leadership fits the description of supportive leader behaviors and enhanced organizational performance. This is significant because servant leadership is viewed by some as a "soft" concept that is not practical and would not be associated with organizational success.[18] Our research suggests that the connection between servant leader behaviors and high performance in a parish could be explained by the fact that the servant leader behaviors are causing an enhancement of organizational citizenship behaviors (OCBs).[19]

Our findings indicate that if the servant leader supports, encourages, empowers, and demonstrates genuine interest in the followers, it is likely that servant leadership will generate trust, commitment, and cohesion among the followers and ultimately will enhance OCBs. Extensive research on OCBs suggests that they drive organizational success.[20] This is the fundamental logic that became the basis for suggesting that parish performance can be measured by exploring our behavioral measures. Our study builds upon this research and a few others that have found servant leadership to be an effective style.[21]

The notion that servant leadership is consistent with the supportive leader behaviors that have been demonstrated to enhance

OCBs can also be explained by reviewing Robert Greenleaf's original descriptions of servant leadership. In his classic essay, Greenleaf states that servant leaders are measured by their ability to pass his "best test," meaning that their followers grow as persons and become healthier, wiser, freer, and more autonomous.[22] In other words, the success of the leader is inextricably bound to the success of the followers. Therefore, one way of answering the question in Greenleaf's "best test" is by exploring the behaviors of the members of the organization. In our case, that meant searching for behavioral measures of helping, initiating, participating, and self-developing.

In addition to describing servant leadership, we also sought to explain how and why it works specifically in a parish. This is of import because the more we can understand the dynamics of servant leadership, the more effective we can be in teaching it. To explain servant leadership, we went through a meticulous process of looking at the behavioral interaction between the leaders and members of our parishes.

Based on that careful study, we found four direct mechanisms and three organizational mechanisms to explain how servant leadership works:

Direct Mechanisms
1. Invitation
2. Inspiration
3. Modeling
4. Affection

Organizational Mechanisms
1. Cultural
2. Structural
3. Strategic

We believe these seven mechanisms explain how and why servant leadership works as it enhances organizational citizenship. They are presented in more detail in chapter 9.

Three Models of Parish Size

We were not specifically looking for differences based on parish size, but they became readily apparent as we observed our parishes. For example, we found that the levels of participating were higher in the larger parishes and that the levels of helping and initiating were higher in the smallest parishes. A prescription for parish life ought to take these differences into consideration.

Theories of organizational structure help to explain these differences based on the formalization, bureaucratization, and standardization that occur when organizations grow in size.[23] While parishes are expected to demonstrate competence and activity in all areas of ministry, the parish structures that enable the parish to be involved in these ministries might look a lot different. Larger parishes may be better suited to follow the Iowa City example of teamwork or the Solon example of community building by creating separate commissions for each area of ministry. Smaller parishes might follow the example of Bloomfield by utilizing the parish council as a committee of the whole for all areas of ministry. Although the parish structures varied from parish to parish, in each case, the bottom line was a high-performing parish doing well in nine areas of ministry.

We attributed the following names to the three parishes in our study as we believe they provide a positive view of the healthy differences based on parish size.

1. *Family*: The smallest parishes
2. *Community*: The medium-sized parishes
3. *Teams*: The largest parishes

Limitations and Suggestions for Future Research

While our models of parish life incorporated the results of only three Catholic parishes in southeast Iowa, we believe that the behaviors described in these churches can be applied to other churches and places. The three parish life measures, the three servant leader behaviors, and the differences we found based on three parish sizes ought to be applicable to other church settings. The interactions described in our model of seven behavioral mechanisms are human dynamics that should be evident in many ecclesial communities, regardless of faith tradition, and in many other not-for-profit organizations. Future research could explore whether our findings can be generalized to other parishes, including those of other Christian denominations, those of other faith traditions, and those in other geographic locations.

As a qualitative study that describes parish behaviors, our research was not able to eliminate alternative explanations to the success of these three parishes. Case research does not intend to prove a theory. Instead, it illustrates important theoretical connections by describing how and explaining why something works. While our study does not pretend to be a rigorous quantitative study, it does help to explain causal factors of an evolving theory. The use of multiple cases, such as the three parishes involved in this study, adds reliability to the study, but does not prove our theory about parish servant leadership. While our study has some obvious limitations, we believe that it also makes a valuable contribution to the study of parish life.

Our model of three servant leader behavioral categories proposes one way to describe *how* servant leadership works in a parish. Our model of seven behavior mechanisms proposes a way to explain *why* servant leadership works as it enhances organizational citizenship. More research is needed to generalize our study beyond its limitations and to test our models of servant leadership more broadly, seeking to confirm the proposed linkages of servant leadership and organizational citizenship in a variety of settings. We hope that our models of parish leadership will help us to better understand how we can improve parish life as we foster the growth and nurture the effectiveness of parish leaders.

Generalizing our results *beyond* a parish setting is a stretch we are not yet prepared to make. However, one of the challenges of living as disciples of Christ is taking his message and trying to apply it to the secular world by living out his teachings every day. If servant leadership can apply to high-performing parishes, perhaps it might also apply to other high-performing organizations.

Leadership Traits versus Behaviors

In the process of studying behaviors in high-performing parishes, we also identified some leadership traits associated with servant leadership. In chapter 1, some of those traits were listed, but further study would help clarify and expand upon the question of what traits are associated with servant leadership.[24] *Traits* are defined as the internal qualities or characteristics that describe the leader.

In the early twentieth century, leadership studies emphasized leadership traits. The point was to identify successful leaders and ask what traits were associated with them. Later, the emphasis switched to leadership *behaviors*, which are defined as what the leader actually does.[25] Both leadership behaviors and leadership traits are critical to understanding the dynamics of leadership.[26] Frances Hesselbein demonstrates the importance of leadership traits when she states, "Leadership is a matter of how to be, not how to do it."[27] In her experiences with the Girl Scouts, she discovered that the quality and character of the leader are what determined the greatest results.

Traits and behaviors are often presented as two sides of the same coin. The study of leadership ethics, for example, falls into two broad categories: the conduct of the leader, which is behavioral, and the character of the leader, which explores the virtues and disposition of the leader.[28] Conduct is seen through the *outward* behaviors of the leader, while character is manifested by an *inward* journey of personal training and self-discipline. The leader is not born with character. Character is established through the routines and practices of the person being trained. The behavioral approach looks at the external conduct of leaders and asks what effective leaders *do*. The traits approach considers the character of the leader and asks what internal qualities are associated with admired leaders. Together, these two approaches explain "the actions of leaders and who they are as people."[29]

In our study, some leader behaviors appeared to be associated with certain leader traits. For example, recognizing behaviors seemed to be associated with hopefulness in the leader, which involves a positive attitude about the potential of the gifts and talents of the parishioners. Serving behaviors seemed to be associated with humility, which involves a virtuous balance between selfishness and selflessness. Empowerment seems to be related to the leadership trait of self-confidence. Leaders who lack confidence are less likely to risk building capacity in others to act and are more likely to command and control everything instead.

Given these possible associations between traits and behaviors, we can suggest that leaders who recognize, serve, and empower are likely be people who are hopeful, humble, and confident. Some support for these associations can be found in scripture. Hopefulness and humility fit into the list of leadership qualities presented in 1 Timothy 3:1–10. That list includes integrity, temperance, humility, respectability, hospitality, nonviolence, gentleness, being positive and unselfish. Timothy's passage on leadership states that the most important leadership skill is to teach, which requires confidence and is related to empowerment.

Other leadership traits, which ought to become the focus of more rigorous study, include:

- Honesty and trustworthiness, which seem to be associated with the credibility that is mandatory for leadership in a community of faith[30]
- Collaboration, which seems to be consistent with empowerment
- Innovation, which includes openness to new ideas and willingness to take risk
- Passion for the mission of the organization, which fuels persistence and dedication in leaders facing increasing challenges

When we practice certain leadership behaviors, we can activate ourselves into a new way of thinking and being. That new way of being is another way to describe leadership traits. Over time, if the leadership behaviors become leadership practices, the leader's traits can change as well. Therefore, practicing certain leadership behaviors can be a means toward developing certain leadership traits. If people can activate themselves into a new way of thinking, and if people can conceive of themselves into a new way of being, more emphasis should be placed on leadership traits.[31] Studying leadership behaviors and traits together gives us a more complete view of leadership.[32] Future research should be conducted to associate the servant leader behaviors studied here with the traits that seem to be most consistent with these behaviors.

Visioning

One of the traits most associated with leadership is being forward-looking or visionary.[33] **Visioning** is a critical area of leadership. Greenleaf said that foresight is "the lead the leader has."[34] He said that visioning is not a means of predicting the future but instead a "step in constructing the future that we want."[35] The process of visioning is more important than the vision statement. The **vision statement** is a hopeful picture of what the future might bring for an organization, given the pursuit of certain goals, strategies, and plans.[36] While the **mission statement** articulates the purpose of a team or organization, the vision statement sets the direction.[37]

Visions have also been described as "dreams with deadlines." An internal vision statement describes how the organization itself would look differently if it addresses its strategic issues, meets its goals, and accomplishes its mission.[38] The external vision statement, which is much more significant, describes how the outside world would look differently if the organization addresses its strategic issues, meets its goals, and accomplishes its mission.[39] A shared vision is one that has been created through a collaborative process between the leader and the members of an organization, thus enhancing a sense of ownership in the vision.

Visionary leadership is a critical part of servant leadership. The servant leader—like the transformational leader—approaches visioning as a process involving as many members of the organization as possible.[40] In contrast, the charismatic leader identifies and articulates the vision in such a compelling way that others are moved to follow that vision.[41] But the vision of the charismatic leader belongs to the leader, whereas the servant leader tries to involve many people in a process of creating a sense of **shared vision**.[42] This has best been described by Marshall Sashkin and Molly Sashkin through four proposed steps: expressing, explaining, extending, and expanding a vision.[43]

Visioning is a continual process that does not end once the vision statement is expressed. Given the pace of change in our society, the leader needs to be continually looking toward the future with an eye toward organizational transformation. As the world changes externally, the organization needs to change internally. A common mistake is thinking that once the vision statement has been expressed, the visioning process is complete. While it may be true that the vision statement might not need to be revisited for a few years after it has been articulated, it is a mistake to assume that once the vision statement is complete, the visioning process is also complete. Visioning is a never-ending process.

Strategic Planning

Strategic planning is a rational, intentional process of identifying strategies and making plans for the future.[44] This is something that most organizations do every two to three years. *Strategic thinking* is the continuous process of adapting to the changes occurring in our world and making adjustments to the strategic plan when change becomes necessary.[45] Both strategic planning and strategic thinking are part of the visioning process. The strategic planning process is the time to consider changes to the vision statement. The vision statement is the public face of the visioning process. It is an expression of the vision that gives hope and inspiration to the people. It helps to set the general direction of the organization, but the visionary leader is always looking to the future and making adjustments to that direction as the world changes.

Like most qualities of a leader, foresight is not seen as a fixed trait but is something that a leader can work on and develop over time.[46] However, some people seem to have cognitive capabilities, creative talents, or personality traits that give them an advantage when it comes to visioning.[47] Those who are very intuitive, for example, might spend more time imagining the future. Those not as intuitive might struggle more with the conceptual side of a visioning process. Some leaders seem to have a knack for visioning while others struggle mightily with their ability to envision. But all leaders can develop skills to improve in this area.

While vision is about the future, the visioning process begins with the present. The first step in the visioning process is doing a

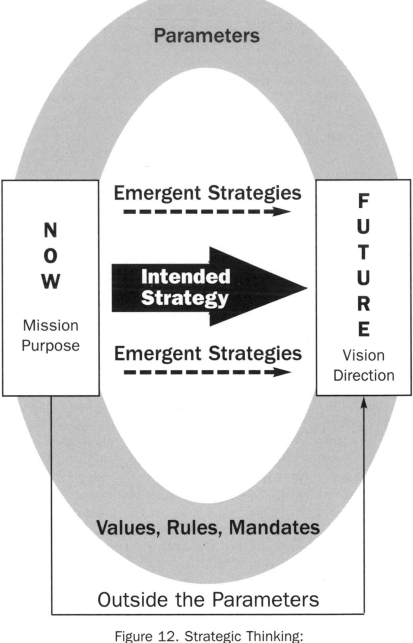

Figure 12. Strategic Thinking:
Outside the Box but Inside the Circle

reality check about the current state of the organization. This includes identifying the mission, core values, and mandates. Together, these can be viewed as a circle that creates certain *parameters* as noted in Figure 12. The strategies developed out of a strategic planning process are the *intended strategies*, noted by the bold arrow in Figure 12. The dotted lines are strategies that *emerge* out of crisis situations or creative thinking. Together, the intended and emergent strategies help provide a sense of direction toward the vision. However, when an organization is limited to its intended strategies, it is like thinking inside a box, such as the one portrayed by the bold arrow in Figure 12. The key to visioning is to think outside the box of intended strategies but inside the circle of parameters set by our mission, values, and mandates. Visionary leaders are those who can stimulate strategic thinking among their followers to *think outside that box but inside that circle*.

Conclusion

In this chapter, we summarized our major contributions to the discussion about parish life and servant leadership. We suggested a model of three measures of parish life: strategic, operational, and behavioral. We proposed a model of three servant leader behavior categories that describe how servant leadership works in a parish. We presented a model of seven behavioral mechanisms that explain why servant leadership works in a parish. And we described a model of three parish sizes: family, community, and teams. We also suggested new ways of looking at servant leadership traits, and we presented a model for strategic thinking and planning as part of the visioning process. Next we discuss the importance of developing new approaches to leadership in the church.

12

DEVELOPING SERVANT LEADERS

The best advice I've received in more than thirty-three years of ministry came from Harry Fagan at a national meeting of the Roundtable Association for Social Action Directors. I was new to diocesan ministry, looking for advice, when Harry stated bluntly, "If you are not developing leaders, you might as well get out of this business." Those words have stayed with me ever since. They have inspired every day of my ministry. And they influenced my decision in 2006 to accept a full-time teaching job in the Masters of Organizational Leadership program at St. Ambrose University while maintaining a part-time leadership position with the Diocese of Davenport.

In thirty-three years of ministry, regardless of the ministry I led, my priority has been to *develop leaders*. As a social action director, I developed an annual statewide social action institute that has brought together more than a hundred parish leaders across Iowa since the early 1990s. As a stewardship director, I developed a statewide stewardship institute that has involved hundreds of participants and dozens of coaches, running for a period of twenty weeks each year since 2005. At the time of this writing, I am starting a leadership development program for diocesan priests at the request of Bishop Martin Amos.

At the conclusion of our liturgies, we hear words such as, "Go in peace to love and serve the Lord." And we respond, "Thanks be to God." That is the call to action for every disciple of Christ to live out their faith seven days a week. Responding to this call to action means that before we come back to the table of the Eucharist the following week, we will be

- Forming our faith in Christ
- Living a life of stewardship
- Evangelizing others to be inspired by Christ

- Participating in the life of our parish
- Practicing our faith in our workplaces and family life
- Reaching out to others with charity and justice

Practicing this level of discipleship would revolutionize the church and society. Encouraging this level of discipleship is required of leaders. To make this happen, we need to create and promote leadership development opportunities for clergy and lay leaders. This chapter focuses on the urgent and important need to develop servant leaders in our church today.

The Urgency of the Leadership Situation

Given the critical need for leadership in the church and society, the development of leaders needs to be framed as a matter of urgency and importance. It is simply not possible to lead and organize ministry without inviting, recruiting, developing, supporting, and training the people. It is easy to get caught up in the day-to-day urgent matters that need to be addressed in a parish. We sometimes forget to devote the energy needed for longer-range, important matters, such as developing future leaders. If the leader is not focused on the important work of developing leaders among the congregation, other urgent matters will demand the attention of the parish.[1]

One of the distinctions between leadership and management is that leaders focus on important issues involving change, visioning, and the future—ones that are not necessarily urgent—while managers spend more time on the urgent day-to-day issues—ones that may not necessarily be important. John Kotter suggests that the most important role of the leader is to create a sense of urgency about the need for change.[2] This is another way of saying that the leader creates a **sense of urgency** about what is important. Leadership development is an issue that is often perceived as important but not necessarily urgent. Robert Greenleaf suggests that leadership development is part of the real test for servant leaders.[3] In order to change the perception that leadership development is not an urgent matter, the leader needs to make the case that without developing new leaders, urgent needs will not be addressed.

The bishop's question that inspired this study—"How do you measure the life of a parish?"—was asked within the context of a diocesan staff meeting discussing the possible closure of parishes. As the shortage of clergy deepens, the issue of measuring parish viability and making prudent decisions about parish closings will become even more critical.[4] Churches of all denominations and faith groups of all traditions are trying to discern how to provide clergy to meet the congregational needs of the faithful, especially when the community of faith is located in a poor neighborhood, a rural community, or a remote location.

This is an urgent and important challenge of leadership. Many churches are experimenting with new forms of parish restructuring and trying to figure out how to implement change when it becomes necessary. More attention needs to be devoted to developing the strategies, plans, and ideas that address how to breathe new life into congregations, to keep them open, and to move them from inactive to active parishes, as well as from good to great parishes. If Harry Fagan was correct, church leaders of all denominations need to re-focus their energy toward developing leaders of tomorrow's church.

Lay leaders are beginning to grasp the urgency of their situation and are making plans to enhance the spiritual, human, and physical capacities of their parishes and to remain viable into the future. Parish leaders are developing a stronger sense of community, training quali-fied leaders for ministry, and remodeling their physical plants so they are capable of holding more people.[5] Some of these changes create more opportunities for lay leadership. All of them require greater par-ticipation in the life of the church by all of the people.

Delegation of
Management Responsibilities

St. Paul describes *leadership* as a spiritual gift and as one of the roles that needs to be fulfilled in the church (1 Cor 12:28). Leadership, or administration of human activities, is mentioned often in the Bible, from the tending of the Garden of Eden by Adam, to the building of the ark by Noah, to the leadership through the desert by Moses, to the use and promotion of delegation by Jethro.[6] Jesus developed the leadership potential among his apostles. Paul became an organizer of the early church under the mentorship of Gamaliel (Acts 22:3).

Similarly, the church today needs to develop administrative abilities among its leaders in order to develop discipleship among its parishioners.[7] Research shows that many clergy are frustrated over the amount of time and energy they have to spend administering the business affairs of the parish.[8] Members of the clergy study theology and philosophy in preparation for parish ministry and then find themselves in a situation where they need to know about leadership, management, finance, and administration.[9] Most have not studied business or leadership theory. Few of them fully grasp the important role that leadership and management play in the performance of parish life.[10]

Most clergy are attracted to ministry because of an interest in working with people, not paperwork.[11] They are motivated by mission, not money.[12] To connect their work back to that mission, clergy need to open up opportunities to utilize their gifts and talents in ministry.[13] Management guru Peter Drucker advises pastors to call forth the laypeople to cover at least some of their management responsibilities so the clergy can dedicate more time toward their strengths in other areas of ministry such as liturgy and faith formation.[14] According to William T. Ditewig, one of the responsibilities delegated to deacons in the earliest days of the church was financial administration.[15]

Laypeople in many parishes today are a source of untapped potential. It is common to hear clergy and staff people in pastoral ministry complain about being too busy. Yet many church leaders are unwilling or unable to delegate more responsibility to laypeople and the diaconate. One way that all pastoral ministers could ease their burdens would be to assign more of the management responsibilities, such as bookkeeping and building maintenance, to laypeople. Many of them already have the business acumen to succeed as managers in the secular world. If laypeople can assume responsibility for managing sophisticated projects in the workplace, we should be able to give them the training, guidance, and support they need to manage some of the parish business as well.

In chapter 1, we described transactional leaders, or managers, as those who value stability, maintain order, and take control, while transformational leaders value creativity, take risks, and inspire people toward a vision. Generally speaking, managers deal with day-to-day operational issues, while leaders inspire a sense of shared vision,[16] challenge the organization to deal with change,[17] and set a future direction for the organization.[18] As explained previously, managers deal with more urgent matters that surface every day while leaders deal with more important issues that others might not see.

Sorting out the urgent from the important is the key to time management for leaders. In order to address the longer-term strategic and important issues like dealing with change and envisioning the future, leaders need to be able to delegate management duties. This enhances the leaders' ability to think more strategically and focus on the shared vision for the future. Delegating managerial responsibilities can create time and space for the leader to address important issues that might not otherwise get addressed.

Nevertheless, pastors cannot and should not delegate all management responsibilities. All leaders have to deal occasionally with some management tasks but not necessarily to perform them directly. For example, the pastor needs to understand how to read financial statements but not necessarily how to produce them. The extent of management attention of the pastor might vary according to parish size and scope of responsibilities. In larger parishes, where the temptation to control the budget and micromanage the staff may be difficult to resist, it is even more critical that pastors focus on leadership duties that can easily go unattended. Once a task is delegated to another manager or leader, the role of the person doing the delegating is to provide support and invite feedback, not to command and control.[19]

When leaders create a sense of urgency about what is important, they change the perception about what requires immediate attention, such as matters that may be seen as important but not urgent. It is important but not necessarily perceived as urgent that the church recruit, develop, train, and assign responsibility to laypeople for leadership and management roles in today's church. Whether the skills and abilities of the laity are fully realized is contingent upon the leadership skills and abilities of the existing parish staff and clergy to recognize that talent, to call it forward, and to empower the laity to con-tribute their talents to the work of the church. The model parishes in our study demonstrated that if a parish wants to enhance the partici-pation, initiative, and other signs of organizational citizenship among the laity, leaders need to devote their attention to recognizing, empowering, and serving the people.

Lao Tsu, writing hundreds of years before the birth of Christ, wrote in the *Tao* about leaders taking a lower profile and delegating responsibilities to others: "A leader is best when people barely know that he exists. Not so good when people obey him. Worse when they despise him. But of a good leader, who talks little, when his task is done, his aim fulfilled, the people will say, 'We did it ourselves.'"[20]

Pastor as Leader, Not Manager

The pastor of a church is responsible for the parish and needs to review, understand, and oversee certain management concerns of the parish. It is important that the pastor understand the urgent manage-rial issues of the parish and ensure consistency between management practices and leadership priorities.

One of the interesting characteristics of our model parishes was the managerial proficiency of the parishes. However, excellence in management does not require the pastors to devote their own time in doing the management or being the managers of the parish. In the parishes we studied, the pastors delegated management responsibili-ties, supervised the managers of the parish, and provided support to them. When the pastor tries to be the leader and the manager of a parish, many of the leadership responsibilities go unattended.

Programmatic Approaches

Much has been written about what projects, programs, or areas of ministry ought to be in place to enhance the quality of life in a parish. One example is the national program called Why Catholic?, which is an evangelical/Catholic faith formation program for adults. Other examples include JustFaith, an adult education program that builds commitment to social justice, and RENEW, which is a parish renewal program. These excellent programs operate with a certain philosophy, usually trying to bring people together around a certain area of ministry in pursuit of the mission of the parish.

Emerging Models of Pastoral Leadership held a series of regional meetings across the United States in 2006–07 and then convened a thousand Catholic leaders to discuss new ways of thinking about leadership in the Catholic Church in 2008.[21] In attending the regional conference in Minnesota in fall 2006 and the national meeting in Orlando in spring 2008, I discovered that while the conference addressed many approaches to parish leadership, it was not focused on behavioral models of parish leadership.[22] Instead, the emphasis was on parish programs, projects, or structures of parish leadership. It seems that the national discussion on the future of the church could be enhanced by directing more attention and research toward parish leadership traits and behaviors.[23]

Several of the critical questions identified by Emerging Models of Pastoral Leadership for today's parishes were similar to the concerns presented in the introduction of this book. They include the declining numbers of priests, the need for collaboration between clergy and laity, the role of the parish council, the training and development of lay leaders, and the most effective models for staffing clustered or mega parishes. While our study addressed many of the same concerns, we took a different approach, focusing on how people behave and treat each other in the day-to-day community life of a high-performing parish.

Collaborative Decisions

One area of overlap between the findings of Emerging Models and our study was the need for parish collaboration, a concern that has been expressed in church ministry for many years.[24] However, it is important to explain what it is and why it is important. *Collaboration* is defined here as working together to meet the needs and settle the interests of more than one parties.[25] It involves understanding and expressing your own needs and interests as well as seeking to understand and express the needs and interests of others.

One of the greatest challenges for pastors and other parish leaders who wish to practice servant leadership and delegate management responsibilities is the question of how to collaborate on decision making. Whether the issue is one of leadership or management, some decisions will be divisive. The leaders of the parishes in our study modeled a more collaborative decision-making style that involved listening to others, being open to their ideas, and building a greater sense of ownership of the final decisions. Collaborative decision making is a necessary feature of servant leadership. It involves recognizing, serving, and empowering the members of the parish. It is more likely to generate greater participation and encourage the initiative of laity.

The collaborative servant leader focuses on needs and interests, not positions, and seeks options that will mutually benefit the needs and interests of both parties.[26] A *position* is where you stand on an issue, while an *interest* explains why you are taking that position.[27] This means being assertive about your own interests and cooperative about the interests of others as you explore ways to integrate your interests with those of others.[28] When collaboration is successful, both parties win, and as a result, the organization also wins. (Literally a "win, win, win"!)

Research shows that collaboration enhances organizational life in multiple ways.[29] For example, collaboration has a reciprocal relationship with trust. It requires trust to collaborate, and it builds trust when you do collaborate.[30] Trust is such an important factor for organizational life that it has been described both as the glue that holds an organization together and the grease that keeps the organization functioning properly. Any factor that can be described in these two apparently contradictory qualities is obviously a key ingredient for successful leadership in organizations.

Guide to Collaborative Meetings

The following list of key principles is a suggested guide for collaborative decision making in a parish.[31]

1. *Respect.* Demonstrate that you value the dignity of others, especially those with whom you disagree. Show that you value the process and the outcome. Separate the person from the problem.[32]

2. *Openness*. Be open to the viewpoints of others, regardless of your relationship to them. Be open to new ideas, regardless of your position on the issue.[33]

3. *Fairness*. Allow equitable time and attention for all viewpoints. Make sure that minority views are well represented in any discussion. Keep comments brief.

4. *Listening*. Listen to understand the needs and interests of others.[34] Focus on what is being said, rather than mentally preparing your own remarks.

5. *Privacy*. Speak from your own experience. After the meeting, do not repeat and attribute comments made by others or allude negatively to their personality or motives.

6. *Presence*. Be fully present to the dynamics of the meeting, not distracted by phone calls, text messages, or other interruptions. Consider the interests of others as worthy of your attention.

7. *Commitment*. Seek options that will be mutually beneficial to other parties in the decision.[35] Keep your commitment to the mission of the parish at the center of your deliberations.

The Future of Church Leadership

Church leadership is a subject that needs further attention in seminaries, clergy seminars, lay ministry formation programs, and other trainings to explore the strengths and weaknesses of different leadership styles and to reflect that upon the gospel. People assuming new positions of leadership in the church need to understand that when they take a command-and-control approach, they stifle lay participation and initiative. Servant leadership offers a radically different approach to church leadership. It may look and sound new to some local parish communities, but it is actually as old as the teachings of Jesus.

The evidence of the declining numbers of priests reported earlier indicates that the church is at a watershed. Unless new models of leadership are discovered, preached, and practiced, many parishes may be closed. The faithful will suffer and many may leave the church, feeling that the church left them.[36] If the parish has added a meaningful contribution to the local community, closing that parish will be a loss to that community. Servant leadership is an approach to parish leadership that carries out the message of *Lumen Gentium*, calling for full empowerment of the gifts and talents of laypeople in the life of the church.

New efforts are needed to promote servant leadership in all denominations and faith traditions. For churches, this might include creating leadership curricula within seminaries that focus specifically on the leadership style of Jesus, infusing servant leadership into the continuing education programs for clergy, creating servant leadership retreats to reflect on leadership attitudes and styles, and adding servant leadership as a special topic for lay ministry formation programs as well.

Greenleaf advised that training in servant leadership should be practitioner oriented. "One does not 'learn' to be a leader the way one learns about most things that are taught in college. Like anything else that is acquired, one will do better with a mentor or a coach."[37] Servant leadership is more than a skill that one can learn through training programs. It involves a conversion to a philosophy of service to others and an approach that considers the needs and interests of others first. It can be enhanced by reading and listening to others as they explain the concepts prescribed by Jesus and articulated by Greenleaf. However, it requires a process of action and reflection that is described by Greenleaf as "growth through experience."[38]

Growing Support for Servant Leadership

A number of authors suggest that servant leadership can improve organizational performance.[39] Bill George, a former chief executive officer of Medtronic, equates servant leadership with what he calls "authentic leadership" and says that "if people feel that you are genuinely interested in serving others, then they will be prepared not just to follow you but to dedicate themselves to the common cause."[40] He tells many stories of exemplary corporate executives who learned that by serving customers, coworkers, and the organization, they can be authentic leaders with successful companies.

However, only a few authors have the empirical evidence to back up those claims.[41] Some are drawn to servant leadership simply because of its association with Jesus. Others are critical of servant leadership because it sounds soft and seems impractical.[42] This study attempts to tie servant leadership to religious principles as well as demonstrating that it works in a parish.

James Autry suggested that servant leadership "will enhance productivity, encourage creativity, and benefit the bottom line."[43] He suggested that some indications of servant leadership would be parking lots without special places for leaders, smaller offices for leaders, women in positions of leadership, pictures of employees receiving excellence awards, and parties held occasionally for employees to celebrate their successes. This study adds to that list of indicators of servant leadership by presenting an extensive list of examples of servant leadership in action.

Bob Briner and Ray Pritchard state:

> *To think that a leader can succeed by putting his or her followers and customers first, both individually and as a group, seems wrong-headed, unworkable, and a formula for failure. In fact and in truth, this leadership lesson of Jesus is the single surest formula for success ever enunciated. It is a guarantee of success in the broadest, most lasting sense.*[44]

This type of sweeping statement reflects the confidence that religious people should have in practicing their religious beliefs, even when they appear to be paradoxical. By finding support for our hypotheses that servant leadership is associated with high performance, this study adds empirical evidence that Briner and Pritchard's statement is true.

Charles Manz advocates servant leadership by stating, "In my broad search I have not found a more powerful yet straightforward philosophy than that offered some 2000 years ago by Jesus."[45] He suggests that servant leadership is the essence of the philosophy of Jesus and adds that the list of businesses embracing servant leadership as a corporate model "reads like a corporate who's who: GM, Ford, Motorola, GE, American Express, Honeywell, P & G, Cummins Engine, Digital Equipment, Boeing, Caterpillar, Texas Instruments, Gaines, AT&T, Xerox, LV Steel, Tektronix—the list goes on and on."[46] Servant leadership has also been embraced as the corporate philosophy of the largest organization in the world, Wal-Mart.[47] While these developments are an encouraging sign and a first step, it seems that servant leadership still stands in contrast to the model of leadership found in most commercial organizations.

As we discussed in our introduction, the institutions of religion and family were the principal institutions influencing society for many centuries. Since about the time of the Industrial Revolution, business has moved closer and closer to the center of influence in society, and religion has become less influential on social, economic, and political decision making. One of the unique characteristics of our study is the integration of religious literature with a rigorous study in the field of business. More work needs to be done to explore what religious leaders can learn from the study of business and what business leaders can learn from the study of religion.[48]

Our Model for Servant Leadership Development

My approach to leadership training has been fundamentally influenced by organizing workshops, conferences, retreats, and seminars in social action ministry. In my experience, the most effective training programs are ones that incorporate some type of experiential learning and the *pastoral planning cycle* that was developed by Joseph Holland and Peter Henriot of the Center of Concern.[49] It is based on the pedagogical work of Paulo Freire, the Brazilian educator who emphasized experiential learning.[50] This is consistent with Robert Greenleaf's philosophy of leadership development: that the servant leader needs a mentor or model for accompaniment during the journey toward servant leadership.[51]

In the servant leader training I have developed for priests in the Diocese of Davenport, we have used the pastoral planning cycle as a general guide for each four-hour session. After opening with a prayer, we read the upcoming Sunday's Gospel to open our meeting. We reflect on the Gospel reading in light of our own leadership experiences by opening up the discussion around a series of reflective questions intended for small group interaction. Examples include:

- What is Jesus doing in this story?
- What is he saying?

- How is he interacting with others in this story?
- How does his message and example speak to our situation today?
- What can we learn from this reading that applies to life in our parishes?

The discussion that begins in scripture usually goes for at least a half-hour, but it might go even longer. We close the theological reflection time with a prayer.

After reflecting on scripture, we focus on one aspect of leadership. It might be conflict resolution, strategic planning, fiscal responsibility, team building, leadership traits, leadership behaviors, or other very specific people skills such as listening, motivation, delegation, or decision making. The leadership area we select is introduced through a ten- to twelve-minute presentation of theory. The theory session incorporates some connections back to servant leadership, such as the relationship between servanthood and power. After a brief session for response or to clarify any questions, we enter into a leadership self-assessment to help the participants reflect on their personal strengths and weaknesses on that leadership area. The self-assessments are discussed one on one or in small groups. Lessons taken from these discussions are reported back to the full group.

The leadership self-assessment usually leads into a full discussion and analysis of the leadership area and about issues of parish life and church leadership. This discussion often flows into reflection on the need for social change, institutional change, and personal growth and development. Suggestions for leadership development lead into a goal-setting session in which all participants are encouraged to set personal goals. Eventually, the discussion about the leadership topic leads us back to scripture, and we conclude with prayer.

A facilitator is helpful to guide the group through these stages. This can be done by asking the right questions, such as:

- What were the takeaways in your small group discussion?
- What does this have to do with parish life and church leadership?
- What are you learning about yourself and your leadership style from this activity?

- What will you change about your leadership when you return to the parish?
- What goals can you set for yourself?

The facilitator also provides the resources, such as the leadership self-assessments, encourages positive group interaction, keeps the process moving within a flexible time schedule, and either presents the leadership theory or asks someone to do so.

Although the process is fluid and rarely follows these steps in exactly this sequence, a summary of the leadership development cycle is illustrated in Figure 13.

Figure 13. Leadership Development Cycle

Implications for Practice: Leadership Development

My best test of leadership is not how many followers you lead but how many leaders you develop. Leadership is not the exclusive purview of clergy and hired staff in a parish. One of the basic elements of servant leadership is the recruitment and development of other servant leaders. It is imperative that lay leadership be developed for the future of the church, especially one with fewer priests. Ken Blanchard and Phil Hodges suggest that the most important role of servant leaders is that of development coach.[52] As servant leaders are developed, the lessons of Jesus and his suggestions about service-oriented leadership should be infused into lay ministry formation programs as well.

Developing leaders is an act of *stewardship* for church leaders. Every new project, every new task, every new problem can be seen as an opportunity to expand lay involvement and leadership. Every new challenge is an opportunity to use the time, talent, and treasure of the laity as a contribution to the work of the church. When parish leaders create more opportunities for others to participate in the church, they are stewarding the gifts and talents of the people in the pews. They are also taking care of themselves, so that they do not overwork themselves by trying to do everything in the parish alone. And they are creating an opportunity for another person to steward their gifts and to practice discipleship.

The practice of servant leadership enhances the stewardship of the leaders and members of a congregation. Stewardship, according to Peter Block, is viewed as "the willingness to be accountable for the well-being of the larger organization in the service, rather than in control, of those around us."[53] Stewardship in a congregation is a partnership between leaders and members, with each party devoted to the mission of the organization instead of serving their own selfish interests.[54] This partnership involves a sharing of power by the leaders so that the gifts and talents of all members can be stewarded toward the accomplishment of the mission.

A number of authors have associated stewardship with servant leadership, suggesting that in both cases, the leader "transcends self-interest to serve the needs of others by helping them grow professionally and personally."[55] Greenleaf teaches that servant leaders are actively involved in developing leadership among the membership of an organization.[56] The question of whether the followers are learning, growing, and developing as leaders is a distinguishing factor in determining whether the leadership is servant leadership. Servant leaders in a parish are concerned not only about their own personal development as leaders, but also for the development of leadership among their parishioners.

Servant Ministry

Many people have asked me what to do when the person in charge of a project—it could be a pastor or a member of the church staff or a committee chairperson—is unwilling to delegate or unable to practice the type of servant leadership we are describing here. What does a person do when their leader is not practicing the recognizing, serving, and empowering behaviors we describe and explain in this book? The answer to this question is what is called "managing up" in business circles. This involves taking care of your relationships with those who have more positional power in the situation.

The servant leader removes obstacles in the way of the followers because he or she wants everyone to succeed. The pedestal leader might place obstacles in the way of others because she wants glory, status, or success for herself. Pedestal leaders take credit for successes of others in the organization while distancing themselves from the failures of others. This can be referred to as "Teflon leadership," which is used in the political arena to describe leaders who are so concerned about image management that problems do not stick to the leader. It is the direct opposite of what Jim Collins calls "the window and the mirror," where the leader looks out the window and gives credit to others when things are going well and looks into the mirror and takes responsibility for mistakes when things are not going well.[57]

The dynamics of the window and the mirror are based on **attribution theory**.[58] Attribution theory suggests that we tend to look at internal factors, such as laziness or incompetence, to explain why *others* fail, and we look for external factors, such as lack of support or assistance from others, to explain why *we* fail.[59] While the servant leader gives credit to others when things are going well (the window) and takes the blame for things when they are not going well (the mirror), the pedestal leader wants all of the credit and none of the blame.

When the person with the positional power in the situation is a pedestal leader, it makes it hard for others to practice servant-oriented ministry, whether leadership or followership. My best suggestion to those who find themselves in this situation is to practice servanthood anyway.[60] Servant ministry can be exercised whether you have positional power or not. Model the way, challenge the process, encourage the heart, and inspire others to act.[61] Place the needs and interests of your parish ahead of your own. Practice the humility of the window and the mirror, allowing the pedestal leader to grab the credit and evade the blame, if necessary. Genuine concern for the welfare of the pedestal leader, even if that person does not seem to care for you at all, will enhance your efforts. In the long run, you *will* change that person, at least in small ways. While you wait for changes to occur, remain dedicated to the mission and the people of your parish.

One mistake that those in church ministry often make is *expecting support from the very people they are trying to change.* When you lack positional power in the situation, and those in power are exercising pedestal leadership, you need to look for other sources of support. When your resources are limited, look for nonpositional forms of power, those that create opportunities to influence people without using positional power.[62] Servant leadership does not require a position. If you practice servant leadership, you will find yourself growing in what is called "referent power."[63] People will refer to you for help and assistance. But when you are trying to change the person in positional power, you cannot realistically expect support from that person.

Conclusion

Our study suggests three servant behaviors for leaders and four servant behaviors for members in religious organizations that are consistent with the traditional teachings of many religious institutions. We connect these religious teachings to recent literature on business, leadership, management, and organizational behavior. Our findings have important ramifications for students of organizations and of parish life, especially for those who wish to improve the performance of religious organizations by integrating the teachings of Jesus and the practices of their congregations with what we can learn from the general research about organizational life.

The public interest in servant leadership seems to be driven, at least in part, by its association with Jesus. Interest from the religious community will grow as people learn more about servant leadership. As more organizations turn to servant leadership, it becomes increasingly important to clarify exactly what it is and how it works. Our study suggests that servant leadership is more than a leadership style that fits Christian norms for leadership. Servant leadership works. It is not only consistent with the leadership style of Jesus. It is an effective style of leadership.

The servant leader in a parish is the one who is more inclined to serve than to be served, to recognize rather than to be recognized, and to empower rather than to flex positional power by commanding and controlling the response of his followers. If leaders place themselves in humble service to their parish, recognize the gifts and talents of their people, and call them forth through empowering actions, then the people will respond with organizational citizenship behaviors. The people will help each other, take initiative, participate in activities, and take responsibility to continuously develop themselves as disciples and as potential servant leaders of their parish.

APPENDICES

The following nine appendices are included here to display some of the materials we used in the major studies that led to this book. The first four appendices, A through D, were part of the parish life study conducted in 2005–06 with eighty-four parishes of the Diocese of Davenport, Iowa. The next five appendices, E through I, were part of the case study that was conducted in 2006–07 with three high-performing parishes in Bloomfield, Solon, and Iowa City. For more information about any of these appendices, contact Dan Ebener, Diocese of Davenport, 2706 North Gaines Street, Davenport, Iowa 52804.

The appendices are

A. Parish Life Self-Assessment
B. Financial Data Analysis
C. Demographic Data Analysis
D. Parish Life Evaluator Survey
E. Focus Group Interview Guide
F. One-on-One Interview Guide
G. Observation Guide with Categorized Behaviors
H. Code Book
I. Comparisons across Cases

Appendix A

PARISH LIFE SELF-ASSESSMENT

Diocese of Davenport
Parish Self-Assessment Tool

Date _____

Parish _____

Address_____

City, State, Zip Code _____

Phone _____ E-mail _____

Persons responsible for completing this assessment:

_____
Name, Title

_____
Name, Title

The first set of twelve questions should be answered "Yes" by a healthy parish. If a parish is not certain that it can respond "Yes" to any of these first questions, that means it should immediately try to strengthen efforts in that area. Parishes are strongly encouraged to contact diocesan staff in pertinent ministry areas for guidance and resources in strengthening their efforts in areas of need.

Please check "Yes" or "No" for each of the first twelve questions. Add comments to clarify your response when necessary.

                                              YES   NO

1. Our parish has a parish pastoral council that meets about once a month with an agenda that addresses all six areas of ministry.
Comments: ❏   ❏

_____

_____

2. Our parish elicits viewpoints from all areas of ministry for decisions made by a finance council that meets monthly or at least quarterly.
Comments: ❏   ❏

_____

_____

3. Our parish has two lay directors/trustees appointed to the parish corporate board.
Comments: ❏   ❏

_____

_____

YES   NO

4. Our parish has a trained coordinator of faith formation, including religious education and sacramental preparation, who is compensated according to the diocesan pay plan, or a fully qualified person who is willing and able to work as a volunteer or with a modest stipend, and has adequate budgets for effective programming for faith formation.

Comments: ❑   ❑

_____

_____

5. Our parish has a trained person assigned responsibility for ministry to the youth in the parish who is compensated according to the diocesan pay plan, or a fully qualified person who is willing and able to work as a volunteer or with a modest stipend, and has adequate budgets for effective programming for youth.

Comments: ❑   ❑

_____

_____

6. Our parish, if we are affiliated with a school, has a principal and staff who are compensated according to the diocesan pay plan and have adequate budgets for effective programming. We have a board of education that meets regularly. (Check "Yes" if you are not affiliated with a school.)

Comments: ❑   ❑

_____

_____

YES   NO

7. Our parish has a trained business manager and/or bookkeeper who provides timely financial statements for the pastor, the councils, board of education (if affiliated with a school), and leaders of all six areas of ministry (family life, liturgy, social action, church life, faith formation, and administration).

Comments: ❏   ❏

_____

_____

8. Our parish maintains all of its buildings and grounds in a manner that provides safety, energy efficiency, and a welcoming environment for all. Regular safety drills are conducted for our youth programs.

Comments: ❏   ❏

_____

_____

9. Our parish has an adequate budget to meet the needs of the parish, publishes that budget within the parish, and conducts an annual financial record review.

Comments: ❏   ❏

_____

_____

	YES	NO

10. Our parish is able to pay its bills on a timely basis and develops strategies to provide for its long-term financial security.
Comments: ❏ ❏

_____

_____

11. Our parish has an active ministry, including a parishioner assigned responsibility for each of the six areas of ministry with adequate budgets for programming.
Comments: ❏ ❏

_____

_____

12. Our parish is actively involved in the diocesan Safe Environment Program (VIRTUS/ Protecting God's Children).
Comments: ❏ ❏

_____

_____

Additional Comments:

_____

_____

_____

The second set of questions is intended to identify areas of strength or weakness in regard to all six areas of parish ministry. Parish leaders using this instrument should circulate this survey to parish pastoral council members, boards of education, and other leaders throughout the parish to get a sense about where they might best direct their energies to become viable or to maintain viability as a parish.

A healthy parish should be able to provide some measurable documentation to give credible evidence of support for its answers to all the questions below. Such documentation might vary from parish to parish but should be attached to this assessment. Attachments might include Sunday bulletins, financial statements, program flyers, or newspaper articles. In addition, you can provide examples of strengths and/or weaknesses on the lines provided following each question. Please type or print.

Check one of the following for each question:

1 = ❏ Strongly agree   4 = ❏ Disagree
2 = ❏ Agree   5 = ❏ Strongly disagree
3 = ❏ Neither agree nor disagree

___

13. Our parish has an active ministry that is adequately funded in the area of family life.

    1 ❏   2 ❏   3 ❏   4 ❏   5 ❏

Examples: _____

_____

14 Our parish has an active ministry that is adequately funded in the area of faith formation.

    1 ❏   2 ❏   3 ❏   4 ❏   5 ❏

Examples: _____

_____

1 = ❏ Strongly agree   4 = ❏ Disagree
2 = ❏ Agree   5 = ❏ Strongly disagree
3 = ❏ Neither agree nor disagree

---

15. Our parish has an active ministry that is adequately funded in the area of finance and administration.

     1 ❏   2 ❏   3 ❏   4 ❏   5 ❏

Examples: _____

_____

16. Our parish has an active ministry that is adequately funded in the area of liturgy.

     1 ❏   2 ❏   3 ❏   4 ❏   5 ❏

Examples: _____

_____

17. Our parish has an active ministry that is adequately funded in the area of social action.

     1 ❏   2 ❏   3 ❏   4 ❏   5 ❏

Examples: _____

_____

18. Our parish has an active ministry that is adequately funded in the area of church life, which includes stewardship, evangelization, and vocations.

     1 ❏   2 ❏   3 ❏   4 ❏   5 ❏

Examples: _____

_____

1 = ❑ Strongly agree   4 = ❑ Disagree
2 = ❑ Agree   5 = ❑ Strongly disagree
3 = ❑ Neither agree nor disagree

---

19. Our parish is welcoming to all, including new-comers, immigrants, refugees, and those with special needs.

1 ❑   2 ❑   3 ❑   4 ❑   5 ❑

Examples: _____

_____

20. Our parish is able to financially support parish leadership and ministries, including leadership training, ongoing leadership formation, and development.

1 ❑   2 ❑   3 ❑   4 ❑   5 ❑

Examples: _____

_____

Comments:

_____

_____

_____

The name, address, phone number, and e-mail address of the parishioner responsible for each of the six areas of ministry should accompany this report. (*Church Life, Faith Formation, Family Life, Finance and Administration, Liturgy,* and *Social Action*)

Parish Signatures, I have reviewed this assessment:

Pastor   Date

Parish Council Chairperson   Date

Finance Council Chairperson   Date

Board of Education Chairperson/Representative
(if applicable)   Date

Lay Trustee of Parish (one of two)   Date

Parish Life Administrator (if applicable)   Date

Please make a copy of this assessment for your parish file.
Mail by DECEMBER 1, 2005 to:
Diocese of Davenport
Bishop Wm. E. Franklin
2706 N. Gaines Street
Davenport, IA 52804

Appendix B

PARISH LIFE STUDY

1. Average annual gift per family was calculated using 2002 and 2004 data that included offertory income + envelope income + other parish envelope income. We divided that number by the number of families appearing on the sacramental records for each parish.
2. The 2004 number above was divided by the 2002 number above, giving each parish a growth rate number for size of family gift.
3. Whether each parish has submitted its financial reports (year-end financial statements on QuickBooks, budgets, and Summary of Financial Data) to the diocese in a timely fashion.
4. Actual numbers of adjusted income over the past five years.
5. The growth rate of the adjusted income over the past five years.
6. The adjusted income was compared to the rate of inflation over the past five years.
7. The total dollar amount of liquid assets for each parish.
8. Using the liquid assets from #7, we divided the liquid assets by the adjusted parish income to calculate a sustainability index.
9. Using the number of parish households receiving the *Catholic Messenger*, we divided that number by the reported number of parish households to calculate the percentage of parishioners who subscribe to the *Catholic Messenger*.
10. We determined whether each of the parishes had paid its bills on time in the current year, using billing records for the *Messenger*, the Annual Diocesan Appeal, and for insurance payments.

Appendix C

DEMOGRAPHIC DATA ANALYSIS
PARISH LIFE STUDY

1. Mass Attendance Percentage
   Mass counts for 2004 divided by the number of individual parishioners for 2004.

2. Growth of Mass Attendance
   Subtracted Mass counts for year 2000 from Mass counts for year 2004.

3. Percentage of Growth in Mass Attendance
   When data was available, Mass counts for the year 2004 minus the Mass counts for the year 2000, divided by the number of individual parishioners for 2004 were used. When data was not provided each year, refer to measure #2 above.

4. Parish Growth—Individual Parishioners
   The number of individual parishioners for 2004 divided by the number of individual parishioners for 2000.

5. Parish Growth—Families
   Number of families for 2004 divided by the number of families for 2000.

6. Total Number of New Catholics
   Total new Catholics for 2000 through 2004 from sacramental records.

7. Increase in New Catholics
   Total number of new Catholics for 2000 through 2004, divided by the number of individual parishioners for 2004 from the sacramental records.

8. Ministry Formation Program Participation
   The total number of graduated and currently participating individuals for the lay ministry formation programs for the years 2000 through 2006, divided by the number of individual parishioners for 2004.

9. First Communion Ratio
   The total number of First Communions for the years 2000 through 2004, divided by the number of individual parishioners for 2004.

10. Confirmation Ratio
    The total number of Confirmations for the years 2000 through 2004, divided by the number of individual parishioners for 2004.

Appendix D

PARISH LIFE EVALUATOR SURVEY

June 5, 2006

Please check one:
_____Diocesan Staff _____Priests' Personnel Board Member

1. How do you define a high-performing parish?

2. Which **5** of the 63 variables (see below) in the Parish Life Study were most important in measuring parish performance? (List in priority order.)

   ## 63 measures of the Parish Life Study

Measuring instrument	Number of measures
Self–assessment report (see attached)	43
Demographics (see attached)	10
Financial (see attached)	10
Total	**63**

3. What other information, either quantitative or qualitative, did you use in making your decision about measuring parish performance?

   _____

   _____

   _____

   _____

4. Name **3** other quantitative measures that would have been useful as measures of parish performance, but were not included in the Parish Life Study. (List in priority order.)

5. Name **3** qualitative or descriptive measures that would have been useful measures of parish performance, but were not included in the Parish Life Study. (List in priority order.)

6. Name 3 behaviors that you would expect to observe in high-performing parishes. (Use verbs to describe these behaviors, and list these in priority order.)

7. Please make any other comments about the usefulness of the Parish Life Study and the process of evaluating the performance of the 84 parishes. Include mention of how long it took you to fill out your score sheet evaluating the 84 parishes of the Diocese.

Your response to this survey implies informed consent to use cumulative data from all responses for the purpose of the dissertation of Dan Ebener and for the benefit of the Diocese of Davenport.

Name (optional):

Return by July 7 to:
Diocese of Davenport
2706 N. Gaines St.
Davenport, IA 52804-1998

Appendix E

FOCUS GROUP INTERVIEW GUIDE

Research questions: (1) What specific behaviors are associated with a high-performing parish? (2) How do the behaviors of the leaders in high-performing parishes have an impact on the behaviors of the members of the parish? (3) What are some other characteristics of the high-performing parish?

Target group: Parish council members, finance council members, lay trustees, and parish staff in three high-performing Catholic parishes in the Diocese of Davenport.

Location: Parish site for each parish.

Size: 8–12 members with one primary investigator (who will serve as the facilitator) and two secondary investigators.

Welcome and introductory remarks: Express thanks, explain purpose, obtain informed consent signatures, and clarify any questions.

Question area #1: Tell me about your most recent parish social event. Walk me through the event. Who is doing what?

Possible follow-up probes to Question #1:

1. Who planned and prepared for the event?

2. Is it the same people all the time or are new people stepping up?

3. What would you see people actually doing?

4, What are the leaders doing?

5. What activities might the leaders and members perform together?

6. What impact do the behaviors of the leaders have on other members of the parish?

Question area #2: All parishes go through some ups and downs as a parish. I would like you to think about the past few years. What sticks out in your memory as some of the high points, when things were going particularly well or when something wonderful happened? Let's pick one of these events to explore more in-depth. (Group selects one.) How did that come about? What were people doing at those times?

Possible follow-up to Question #2:

1. Why does this event stand out in your mind?

2. What were the parish leaders doing during these times?

3. What were members of the parish doing in those situations?

4. Who were other players in that situation and what were they doing?

5. Was there anything that the leaders of the parish were doing that had a direct impact on what the other members of the parish were doing?

Please be as detailed as possible in explaining what else was happening.

Question area #3: Now I would like you to think about the past few years and ask, what sticks out in your memory as a very difficult time, when things were NOT going particularly well? (Eventually, pick one to focus on.) Let's explore one of these cases in depth. How did that come about? What were people doing at those times?

Same follow-up sub-questions as Question #2.

Question area #4: Tell me about the faith formation ministry in your parish.

Possible follow-up probes for Questions #4 through 11:

1. How involved do laypeople get in this ministry?

2. How do laypeople get involved if they are interested?

3. What do the leaders do to create that interest?

4. Do the laypeople tend to take the initiative or do they wait to be asked?

5. How are the laypeople involved trained for this ministry?

6. How do people respond when things are not quite working out?

7. What about the role of the leaders? What impact do they have on others?

8. Who are the leaders in this parish?

9. Whom do people of the parish look to for leadership in this ministry?

10. How do the leaders call forth new talent from the parish?

11. How do the leaders make sure that laypeople are getting trained for ministry?

12. How do the leaders thank, appreciate, and recognize the laity involved?

13. How do the leaders contribute to this ministry effort?

Question area #5: Tell me about the family life ministry in your parish.

Question area #6: Tell me about the finance and administration ministry in your parish.

Question area #7: Tell me about the liturgical ministry in your parish.

Question area #8: Tell me about the social action ministry in your parish.

Question area #9: Tell me about the evangelization ministry in your parish.

Question area #10: Tell me about the stewardship ministry in your parish.

Question area #11: Tell me about the vocations ministry in your parish.

Question area #12: Your parish was asked to participate in part because some evaluators at the Diocese thought you were doing pretty well as a parish. Was it always this way? How and why did things change?

Possible follow-up sub-questions:

1. What was the turning point?

2. How did you know you were doing better?

3. What were your indicators of success?

Question area #13: What else is going on in your parish? What else do I need to know to paint a picture and tell the story about life in this parish?

Possible follow-up questions:

1. What are some of the trademarks of your parish?

2. What is the reputation that you have with outsiders?

Question area #14: Do you have any questions or final comments?

General probing questions (for each of the 14 question areas above) include:

1. Can you provide an example of that?

2. Can you describe an incident where that has happened?

3. Tell me about the most recent time that happened.

4. Does anyone have an example of that?

5. Do you have a similar perspective as that?

Wrap-up and Next steps: Express thanks, explain next steps and answer any questions.

Appendix F

ONE-ON-ONE INTERVIEW GUIDE

Introduction: Express thanks, explain purpose, obtain informed consent signature, and clarify any questions.

List of interview questions (with some possible probes):

1. Walk me through a typical day in the life of a pastor/parish leader here at Parish X. (Possible probes: What activities fill your usual day? Whom do you meet with? Who is calling you on the phone?)
2. What are Saturday and Sunday like in this parish? Describe what I would expect to see you doing on the weekends in this parish. (Possible probes: Please be very specific about what you are doing.)
3. Tell me about a typical parish council meeting. What are you doing during the meeting and what are other people doing? (Possible probes: Who sets the agenda? Who runs the meeting? Please be very specific.)
4. Let's go through each of the areas of parish ministry, one by one, and do a brief assessment of how this parish is doing. First, walk me through a typical social event in your parish. What would you say are the observable behaviors that I would most likely see among the leaders and the members of this parish? (Possible probe: What would people actually be doing that is observable?)
5. Thank you very much. Tell me next about faith formation ministry in Parish X.

Possible follow-up probes for Questions #5 through 12:

a. How are laypeople involved in this ministry?
b. What is the role of the laypeople in this ministry?
c. If people want to get involved in this area of ministry, how do they do it?

    d. Do the laypeople take the initiative or is it difficult to find recruits?

    e. How are the laypeople involved in ministry trained for their ministry?

    f. How do people respond when things are not quite working out?

    g. How do you view your role in this area of ministry?

    h. How do you see people responding to your role as a parish leader?

    i. What impact does your role have on other members of the parish?

    j. What are your thoughts about how people respond to your efforts?

    k. How do you as a leader get more people involved in this ministry?

6. Thank you. Tell me also about family life ministry in this parish.

7. Thank you. Let's look next at finance and administration and how that ministry is organized in your parish.

8. Thank you. Let's discuss liturgy next. Tell me first about your liturgical ministry.

9. Thank you. Let's discuss social action next. Tell me about social action in this parish.

10. Thank you. Tell me also about evangelization ministry here.

11. Thank you. Tell me about the stewardship ministry in your parish.

12. Thank you. And finally, tell me also about vocations ministry in your parish.

13. We have reviewed many of the behaviors of the pastor, leaders, and members of your parish. I would like to ask you to reflect one more time on the impact that your behaviors have on others in the parish. What do you see as the relationship between what you do as pastor/parish leader and the behaviors of the members of the parish?

Possible probes for Question #13:

    a. Can you describe that in specific behavioral terms?

    b. Can you give me a specific example?

    c. What are your precise behaviors and what are the parishioners
      actually doing in response?

14. Do you have any other comments that you want to add to this
     interview?

Other possible probes:

1. Say more about that.
2. Tell me how that happened.
3. Give me an example of how that works.
4. Walk me through the last time that happened.

Closing remarks: Express thanks, explain next steps, and clarify any
questions.

Appendix G

OBSERVATION GUIDE WITH CATEGORIZED BEHAVIORS

Key to Categorized Behaviors:
R = Recognizing
S = Serving
E = Empowering
H = Helping
I = Initiating
P = Participating
SD = Self-Developing

Observation Check List before, during, and after Mass

1. (E) Was there a church sign that was visible and inviting?
2. (E) Were the church buildings and grounds attractive and well maintained?
3. (E) Was the entrance to the church bright and inviting?
4. (E) Were the buildings accessible to the handicapped?
5. (P) Did the greeters offer a warm welcome to the parish?
6. (E) Was the hymnal accessible and available?
7. (E) Was the missalette accessible and available?
8. (E) Was handout information about the Catholic faith available for the taking?
9. (E) Was there an effective system for recording the names and addresses of visitors to the parish?
10. (E) Did the acoustics and sound system of the church allow for easy understanding of what was being said?
11. (P) Were laypeople involved in the liturgy as lectors?
12. (P) Were children or youth involved in any way in the liturgy?

13. (H) Did anyone in the congregation offer to care for a child that was not sitting with them?

14. (E) Did anyone lead the music in a way that invited others to participate?

15. (P) Did the congregation participate enthusiastically in the music?

16. (P) Did the congregation participate enthusiastically in the prayer responses?

17. (E) Did the liturgy make any special efforts to reach out to those of a different culture or language?

18. (P) Did the congregation pay close attention to the homily?

19. (E) Did the homily involve the congregation in any observable way?

20. (S) Did the pastor illustrate any servant leader behaviors in the homily?

21. (H) Did people in the pews extend a handshake during the kiss of peace?

22. (H) Did anyone in the congregation go out of their way to extend a handshake to someone more than about 6–8 feet away?

23. (P) Were laypeople involved as Eucharistic ministers?

24. (E) Did anyone announce parish activities after the Mass?

25. (S) Did these announcements exemplify servant leader behaviors in any way?

26. (SD) Was there any mention of training or educational opportunities in the announcements of the parish bulletin?

27. (R) Did any parish leaders thank the people for any of their efforts?

28. (H) Did anyone come up and initiate speaking to you after the Mass?

29. (E) Was there a fellowship time organized after the Mass?

30. (H) Did anyone encourage you to attend that fellowship?

31. (H) Were there observable signs of people helping people during the visit?

32. (P) Were there observable signs of people attending meetings during the visit?

33. (P) Were there observable signs of laypeople volunteering in any other way?

Observation Guide during the Focus Group Interviews

1. (E) Was the room set up for the focus group interviews before we got there?
2. (S) Did anyone arrange for hospitality for the focus group interview?
3. (P) Did the people who said they would be there show up?
4. (P) Was there a good cross-section of lay leaders represented in the focus group?
5. (P) Did at least 8 people participate in the focus group?
6. (H) Did any layperson from the parish go out of their way to initiate introductions?
7. (H) Did any layperson from the parish go out of their way to help get the focus group started?
8. (P) Was the group at least one-third female?
9. (P) Was the group at least one-third male?
10. (P) Was the group approximately one-half male and one-half female?
11. (P) Did it seem that at least one-third of the group was under the age of 60?
12. (P) Did it seem that at least one-third of the group was under the age of 50?
13. (P) Did it seem that at least one-third of the group was under the age of 40?
14. (P) Did it seem like the contribution of anyone in the group was being diminished or marginalized by the group in any way?
15. (H) If so, did anyone in the parish speak up on behalf of that person?
16. (P) Did any one person dominate the discussion of the focus group?
17. (H) If so, did any member of the parish respond appropriately to this domination?
18. (P) Were some participants in the focus group particularly quiet?
19. (H) If so, did any member of the parish invite any quiet members of the parish to speak up during the focus group interview?
20. (P) Did some participants in the focus group seem disinterested?
21. (H) If so, did any member of the parish reach out to pique that person's interest?
22. (H) Did any member of the parish facilitate and enhance the participation of others in the group in any observable way?

23. (P) Were any lay women actively engaged in the focus group?
24. (P) Were any lay men actively engaged in the focus group?
25. (P) Were any young people actively engaged in the focus group?
26. (P) Did anyone leave the focus group interview early?
27. (R) Did anyone from the parish thank us for coming?

Appendix H
CODE BOOK

Leader Behaviors

a. Recognizing: Leaders affirming the gifts and talents of the members; showing appreciation for the work of parishioners; sending thank you cards and notes; acknowledging the efforts of parishioners from the pulpit or in the bulletin; expressing thanks.
b. Serving: Leaders offering humble assistance with menial tasks in the parish; giving credit to others and taking blame themselves; putting the needs, interests, and ideas of others ahead of one's own; willing to admit mistakes or change one's mind about the ideas of others.
c. Empowering: Leaders clearing the obstacles to enable members to fully participate; developing parish structures that increase the likelihood that others will get involved; building capacity by teaching, inviting, and supporting the members of the parish; encouraging parishioners to take initiative on their own; being supportive of the projects, ideas, and initiatives of parishioners; allowing others to act on their own behalf.

Member Behaviors

a. Helping: Members providing informal assistance to each other, or to leaders, or to the parish (in a less formal way than "participating"); building a sense of community and teamwork by working collaboratively and cooperatively together; welcoming new members; responding to the informal requests for help.
b. Initiating: Members taking action on their own, without waiting for parish leaders to tell them what needs to be done; presenting new ideas about what the parish needs to do; launching new

215

parish initiatives that are led by laypeople; stepping up to take leadership on a project, program, or commission.

c. Participating: Members getting involved in any of the nine areas of ministry; being active in the life of the parish (in a more formal way than "helping"); attending parish functions; joining parish programs; receiving the sacraments; contributing financially to the parish; being actively involved in parish commissions.

Leader or Member Behavior

a. Self-developing: Members or leaders taking responsibility for their own personal growth and development; attending programs or trainings that make that person more qualified for parish ministry; developing one's own spirituality; training other members of the parish to take their place in ministry.

Appendix I
COMPARISONS ACROSS CASES

Behavior	Level of Evidence			Mean	Rank
	St. Mary Magdalen's, Bloomfield St. Mary's, Solon St. Mary's, Iowa City				
	Bloomfield	Solon	Iowa City		
Recognizing	2.8	2.1	3.0	2.6	6
Serving	4.1	3.1	4.0	3.7	3
Empowering	4.9	5.8	5.3	5.3	1
Helping	5.1	3.3	2.4	3.6	4
Initiating	5.0	3.3	2.0	3.4	5
Participating	4.0	4.0	5.1	4.4	2
Self-Developing	2.6	1.9	2.8	2.4	7

Note. 1.5–2.4 = moderately low; 2.5–3.4 = moderate; 3.5–4.4 = moderately high; 4.5–5.4 = high; 5.5–6 = very high.

NOTES

Foreword

1. Henri Nouwen, *In the Name of Jesus: Reflections on Christian Leadership* (New York: Crossroad, 1989). Nouwen was an early advocate of servant leadership as the foundation for leadership in the church.

2. Dan R. Ebener, "The Servant Parish: A Case Study of Servant Leadership and Organizational Citizenship Behaviors in High-Performing Catholic Parishes." Doctoral dissertation, College of Business, St. Ambrose University, 2007.

3. Conference for Pastoral Planning and Council Development, *Pathways for the Church of the 21st Century: A National Study of Recent Diocesan Efforts at Parish Reorganization in the United States* (Mt. Laurel, NJ: Conference for Pastoral Planning and Council Development, 2003), 1.

4. Emerging Models of Pastoral Leadership is a joint project of six national Catholic organizations. These groups have joined together to examine areas of pastoral excellence and to identify emerging models of pastoral leadership in the Catholic church. Their primary area of focus has been collaboration in ministry at all structural levels of the church. The six national partners are the National Association for Lay Ministry, the Conference for Pastoral Planning and Council Development, the National Association for Church Personnel Administrators, the National Association of Diaconate Directors, the National Catholic Young Adult Ministry Association, and the National Federation of Priest Councils.

Introduction:
Who Are the Servant Leaders?

1. One of my doctoral classes in business was taught by a sociologist who used an exercise in which he asked the class to rank these five institutions in the present, a hundred years ago, two hundred years ago, and five hundred years ago. This led to a fascinating discussion. Since then, I have used the same exercise several times in my own classes, with interesting discussions each time. Generally speaking, nearly everyone ranks religion and family as number 1 or number 2 in each of the past categories while ranking business as number 1 in the present, with family and religion moving down to number 4 and number 5. It is a great exercise for demonstrating how the influence of family and religion has been replaced by the institution of business.

2. Pope Benedict XVI has repeatedly warned about the dangers of consumerism and secularism. In his 2008 World Day of Peace Message, "The Human Family, a Community of Peace," on January 1, 2008, he emphasized the need to revive the institutions of family and social community.

3. Larry C. Spears and Michele Lawrence, eds., *Focus on Leadership: Servant-Leadership for the Twenty-First Century* (New York: Wiley, 2002).

4. The number of empirical studies that are exploring servant leadership are increasing as this book is being written. Two notable studies are a good fit with ours. The first is Mark Ehrhart, "Leadership and Procedural Justice Climate as Antecedents of Unit-Level Organizational Citizenship Behavior," *Personnel Psychology* 57 (2004): 61–94. A second is Robert C. Liden, Sandy J. Wayne, Hao Zhao, and David Henderson, "Servant Leadership: Development of a Multidimensional Measure and Multi-Level Assessment," *Leadership Quarterly* 19 (2008): 161–77.

5. The search for key indicators of parish success has led to a number of recent studies, most of which look at certain areas of ministry, parish structures, and demographic and financial measures of success. See David DeLambo, "In Search of Pastoral Excellence," *Church* (Summer 2007). DeLambo suggests that the most common demographic measures include growth in membership and attendance at liturgies.

6. Spears and Lawrence, *Focus on Leadership*.

7. We occasionally refer to the high-performing parishes of our study as "model parishes."

8. The current director of the Greenleaf Center for Servant Leadership has written an excellent book: Kent M. Keith, *The Case for Servant Leadership* (Westfield, IN: Greenleaf Center for Servant Leadership, 2008).

9. Peter G. Northouse, *Leadership: Theory and Practice* (Thousand Oaks, CA: Sage, 2007).

10. Ibid.

11. Ibid.

12. The original essay on servant leadership by Robert K. Greenleaf can be found in Robert K. Greenleaf, *The Servant Leader Within: The Transformative Path*, ed. Hamilton Beazley, Julie Beggs, and Larry C. Spears (Mahwah, NJ: Paulist Press, 2003). Greenleaf says that he wrote the original essay in 1969; it was first published in 1970. Greenleaf circulated a revised edition, which was published by Paulist Press in 1977. The revised version can be found in Robert K. Greenleaf, *Servant Leadership* (Mahwah, NJ: Paulist Press, 1977) and in Robert K. Greenleaf, *Servant Leadership*, 25th anniversary ed. (Mahwah, NJ: Paulist Press, 2002). See also Robert K. Greenleaf, "The Servant as Leader," *Journal of Religion and Applied Behavioral Sciences* 3 (1982): 7–10.

13. Dennis W. Organ, Philip M. Podskakoff, and Scott B. MacKenzie, *Organizational Citizenship Behavior: Its Nature, Antecedents, and Consequences* (Thousand Oaks, CA: Sage, 2006). This book summarizes the research demonstrating that OCBs are instrumental in obtaining high performance in a variety of organizations.

14. Philip M. Podsakoff and Scott B. MacKenzie, "The Impact of Organizational Citizenship Behavior on Organizational Performance: A Review and Suggestions for Future Research," *Human Performance* 10, no. 2 (1997): 133–51.

15. Ibid.

16. Ibid.

17. These are the three names that we give to the three parishes in our study. We call the smallest parish a *family*, the medium-sized parish a *community*, and the large parish a *team*. See chapter 9 for more information.

18. Greenleaf, *Servant Leader*, 25th anniversary (Mahwah, NJ: Paulist Press, 2002), 27.

19. Tertullian, "Apology" (second century), in *The Ante-Nicene Fathers*, ed. Alexander Roberts and James Donaldson, vol. 3, *Latin Christianity: Its Founder, Tertullian*, arranged by A. Cleveland Coxe (Grand Rapids: Eerdmans, 1976), 46.

Chapter 1: Servant Leadership

1. Robert K. Greenleaf, *The Servant Leader Within: The Transformative Path*, ed. Hamilton Beazley, Julie Beggs, and Larry C. Spears (Mahwah, NJ: Paulist Press, 2003).

2. See list in Ken Blanchard and Phil Hodges, *Lead Like Jesus: Lessons from the Greatest Role Model of All Time* (Nashville: Thomas Nelson, 2003).

3. Greenleaf, *Servant Leader Within*, 32.

4. Ibid., 32.

5. Ibid., 27.

6. Ibid., 30.

7. Ibid.

8. Blanchard and Hodges. *Lead Like Jesus*.

9. Peter G. Northouse, *Leadership: Theory and Practice* (Thousand Oaks, CA: Sage, 2007).

10. Hermann Hesse, *Journey to the East* (London: P. Owen, 1956).

11. Greenleaf states that power will always be a part of the leadership equation. "Sometimes it will be a servant's power of persuasion and example. Sometimes it will be coercive power used to dominate and manipulate people. The difference is that in the former, power is used to create opportunity and alternatives so that people may choose and build autonomy. In the latter, individuals are coerced into a predetermined path. Even if it is good for them, if they experience nothing else, ultimately their autonomy will be diminished." See Greenleaf, *Servant Leader*, 25th anniversary (Mahwah, NJ: Paulist Press, 2002), 55.

12. J. R. French and B. Raven, "The Bases of Social Power," in *Studies in Social Power*, ed. D. Cartwright (Ann Arbor, MI: Institute for Social Research, 1959).

13. A zero-sum game means that the sum of our efforts is finite and the resources that we have are limited to a fixed pie.

14. Much has been written about empowerment, but the term often goes undefined. Here we are talking about the process of building capacity and sharing power with others in the leadership process. See Gary A. Yukl and W. S. Becker, "Effective Empowerment in Organizations," *Organizational Management Journal* 3, no. 3 (2006): 210–31.

15. James M. Kouzes and Barry Z. Posner, *The Leadership Challenge: How to Keep Getting Extraordinary Things Done in Organizations* (San Francisco: Jossey-Bass, 2002), 381.

16. Ken Collier and Matt Williams, *Biblical Leadership: Becoming a Different Kind of Leader* (Greenville, SC: Ambassador Emerald International, 2004).

17. Greenleaf, *Servant Leadership*, 25th anniversary, 27.

18. Greenleaf says that "some coercive power is overt and brutal. Some is covert and subtly manipulative. The former is open and acknowledged; the latter is insidious and hard to detect. Most of us are more coerced than we know....Part of our dilemma is that all leadership is, to some extent, manipulative. Those who follow must be strong!" Greenleaf, *Servant Leadership*, 25th anniversary, 55.

19. Northouse, *Leadership*. The initial studies on leadership behaviors were carried out primarily among researchers at the University of Michigan, where task and relationship were measured on opposite ends of a one-dimensional model, and Ohio State University, where the two-dimensional model was proposed.

20. This model was originally conceived by Robert R. Blake and Jane S. Mouton in *The Managerial Grid* (Houston: Gulf Publishing, 1964) and has been expanded greatly by Dimensional Management Systems through a program called "Leadership through People Skills."

21. See Northouse, *Leadership*, for more discussion on this.

22. Ibid.

23. Don Cohen and Laurence Prusak, *In Good Company: How Social Capital Makes Organizations Work* (Boston: Harvard Business School Press, 2001).

24. This language is used in the training sessions by Leadership through People Skills. See Robert E. Lefton and Victor R. Buzzotta,

Leadership through People Skills: Using the Dimensional Model of Behavior to Help Managers (New York: McGraw-Hill, 2004).

25. Ibid.

26. Ibid.

27. Ibid.

28. Richard L. Daft, *Essentials of Organizational Theory and Design* (Cincinnati: Southwestern Thomson Learning, 2005).

29. Martin Luther King Jr., *I Have a Dream: Writings and Speeches That Changed the World* (New York: HarperCollins, 1992), 189.

30. John R. Wooden and Steve J. Jamison, *Wooden on Leadership* (New York: McGraw-Hill, 2005).

31. Shelly A. Kirkpatrick and Edwin A. Locke, "Leadership: Do Traits Matter?" *Executive* 5 (1991): 48–60. Kirkpatrick and Locke have conducted extensive research on leadership traits. Confidence is among six traits identified as most important for leaders. The other five are drive, desire to lead, honesty and integrity, intelligence, and knowledge of the business.

32. Trust can be described as both the grease that keeps organizations running smoothly and the glue that holds organizations together. Trust is the basis for many models of organizational effectiveness, including Patrick Lencioni's *Five Dysfunctions of a Team* (San Francisco: Jossey-Bass, 2002).

33. This is a key factor explained in the classic book, *Getting to Yes*, which was part of the Harvard Negotiation Project. See *Getting to Yes: Negotiating Agreement without Giving In*, 2nd ed. (New York: Penguin, 1991).

34. Kouzes and Posner, *Leadership Challenge*.

35. Northouse, *Leadership*.

36. Frances Hesselbein is the former director of Girl Scouts USA, and she emphasizes leadership traits as answering the question of "how to be" a leader. See Frances Hesselbein, *Hesselbein on Leadership* (San Francisco: Jossey-Bass, 2002).

37. John Kotter emphasizes leadership behaviors as answering the question of "what leaders do." See John P. Kotter, "What Leaders Really Do," in *Business Leadership: A Jossey-Bass Reader* (San Francisco: Jossey-Bass, 2003), 29–43.

38. Ibid.

39. Ibid.

40. Mark Ehrhart identified fourteen such behavioral items that were later useful in selecting servant leader behaviors for our study.

41. Jim Collins in *Good to Great* is an example of this. See Jim Collins, *Good to Great: Why Some Companies Make the Leap...and Others Don't* (New York: HarperCollins, 2001).

42. Some research is showing that transformational leadership is more effective than transactional leadership in motivating people to go above and beyond the call of duty. This is a concept called "organizational citizenship" that is becoming the focus of many studies. See Podsakoff and MacKenzie, "Impact of Organizational Citizenship Behavior," 133–51.

43. Bass, *Leadership and Performance*.

44. James MacGregor Burns, *Leadership* (New York: Harper & Row, 1978); Bass, *Leadership and Performance*.

45. Bass, *Leadership and Performance*.

46. Abraham Zaleznik, "Managers and Leaders: Are They Different?" *Harvard Business Review* (January 2004).

47. Ibid.

48. John P. Kotter, *Leading Change* (Boston: Harvard Business School Press, 1996), 28.

49. Afsenah Nahavandi, *The Art and Science of Leadership*, 4th ed. (Upper Saddle River, NJ: Pearson, 2006).

50. Max Weber, *A Theory of Economic and Social Organizations*, ed. A. H. Henderson and Talcott Parsons (Glencoe, IL: Free Press, 1947).

51. Ibid.

52. Marshall Sashkin and Molly G. Sashkin, *Leadership That Matters: The Critical Factors for Making a Difference in People's Lives and Organizations' Success* (San Francisco: Berrett-Koehler, 2003).

53. Northouse, *Leadership*.

54. Bass, *Leadership and Performance*, 5.

55. Northouse, *Leadership*.

56. Ibid.

57. The published version of Greenleaf's essay can be found in *Servant Leader Within*, ed. Beazley, Beggs, and Spears.

58. Bass, *Leadership and Performance*.

59. Greenleaf, *Servant Leader Within*, 54. In the revised version of his essay, Greenleaf says, "Foresight is seen as a wholly rational process, the product of a constantly running computer that deals with

intersecting series and random inputs and is vastly more complicated than anything that technology has yet produced. Foresight means regarding the events of the instant moment and constantly comparing them with a series of projections made in the past and at the same time projecting future events—with diminishing certainty as projected time runs out into the indefinite future." Greenleaf, *Servant Leadership*, 39.

60. In the revised edition of his essay, Greenleaf states, "The trouble with coercive power is that it only strengthens resistance. And if successful, its controlling effect lasts only as long as the force is strong. It is not organic. Only persuasion and the consequent voluntary acceptance are organic." Greenleaf, *Servant Leadership*, 55–56.

61. Joseph Rost, *Leadership for the Twenty-First Century* (Westport, CT: Praeger, 1991).

Chapter 2: Parish Behaviors

1. The Good Samaritan story is often referred to in describing "helping" as an organizational citizenship behavior. However, in the business literature, the protagonist of the story is sometimes referred to simply as "Good Sam." See Dennis W. Organ, Philip M. Podskakoff, and Scott B. MacKenzie, *Organizational Citizenship Behavior: Its Nature, Antecedents, and Consequences* (Thousand Oaks, CA: Sage, 2006).

2. Tertullian, "Apology" (second century), in *The Ante-Nicene Fathers*, ed., Alexander Roberts and James Donaldson, vol. 3, *Latin Christianity: Its Founder, Tertullian*, arranged by A. Cleveland Coxe (Grand Rapids: Eerdmans, 1976), 46.

3. Larry C. Spears and Michele Lawrence, eds., *Focus on Leadership: Servant-Leadership for the Twenty-First Century* (New York: Wiley, 2002).

4. Mark G. Ehrhart, "Leadership and Procedural Justice Climate as Antecedents of Unit-Level Organizational Citizenship Behavior," *Personnel Psychology* 57 (2004).

5. Robert K. Greenleaf, *The Servant Leader Within: The Transformative Path*, ed. Hamilton Beazley, Julie Beggs, and Larry C. Spears (Mahwah, NJ: Paulist Press, 2003).

6. Dennis W. Organ, *Organizational Citizenship Behavior: The Good Soldier Syndrome* (Lexington, MA: Lexington Books, 1988). This early book by Dennis Organ shows that successful organizations are ones that tie organizational citizenship to supportive leadership. In our study, we make the case that supportive leadership has similar features to servant leadership. If true, then servant leadership can be expected to create conditions that will enhance organizational performance, much the same as the research shows that supportive leadership does.

7. Ehrhart, "Leadership and Procedural Justice Climate."

8. Don F. Frick and Larry C. Spears, eds., *On Becoming a Servant Leader: The Private Writings of Robert K. Greenleaf* (San Francisco: Wiley, 1996).

9. Greenleaf, *Servant Leader Within*, 27.

10. Ehrhart, "Leadership and Procedural Justice Climate."

11. Greenleaf, *Servant Leader Within*.

12. As explained in chapter 1.

13. Many leadership theories emphasize the need to involve others in decision making. For example, the situational leadership theory of Paul Hersey and Ken Blanchard suggests that as followers are more willing and able, the leader becomes more participative or delegates responsibility to the follower. The path-goal theory of Robert House and Terence Mitchell suggests that the leader becomes more participative in order to motivate the follower who expects to be involved in decision making. Both of these theories are presented in Jon L. Pierce and John W. Newstrom, *Leaders and the Leadership Process*, 4th ed. (New York: McGraw-Hill, 2006).

14. Peter G. Northouse, *Leadership: Theory and Practice* (Thousand Oaks, CA: Sage, 2007).

15. James MacGregor Burns, *Transforming Leadership* (New York: Grove, 2003).

16. The definition of *consensus* here is not unanimity but rather a sense of agreement among those making the decision. The best test of consensus is that everyone in the room either supports the decision or is at least willing to live with the decision. Trying to reach consensus builds more ownership in group decisions. To reach consensus, the group first listens to each member and then tries to integrate the interests of all parties into a collaborative solution. This is best done

by seeking first to understand the needs and interests of others before trying to shape an agreement.

17. Organ et al., *Organizational Citizenship Behavior*.

18. Ibid.

19. This is the essence of our definition of leadership, explained as an influence process by Northouse.

20. Bateman and Organ (1983) state that supportive leader behaviors "lubricate the social machinery of the organization" (p. 588) as they enhance citizenship behaviors. See T. S. Bateman and Dennis W. Organ, "Job Satisfaction and the Good Soldier," *Academy of Management Journal* 26, no. 4 (1983).

21. Ehrhart, "Leadership and Procedural Justice Climate."

22. Of the four leader behaviors explained in path goal theory—supportive, directive, participative, and achievement-oriented—the *supportive* behaviors were the strongest antecedents of OCB. This research finding was presented in Philip M. Podsakoff, Scott B. MacKenzie, J. B. Paine, and D.G. Bachrach, "Organizational Citizenship Behaviors: A Critical Review of the Theoretical and Empirical Literature and Suggestions for Future Research," *Journal of Management* 26, no. 3 (2000): 513–63.

23. Organ et al., *Organizational Citizenship Behavior*.

24. Ibid.

25. Ibid.

26. Ibid., 26.

27. Second Vatican Council, *Lumen Gentium*, in *The Documents of Vatican II*, ed. Walter M. Abbot (New York: America Press, 1966), 58. We particularly looked at the ideas and values of the Vatican II document, *Lumen Gentium*, which means "Light of the World," promulgated by Pope Paul VI in 1964. It is considered a major contribution to church teaching on the involvement of the laity in the life of a parish and is an important part of the Vatican II documents.

28. Pope Benedict XVI, *God Is Love* (Washington, DC: United States Conference of Catholic Bishops, 2006).

29. The works of mercy are charitable actions by which we come to the aid of our neighbor in his spiritual and bodily necessities. Instructing, advising, consoling, comforting are spiritual works of mercy, as are forgiving and bearing wrongs patiently. The corporal works of mercy consist especially of feeding the hungry, sheltering

the homeless, clothing the naked, visiting the sick and imprisoned, and burying the dead. See *Catechism of the Catholic Church*, 2nd ed. (Washington, DC: United States Catholic Conference, 1997), no. 2447. See also Matthew 25:31–46.

30. Ibid. Again, we were looking especially to scripture, such as the Sermon on the Mount, and the Vatican II documents, such as *Lumen Gentium, Gaudium et Spes*, and *Apostolicam Actuositatem*.

31. Organ et al., *Organizational Citizenship Behavior*.

32. Organ, *Organizational Citizenship Behavior*.

33. Organ et al., *Organizational Citizenship Behavior*.

34. Paul Wilkes, *Excellent Catholic Parishes: The Guide to Best Places and Practices* (Mahwah, NJ: Paulist Press, 2001).

35. Ibid.

36. Collaboration is the integration of the needs and interests of various parties into a solution that is a win-win for all parties. For more information on collaboration, refer to Roger Fisher and William Ury, *Getting to Yes: Negotiating Agreement without Giving In* (New York: Penguin, 1981).

37. "Further, let them [pastors] encourage the layman so that he may undertake tasks on his own initiative." Second Vatican Council, *Lumen Gentium*, no. 37.

38. Research has found that participation is a route to greater organizational effectiveness in the workplace. See James L. Bowditch and Anthony F. Buono, *A Primer on Organizational Behavior*, 6th ed. (Hoboken, NJ: Wiley, 2005).

39. Ibid.

40. Ibid.

41. "Consequently, let every opportunity be given them [the laity] so that, according to their abilities and the needs of the times, they may zealously participate in the saving work of the Church." Second Vatican Council, *Lumen Gentium*, no. 33.

42. Wilkes, *Excellent Catholic Parishes*.

Chapter 3: Measures of Parish Life

1. Figures taken from the *Official Catholic Directory* over the past forty years show that between 1967 and 2008, the number of U.S.

Catholic priests dropped from 59,892 to 41,406. During the same period, the number of U.S. Catholics grew from 46.9 million to 67.4 million. This means that 18,486 *fewer* priests were serving about 20 million *more* Catholics. See Katarina Smith, "Structuring a Viable Future for Parishes," *Church* (Spring 2009), 29–33.

2. A number of excellent books have been written about the struggles of restructuring and closures of parishes. See Michael Weldon, *A Struggle for Holy Ground: Reconciliation and the Rite of Parish Closure* (Collegeville, MN: Liturgical Press, 2004).

3. T. Keenan, "Church Health: Finding the Focal Point," *Leadership* (Summer 1997). As Keenan points out, "Church health is a matter of focus: Focus on Christ, not the church," 35.

4. Many of our qualitative research methods were based on M. B. Miles and A. M. Huberman, *Qualitative Data Analysis: An Expanded Sourcebook*, 2nd ed. (Thousand Oaks, CA: Sage, 1994).

5. From 2000 to 2008, the number of Catholic priests dropped about five thousand and the number of Catholic parishes dropped by about 737. See Smith, "Structuring a Viable Future for Parishes."

6. The case study methods were based upon Robert K. Yin, *Case Study Research*, 3rd ed. (Thousand Oaks, CA: Sage, 2003). The other characteristics found in the study are presented in chapter 10.

7. We eliminated twenty-eight parishes from consideration in this study due to the recent changes of pastor (over a two-year period).

8. Richard E. Boyatzis, *Transforming Qualitative Information: Thematic Analysis and Code Development* (Thousand Oaks, CA: Sage, 1998).

9. Ibid.

10. David W. Stewart and Prem N. Shamdasani, *Focus Groups: Theory and Practice* (Newbury Park, CA: Sage, 1990).

11. Yin, *Case Study Research*.

12. Ibid.

13. Ibid.

14. Churches United of the Quad City Area, *Shopper's Guide for Visiting Parishes* (Rock Island, IL: Churches United of the Quad City Area, 2005).

15. Miles and Huberman, *Qualitative Data Analysis*, 64.

16. The intercoder reliability (ICR) for the focus groups and interviews was calculated for each of the three cases and for an overall rating. This number reports the number of times the two coders looked at the same data and coded it the same way. In Solon, the first case that was coded, the ICR rating was 76.4 percent. In Iowa City, the ICR rating was 87.4 percent. In Bloomfield, the ICR rating was 86.6 percent. The overall ICR rating was 84.5 percent. This was considered a highly reliable figure. It meant we could move forward to analyze the data. In each instance when the two coders initially disagreed on coding a segment of the transcripts, we discussed various options until we agreed on which way to code the data.

17. The observation guide we developed was based on one designed by Churches United of the Quad Cities.

18. As we categorized the observation guide, we went through another round of calculating our intercoder reliability rate, which was calculated at 88.3 percent. The same two coders eventually agreed on the categorization of all sixty variables.

19. In order to calculate the level of evidence for the seven behaviors in the archival data, the evidence in the parish life study was categorized in consultation with the same second coder.

20. This was step 1 of the parish life study.

21. This was steps 2 and 3 of the parish life study.

22. The behavioral measures became the focus of step 7, the case study.

Chapter 4: The Family Approach

1. Why Catholic? Journey through the Catechism is an adult faith formation process of RENEW International. It is based on scripture and the *Catechism of the Catholic Church*.

Chapter 7: Parish Results

1. C. Gene Wilkes, *Jesus on Leadership: Discovering the Secrets of Servant Leadership from the Life of Christ* (Wheaton, IL: Tyndale, 1998).

2. Dan R. Ebener, "The Servant Parish: A Case Study of Servant Leadership and Organizational Citizenship Behaviors in

High-Performing Catholic Parishes." Doctoral dissertation, College of Business, St. Ambrose University, 2007.

3. Second Vatican Council, *Lumen Gentium*, in *The Documents of Vatican II*, ed. Walter M. Abbot (New York: America Press, 1966), 58.

4. Dennis W. Organ, Philip M. Podskakoff, and Scott B. MacKenzie, *Organizational Citizenship Behavior: Its Nature, Antecedents, and Consequences* (Thousand Oaks, CA: Sage, 2006).

5. James M. Kouzes and Barry Z. Posner, *The Leadership Challenge*, 3rd ed. (San Francisco: Jossey-Bass, 2002), 11.

6. Larry C. Spears and Michele Lawrence, eds., *Focus on Leadership: Servant-Leadership for the Twenty-First Century* (New York: Wiley, 2002).

7. Robert K. Greenleaf, *The Servant Leader Within: The Transformative Path*, ed. Hamilton Beazley, Julie Beggs, and Larry C. Spears (Mahwah, NJ: Paulist Press, 2003).

8. Organ et al., *Organizational Citizenship Behavior*.

9. Ibid.

10. Kenneth W. Thomas, "Conflict and Negotiation Processes in Organizations," in *Handbook of Industrial and Organizational Psychology*, 2nd ed., ed. M. D. Dunnette and L. M. Hough, vol. 3 (Palo Alto, CA: Consulting Psychologist Press, 1992), 651–717. This article presents an excellent model of collaboration based on various approaches to conflict negotiations.

11. Greenleaf, *Servant Leader Within*, 27.

12. Ibid., 37.

13. Ken Blanchard and Phil Hodges, *Lead Like Jesus: Lessons from the Greatest Leadership Role Model of All Time* (Nashville: Thomas Nelson, 2005).

14. Organ et al., *Organizational Citizenship Behavior*.

15. Dennis W. Organ, *Organizational Citizenship Behavior: The Good Soldier Syndrome* (Lexington, MA: Lexington Books, 1988).

16. Organ et al., *Organizational Citizenship Behavior*.

17. Ibid.

18. Ibid., 310.

19. Jon R. Katzenbach and Douglas K. Smith, *The Wisdom of Teams: Creating the High-Performing Organization* (New York: HarperCollins, 1999).

20. "Problems of coordination and communication magnify, new functions emerge, levels in the management hierarchy multiply and jobs become more interrelated." Larry E. Greiner, "Evolution and Revolution as Organizations Grow," *Harvard Business Review* (1998): 56.

21. Ibid., 64.

22. Organ et al., *Organizational Citizenship Behavior*.

23. Philip M. Podsakoff, Scott B. MacKenzie, J. B. Paine, and D. G. Bachrach, "Organizational Citizenship Behaviors: A Critical Review of the Theoretical and Empirical Literature and Suggestions for Future Research," *Journal of Management* 26, no. 3 (2000): 513–63. This article summarized OCBs into seven categories, and those same seven categories are used in Organ et al., *Organizational Citizenship Behavior*.

24. Greenleaf, *Servant Leader Within*, 41.

25. While we did not include the causal relationship between OCBs and parish performance as a separate hypothesis, it was inferred from the literature cited here that OCB can increase organizational performance. After our case study, we went back into all of the evidence and inductively put together a set of seven leadership mechanisms that we think explain how servant leadership motivates parishioners to respond with organizational citizenship (as explained in chapter 9). We can infer from the literature that OCB increases the success of the parish.

26. Mark Bolino, William Turnley, and J. M. Bloodgood, "Citizenship Behavior and the Creation of Social Capital in Organizations," *Academy of Management Review* 27, no. 4 (2002): 505–22.

27. Philip M. Podsakoff and Scott B. MacKenzie, "The Impact of Organizational Citizenship Behavior on Organizational Performance: A Review and Suggestions for Future Research," *Human Performance* 10, no. 2 (1997): 133–51.

28. Organ et al., *Organizational Citizenship Behavior*.

29. Bolino et al., "Citizenship Behavior and Social Capital."

30. Organ et al., *Organizational Citizenship Behavior*.

31. The OCB literature suggests many possible reasons linking OCBs to high performance but to my knowledge these ideas have not yet been tested in the context of parish life.

32. Don Cohen and Laurence Prusak, *In Good Company: How Social Capital Makes Organizations Work* (Boston: Harvard Business School Press, 2001).

33. It is important to emphasize that volumes of research show that organizational citizenship does indeed generate high levels of organizational performance. The servant leadership behaviors do not necessarily enhance performance directly. According to the OCB research, supportive leader behaviors enhance the organizational citizenship, and that in turn drives the organization to high performance. Our study found strong evidence that all three leader behaviors and all four member behaviors that we selected and studied were present in our three high-performing parishes.

Chapter 8: Servant Leadership

1. Dennis W. Organ, Philip M. Podsakoff, and Scott B. MacKenzie, *Organizational Citizenship Behavior: Its Nature, Antecedents, and Consequences* (Thousand Oaks, CA: Sage, 2006).

2. Second Vatican Council, *Lumen Gentium, The Documents of Vatican II*, ed. Walter M. Abbot (New York: America Press, 1966), no. 33.

3. Ibid, no. 37.

4. Robert K. Greenleaf, *The Servant Leader Within: The Transformative Path*, ed. Hamilton Beazley, Julie Beggs, and Larry C. Spears (Mahwah, NJ: Paulist Press, 2003).

5. Greenleaf also wrote, "Servants, by definition, are fully human. Servant-leaders are functionally superior because they are closer to the ground——they hear things, see things, know things, and their intuitive insight is exceptional. Because of this they are dependable and trusted." Robert K. Greenleaf, *Servant Leadership*, 25th anniversary ed. (Mahwah, NJ: Paulist Press, 2002), 56.

6. One of the catch phrases of the Vatican II Council is "Mother Church earnestly desires that all the faithful be led to that full, conscious and active participation in liturgical celebrations." See Second Vatican Council, *"Sacrosanctum Concilium*, para. 14 in Abbot, *Documents of Vatican II*. Similar sentiments about the full, conscious, and active participation of the laity in other areas of ministry are expressed in other documents of the Vatican II Council as well,

although not exactly in those same words. See chapter 4 on "The Laity," in *Lumen Gentium*, in paras. 30–38.

7. Jim Collins, *Good to Great: Why Some Companies Make the Leap...and Others Don't* (New York: HarperCollins, 2001), 34.

8. A. Bandura, *Social Foundations of Thought and Action: A Social-Cognitive View* (Englewood Cliffs, NJ: Prentice-Hall, 1986).

9. James M. Kouzes and Barry Z. Posner, *The Leadership Challenge*, 3rd ed. (San Francisco: Jossey-Bass, 2002).

10. Organ et al., *Organizational Citizenship Behavior*.

11. Ibid., 105.

12. Terence E. Deal and Alan A. Kennedy, *Corporate Culture: The Rites and Rituals of Corporate Life* (Reading, MA: Addison-Wesley, 1982).

13. Edgar H. Schein, *Organizational Culture and Leadership*, 3rd ed. (San Francisco: Jossey-Bass, 2002).

14. Karl E. Weick, *Sensemaking in Organizations* (Newbury Park, CA: Sage, 1995).

15. James MacGregor Burns, *Leadership* (New York: Harper & Row, 1978).

16. Organ et al., *Organizational Citizenship Behavior*.

17. See chapter 4, on "The Laity" in paras. 33–37 in *Lumen Gentium*.

18. Organ et al., *Organizational Citizenship Behavior*.

Chapter 9: Servant Parishes

1. Organizational theorists teach us that as organizations get larger, they have to figure out ways to become smaller in order to reach people. People can get lost in large parishes unless they personalize their outreach to their members. See Larry E. Greiner, "Evolution and Revolution as Organizations Grow," *Harvard Business Review* (May–June 1998).

2. One might expect that the OCBs measured in this study—initiative, helping, participation, and self-development—would be less evident as organizations grow larger, especially if the growth in size is accompanied by decreasing commitment and increasing reliance on structured routines.

3. After we named our three parish size categories, we discovered that several other studies have produced similar names to ours. For example, the Center for Applied Research in the Apostolate (CARA) at Georgetown groups parishes into the four following categories: 31 percent of parishes are "mega" parishes with more than 3,000 members; 28 percent are "corporate" parishes with 550–1,200 registered parishioners; 25 percent are "community" parishes with 450–1,199 members; and 16 percent are "family" parishes with fewer than 450 parishioners. See Katarina Schuth, "Structuring a Viable Future for Parishes," *Church* (Spring 2009), 29–33.

4. Dan R. Ebener, "The Servant Parish: A Case Study of Servant Leadership and Organizational Citizenship Behaviors in High-Performing Catholic Parishes." Doctoral dissertation, College of Business, St. Ambrose University, 2007.

5. Jon R. Katzenbach and Douglas K. Smith, "The Discipline of Teams," chap. 1 in *Harvard Business Review on Teams That Succeed* (Boston: Harvard Business School Publishing, 1993).

6. Crow's study of Nazarene congregations distinguished between the "family type" and the "enterprise type." See Kenneth Crow, "A Network of Congregations: Congregation Size in the Church of the Nazarene." A research paper from the Church of the Nazarene Research Center, October 5, 2004.

7. Stonebraker says the "family church" has fewer than fifty active members and the pastor is like a parent or family chaplain. The clergy is expected to provide pastoral care and befriend the powerful lay members of the parish. The pastor delegates some authority and is expected to be available at times of crisis. In a small church, the interpersonal skills of the clergy make a big difference. The "program church" is from 150 to 350 active members, with lay leaders heading up a number of committees. The pastor devotes a lot of time to recruiting people to head up ministries, training, supervising, and evaluating them as they lead the ministries. The "corporate church," with 350 or more active members, can focus a lot of energy on making the Sunday worship "a rich experience." Those who enjoy this type of church are willing to sacrifice a personal connection with the pastor in favor of the variety and quality of program offerings. See Roy M. Oswald, *How to Minister Effectively in Family, Pastoral, Program, and Corporate Sized Churches* (Herndon, VA: Alban Institute, 2007). A key

for this size of church is the ability to manage diverse ministries collegially. Robert J. Stonebraker, "Optimal Church Size: The Bigger the Better?" *Journal for the Scientific Study of Religion* 32, no. 3 (1993): 231.

8. Stonebraker, "Optimal Church Size."

9. P. H. Wilken, "Size of Organizations and Member Participation in Church Congregations," *Administrative Science Quarterly* 16, no. 2 (1971): 173.

10. Ibid.

11. Ibid.

12. Wilken noted that some larger congregations have found ways to compensate for their handicaps connected with large size, and some smaller congregations are not taking advantage of the opportunities of small size. See Wilken, "Size of Organizations and Member Participation," 173.

13. Pinto and Crow found that size was negatively related to activating the membership and the enforcement of high membership standards. Hougland and Wood studied fifty-eight churches in Indianapolis and found that large church size had a negative effect on organizational involvement and identification. See L. J. Pinto and Kenneth E. Crow, "The Effects of Size and Other Structural Attributes of Congregations within the Same Denomination," *Journal for the Scientific Study of Religion* 21 (1982): 304–16; and J. G. Hougland and J. R. Wood, "Participation in Local Churches, An Exploration of its Impact on Satisfaction, Growth, and Social Action," *Journal for the Scientific Study of Religion* 21, no. 4 (1982): 338–52.

14. Roger Finke, "The Quiet Transformation: Changes in Size and Leadership of Southern Baptist Churches," *Review of Religious Research* 36, no.1 (1994): 3.

15. Ibid.

16. Ibid.

17. Stonebraker, "Optimal Church Size."

18. Finke, "Quiet Transformation."

19. Ibid.

20. Ibid.

21. Ibid.

22. M. V. Tidwell, "A Social Identity Model of Prosocial Behaviors within Nonprofit Organizations," *Nonprofit Management & Leadership* 15, no. 4 (2005): 449–67.

238 ~ SERVANT LEADERSHIP MODELS FOR YOUR PARISH

23. Ibid., 451.

24. Don Cohen and Laurence Prusak, *In Good Company: How Social Capital Makes Organizations Work* (Boston: Harvard Business School Press, 2001).

25. Wilken, "Size of Organizations and Member Participation," 176. Wilken speculates that "larger congregations are apparently able to overcome some of the negative effects related to their size, possibly through effective leadership."

Chapter 10: Six Other Characteristics of Servant Parishes

1. These distinctions between management and leadership fit the definitions by John Kotter. Management behaviors identified by Kotter include financial accounting, budgeting, organizing, hiring, and implementing strategic plans, while leaders are responsible for visioning, inspiring, motivating, aligning, and empowering. The essential difference is that leaders provide a sense of direction to create change and managers promote a sense of order to provide stability. See John P. Kotter, "What Leaders Really Do," in *Business Leadership: A Jossey-Bass Reader* (San Francisco: Jossey-Bass, 2003), 29–43.

2. Ibid.

3. Ibid.

4. Peter F. Drucker, "Sticking to Your Mission: The Importance of Saying No," *Leadership Journal*, Christianity Today International (2000).

5. John P. Kotter, *Leading Change* (Boston: Harvard Business School Press, 1996), 26.

6. F. W. Gluck, "Can the Church Learn from Wal-Mart?" *America* 190, no. 17 (2004): 14.

7. Ibid., 15.

8. James M. Kouzes and Barry Z. Posner, *The Leadership Challenge*, 3rd ed. (San Francisco: Jossey-Bass, 2002), 288.

9. Daniel Katz and Robert Kahn, *The Social Psychology of Organizations*, 2nd ed. (New York: Wiley, 1978).

10. W. Richard Scott, *Organizations: Rational, Natural, and Open Systems*, 5th ed. (Upper Saddle River, NJ: Prentice-Hall, 2003).

11. Catholic social teaching is a rich source of wisdom about the social responsibilities of Christians. In the 1960s, Fr. Marv Mottet of Davenport created a social action model of "two feet"—charity and justice—that is used by many churches. Specific statements of the U.S. bishops and the Vatican can easily be accessed via the Internet, such as the Web site of the U.S. Conference of Catholic Bishops at www.usccb.org. See also Joe Holland, *Modern Catholic Social Teaching: The Popes Confront the Industrial Age, 1740-1958* (Mahwah, NJ: Paulist Press, 2003).

12. One of the best kept secrets in the Catholic church is the exemplary service provided around the world by Catholic Relief Services (CRS). With offices in more than ninety countries around the world, CRS is addressing the causes and symptoms of global poverty and injustice. One way that Catholics can support CRS is through Operation Rice Bowl, through which CRS develops sustainable projects that feed people around the world. See www.crs.org.

13. James A. Autry, *The Servant Leader: How to Build a Creative Team, Develop Great Morale, and Improve Bottom-Line Performance* (Roseville, CA: Prima, 2001), 42.

14. James M. Kouzes and Barry Z. Posner, *The Encouraging the Heart Workbook* (San Francisco: Jossey-Bass, 2006), 32.

15. Robert K. Greenleaf, *The Servant Leader Within: The Transformative Path*, ed. Hamilton Beazley, Julie Beggs, and Larry C. Spears (Mahwah, NJ: Paulist Press, 2003).

16. Charles Manz, *The Leadership Wisdom of Jesus: Practical Lessons for Today* (San Francisco: Berrett-Koehler, 1999), 24.

17. Jim Collins, *Good to Great: Why Some Companies Make the Leap...and Others Don't* (New York: HarperCollins, 2001), 34.

18. Ibid.

19. Ibid.

20. Many of the studies on parish excellence gravitate toward certain areas of ministry and suggest that the presence of certain ministries is an indication of success. For example, a survey conducted by the Emerging Models of Pastoral Leadership project found that parish leaders identified the following five marks of parish excellence: (1) Preaching that applies the gospel to daily life, (2) pastoral ministry to the sick and bereaved, (3) having an enthusiastic pastor, (4) liturgies that are prayerful and spirit moving, (5) outreach to the poor. Four of

these five marks are indicative of certain areas of ministry. See David DeLambo, "In Search of Pastoral Excellence," *Church* (Summer 2007), 5–9. We suggest that high-performing parishes perform well in nine areas of ministry because of the presence of servant leadership and organizational citizenship.

Chapter 11:
Four Models from Our Study

1. Thomas Merton's letter of February 21, 1966, now entitled "A Letter to a Young Activist," was sent to Jim Forest, who was a member of the New York Catholic Worker community and later editor of *Fellowship* magazine. Excerpts of this letter from Merton to Forest were published in the September/October 1997 issue of *Fellowship*.

2. John M. Bryson, *Strategic Planning for Public and Nonprofit Organizations: A Guide to Strengthening and Sustaining Organizational Achievement*, 3rd ed. (San Francisco: Jossey-Bass, 2004).

3. Ibid.

4. Jon R. Katzenbach and Douglas K. Smith, *The Wisdom of Teams: Creating the High-Performing Organization* (New York: HarperCollins, 1999).

5. Bryson, *Strategic Planning for Public and Nonprofit Organizations*.

6. Ibid.

7. Ibid.

8. Bob Briner and Ray Pritchard, *Leadership Lessons of Jesus: Timeless Wisdom for Leaders in Today's World* (New York: Random House Value Publishing, 1998).

9. Ibid.

10. Robert Short, "The Pope's Divisions," *Times Literary Supplement*, April 10, 2009, pp. 23–24.

11. Ibid.

12. Robert K. Greenleaf, *The Servant Leader Within: The Transformative Path*, ed. Hamilton Beazley, Julie Beggs, and Larry C. Spears (Mahwah, NJ: Paulist Press, 2003). The term *servant leadership* was coined by Robert K. Greenleaf in his essay in 1970, and while he refers to Jesus in the essay, he does not present servant leadership as

the leadership style of Jesus. That distinction has emerged since Greenleaf's essays.

13. Briner and Pritchard, *Leadership Lessons of Jesus*, 205.

14. Ibid., 294.

15. Ibid., 295.

16. USCCB, *Stewardship: A Disciple's Response* (Washington, DC: United States Catholic Conference of Bishops, 1992).

17. Mark G. Ehrhart, "Leadership and Procedural Justice Climate as Antecedents of Unit-Level Organizational Citizenship Behavior," *Personnel Psychology* 57 (2004).

18. In *Good to Great*, Jim Collins reports that his research team considered using the title "servant leadership" to describe the leadership they discovered in the "good to great" companies, but he thought it sounded too soft and too religious. He decided to create his own term of "Level Five Leadership" to describe it instead.

19. Dennis W. Organ, Philip M. Podskakoff, and Scott B. MacKenzie, *Organizational Citizenship Behavior: Its Nature, Antecedents, and Consequences* (Thousand Oaks, CA: Sage, 2006). These authors summarize the empirical findings that supportive leader behaviors enhance OCBs.

20. Ibid.

21. Ehrhart, "Leadership and Procedural Justice Climate."

22. Greenleaf, *Servant Leader Within*, 41.

23. Larry E. Greiner, "Evolution and Revolution as Organizations Grow," *Harvard Business Review* 50, no. 4 (July–August 1972): 37–46.

24. John Maxwell, a former minister and author of many leadership books, suggests that the five most important traits for leaders are competence, courage, passion, character, and charisma. See John C. Maxwell, *The 21 Indispensable Qualities of a Leader* (Nashville: Thomas Nelson, 1999).

25. Afsenah Nahavandi, *The Art and Science of Leadership*, 4th ed. (Upper Saddle River, NJ: Pearson, 2006).

26. Peter G. Northouse, *Leadership: Theory and Practice* (Thousand Oaks, CA: Sage, 2007).

27. Frances Hesselbein, *Hesselbein on Leadership* (San Francisco: Jossey-Bass, 2002), 3.

28. Ibid.

29. Ibid., 343.

30. James M. Kouzes and Barry Z. Posner, *Credibility: How Leaders Gain and Lose It, Why People Demand It* (San Francisco: Jossey-Bass, 2003).

31. Marshall Sashkin and Molly G. Sashkin, *Leadership That Matters: The Critical Factors for Making a Difference in People's Lives and Organizations' Success* (San Francisco: Berrett-Koehler, 2003).

32. Northouse, *Leadership*.

33. James M. Kouzes and Barry Z. Posner, *The Leadership Challenge*, 3rd ed. (San Francisco: Jossey-Bass, 2002). The research of Kouzes and Posner lists forward-looking as the second most important trait of leadership, with honesty or integrity being the first.

34. Greenleaf, *Servant Leader Within*.

35. Ibid., 93.

36. Mission and vision statements should be written to promote something in the interests of society, not just the organization. For example, when a vision statement suggests that an organization will be recognized as a "premier," "first rate," "best," or "top quality" organization, it is not answering the question of *how* the organization will contribute to society.

37. Michael Allison and Jude Kaye, *Strategic Planning for Nonprofit Organizations: A Practical Guide and Workbook* (New York: Support Center for Non-Profit Management, Wiley, 2005).

38. Bryson, *Strategic Planning for Public and Nonprofit Organizations*.

39. Ibid.

40. Sashkin and Sashkin, *Leadership That Matters*.

41. Ibid.

42. "Inspiring a shared vision" is one of five practices of the leader as described by Kouzes and Posner in *Leadership Challenge*.

43. Sashkin and Sashkin, *Leadership That Matters*.

44. Bryson, *Strategic Planning for Public and Nonprofit Organizations*.

45. Ibid.

46. Sashkin and Sashkin, *Leadership That Matters*.

47. Ibid.

Chapter 12:
Developing Servant Leaders

1. A number of leadership programs have used a time management model that suggests that the ineffective leader focuses on activities that are urgent but not important while the effective leader focuses on issues that are not urgent but important. The question is how the leader makes the distinction between urgency and importance, and once that is determined, how the leader directs attention away from the urgent but not important activities in order to spend more time on matters that are important but not urgent. The need to focus on importance rather than urgency gets at the essence of the third habit in Stephen Covey's *Seven Habits of Highly Effective People,* where he insists that effective leaders "put first things first."

2. John P. Kotter, *A Sense of Urgency* (Boston: Harvard Business School Press, 2008).

3. Robert K. Greenleaf, *The Servant Leader Within: The Transformative Path,* ed. Hamilton Beazley, Julie Beggs, and Larry C. Spears (Mahwah, NJ: Paulist Press, 2003).

4. For a full discussion of these issues, see Charles E. Zech and Robert J. Miller, *Listening to the People of God: Closing, Rebuilding and Revitalizing Parishes* (Mahwah, NJ: Paulist Press, 2008).

5. As the priest shortage increases, priests are traveling from town to town and parish to parish as parishes are clustered or consolidated together. At some point, difficult decisions are made about how far a priest can travel and how many Masses a priest can say on a weekend. Eventually, one ramification of this cycle is fewer Masses. As the number of Masses is decreased within a geographic area, the churches that have the greatest capacity and the easiest access for people to attend Mass will most likely be selected as the location for those Masses. Enhancing the size, modernizing the buildings, updating the technology, and improving the access to a church building can increase the odds that it will become the site for Masses in a future church that will see fewer Masses with larger crowds for weekend liturgies.

6. G. D. Sands, "A Study of the Difference between the Effectiveness of the Church of God Pastoral Leaders in Texas According to Their Situational Leadership Score." Unpublished doc-

toral dissertation, Southwest Baptist Theological Seminary, 2004. (Dissertation No. 01020308253349)

7. Henri Nouwen, "Moving from Solitude to Community to Ministry," *Leadership* 16, no. 2 (1995): 62–80. Nouwen recommends that the church of the future focus more clearly on leadership development. If pastors are not willing to delegate responsibility to the laypeople, it creates a void in that parish for lay involvement.

8. G. Barna, *Today's Pastors: A Revealing Look at What Pastors are Saying about Themselves, Their Peers and the Pressures They Face* (Ventura, CA: Regal Books, 1993). Barna states that "many pastors, by their own admission, are neither gifted nor trained to be leaders," 14.

9. M. Woodley, "Good Pastor, Lousy Leader," *Leadership* 20, no. 3 (1999): 35–39.

10. Ibid.

11. S-E Kim, "Balancing Competing Accountability Requirements: Challenges in Performance Improvement of the Nonprofit Human Services Agency," *Public Performance & Management Review* 29, no. 2 (2005): 145–63.

12. Peter C. Brinckerhoff, *Mission-Based Management* (Dillon, CO: Alpine Guild, 1994); Peter C. Brinckerhoff, *Financial Empowerment: More Money for More Mission* (New York: Wiley, 1996); Peter C. Brinckerhoff, *Faith-Based Management: Leading Organizations That Are Based on More Than Just Mission* (San Francisco: Jossey-Bass, 1999).

13. Richard P. McBrien, *Catholicism* (New York: HarperCollins, 1994).

14. Peter F. Drucker, "Sticking to Your Mission: The Importance of Saying No," *Leadership Journal*, Christianity Today International (2000).

15. William T. Ditewig, *The Emerging Diaconate: Servant Leaders in a Servant Church* (Mahwah, NJ: Paulist Press, 2007). In addition, William Ditewig retells the following story of St. Lawrence, a deacon of Rome who was responsible for financial management of the church. As a result of these actions, Lawrence was martyred in AD 258. "Lawrence was ordered by the Roman authorities to surrender the wealth of the Church. He returned a few days later with the poor of Rome, telling the Roman officials that the poor were the true treasure of the Church." See William T. Ditewig, *101 Questions and Answers on Deacons* (Mahwah, NJ: Paulist Press, 2004), 16. See also Owen F. Cummings, *Saintly Deacons* (New York and Mahwah, NJ: Paulist Press, 2005).

16. This is one of the five practices of Kouzes and Posner. James M. Kouzes and Barry Z. Posner, *The Leadership Challenge: How to Keep Getting Extraordinary Things Done in Organizations*, 3rd ed. (San Francisco: Jossey-Bass, 2002).

17. John P. Kotter, *Leading Change* (Boston: Harvard Business School Press, 1996).

18. John M. Bryson, *Strategic Planning for Public and Nonprofit Organizations: A Guide to Strengthening and Sustaining Organizational Achievement*, 3rd ed. (San Francisco: Jossey-Bass, 2004).

19. James Sipes and Don Frick provide an excellent guideline for providing feedback, suggesting that feedback should be "timely, supportive, nonjudgmental, specific, well-paced, directive, presented with a request for clarification and offered by permission." See James W. Sipes and Don M. Frick, *Seven Pillars of Servant Leadership: Practicing the Wisdom of Leading by Serving* (Mahwah, NJ: Paulist Press, 2009), 70.

20. Lao Tsu, "The Tao," in *Leaders and the Leadership Process: Readings, Self-Assessments and Applications*, 4th ed., by Jon L. Pierce and John W. Newstrom (Boston: McGraw-Hill, 2006).

21. "Emerging Models of Pastoral Leadership" is the joint project of six national Catholic ministerial organizations examining areas of pastoral excellence and identifying successful models of pastoral leadership in the Catholic church.

22. In 2008, the Emerging Models of Pastoral Leadership released a report that included the results of their research into "a variety of structural models that are being created to provide for parish life in the United States," Carole Ganin, ed., *Shaping Catholic Parishes: Pastoral Leaders in the Twenty-First Century* (Chicago: Loyola Press, 2008), xiv. The marks of excellence in a parish are summarized by Ganin into these five categories: welcoming, collaboration, ethical, pastoral, and prophetic.

23. As this book is being written, Emerging Models of Pastoral Leadership is releasing a request for proposals to do further research into parish leadership models, especially for those involving multicultural parishes and multiparish structures. This research is being made possible by a grant from the Lily Foundation. See Mark Mogilka and Kate Wiskus, *Pastoring Multiple Parishes: Emerging Models of Parish Leadership* (Chicago: Loyola Press, 2009) for insight into leading in the context of multiparish structures.

24. Ganin, *Shaping Catholic Parishes*.

25. Roger Fisher and William Ury, *Getting to Yes: Negotiating Agreement without Giving In* (New York: Penguin, 1981).

26. Ibid.

27. Ibid.

28. Kenneth W. Thomas, "Conflict and Negotiation Processes in Organizations," in *Handbook of Industrial and Organizational Psychology*, 2nd ed., ed. M. D. Dunnette and L. M. Hough (Palo Alto, CA: Consulting Psychologist Press, 1992), vol. 3, 651–717.

29. Ibid.

30. Ibid.

31. These principles were gleaned from the work of Mark Gerzon, *Leading through Conflict: How Successful Leaders Transform Differences into Opportunities* (Boston: Harvard Business School Press, 2006).

32. Separating the person from the problem, according to Fisher and Ury in *Getting to Yes*, means detaching from any personal animosity we might feel toward others and looking at the merits of the problem itself.

33. Focusing on the interests of all parties, instead of being wedded to our own positions, is another major principle of Fisher and Ury in *Getting to Yes*.

34. *Interests*, according to Fisher and Ury in *Getting to Yes*, are the reasons behind the positions we take.

35. Seeking options for mutual gain is the essence of collaboration, as suggested by Fisher and Ury in *Getting to Yes*.

36. See Michael Weldon, *A Struggle for Holy Ground: Reconciliation and the Rise of Parish Closure* (Collegeville, MN: Liturgical Press, 2004).

37. Greenleaf, *Servant Leader Within*, 41.

38. Ibid.

39. James A. Autry, *The Servant Leader: How to Build a Creative Team, Develop Great Morale, and Improve Bottom-Line Performance* (Roseville, CA: Prima, 2001); Bob Briner and Ray Pritchard, *Leadership Lessons of Jesus: Timeless Wisdom for Leaders in Today's World* (New York: Random House Value Publishing, 1998); Charles C. Manz, *The Leadership Wisdom of Jesus: Practical Lessons for Today* (San Francisco: Berrett-Koehler, 1999).

40. Bill George, *Authentic Leadership: Rediscovering the Secrets to Creating Lasting Value* (San Francisco: Jossey-Bass, 2003).

41. Empirical studies that explore the effectiveness of servant leadership include Mark Ehrhart, "Leadership and Procedural Justice Climate as Antecedents of Unit-Level Organizational Citizenship Behavior," *Personnel Psychology* 57 (2004): 61–94; and Robert C. Liden, Sandy J. Wayne, Hao Zhao, and David Henderson, "Servant Leadership: Development of a Multidimensional Measure and Multi-Level Assessment," *Leadership Quarterly* 19 (2008): 161–77.

42. Jim Collins, *Good to Great: Why Some Companies Make the Leap...and Others Don't* (New York: HarperCollins, 2001). Jim Collins looked at possibly naming the leadership style of the "good to great companies" as servant leadership, but instead decided to come up with his own unique title of "Level Five Leadership."

43. Autry, *The Servant Leader*, xv.

44. Briner and Pritchard, *Leadership Lessons of Jesus*, 241.

45. Manz, *Leadership Wisdom of Jesus*, 37.

46. Ibid., 93.

47. Ibid.

48. As reported by McCallum and O'Connell, businesses in the United States were spending $50 billion annually on leadership training in 2000, and an increasing emphasis is being placed on enhancing relationship skills and building social capital. See Shelly McCallum and David O'Connell, "Social Capital and Leadership Development: Building Stronger Leadership through Enhanced Relational Skills," *Leadership & Organizational Development Journal* 30, no. 2, (2009):152–66.

49. Joseph Holland and Peter Henriot, *Social Analysis: Linking Faith and Justice* (Maryknoll, NY: Orbis, 1983).

50. The pastoral planning cycle is based on the works of Paulo Freire, the Brazilian educator who wrote *Pedagogy of the Oppressed* (New York: Herder & Herder, 1970), and *Education for Critical Consciousness* (New York: Seabury, 1973). Freire spent a week with a group of us through the Catholic Campaign for Human Development in 1988 in Los Angeles, in order to teach his pedagogical methods and discuss how to use them in the United States. One result was an increasing emphasis on the pastoral planning cycle, which takes the learner through the process of experience, social analysis, theological reflection, pastoral planning, and action, which becomes the experience in the next round of the cycle. See Tom Ulrich, *Strategies for Success: Parish Social Ministry* (Notre Dame, IN: Ave Maria Press, 2001). The essence

of Paulo Freire's work involves "praxis," the practice of action and reflection as a cycle for learning. Freire's work has made an international impact as it can be seen in action in the work of Catholic Relief Services (CRS) all over the world. But the power of his pedagogy has not been used as effectively in the United States as it has elsewhere.

51. Greenleaf, *Servant Leader Within*.

52. Ken Blanchard and Phil Hodges, *Lead Like Jesus: Lessons from the Greatest Leadership Role Model of All Time* (Nashville: Thomas Nelson, 2005).

53. Peter Block, *Stewardship: Choosing Service over Self-Interest* (San Francisco: Berrett-Koehler, 1993).

54. Keith, *Case for Servant Leadership*.

55. Robert N. Lussier and Christopher F. Achua, *Leadership: Theory, Application, Skill Development*, 3rd ed. (Mason, OH: Thomson Higher Education, 2007).

56. Greenleaf, *Servant Leader Within*.

57. Collins, *Good to Great*, 34.

58. Attribution theory is explained in Afsenah Nahavandi, *The Art and Science of Leadership*, 4th ed. (Upper Saddle River, NJ: Pearson, 2006).

59. Ibid.

60. Kent M. Keith, *Do it Anyway: The Handbook for Finding Personal Meaning and Deep Happiness in a Crazy World* (Makawao, Maui, HI: Inner Ocean, 2003).

61. These are leadership practices of Kouzes and Posner that do not rely heavily upon positional power.

62. J. R. French and B. Raven, "The Bases of Social Power," in *Studies in Social Power*, ed. D. Cartwright (Ann Arbor, MI: Institute for Social Research, 1959). French and Raven suggest there are five sources of leadership power: expert, referent, reward, coercion, and legitimate authority. The first three of these can be positive sources of influence that do not require positional power.

63. Ibid.

GLOSSARY

"Agape" Unconditional love.

Attribution theory Suggests that people attribute internal factors (such as laziness or incompetence) when someone else makes a mistake, while attributing external factors (such as lack of time or support) for their own mistakes.

Behavioral measures Observable, countable, and changeable indicators of success based upon the actions of the people in an organization.

Charisma The attraction of the follower toward the leader, usually based on unique characteristics and communication skills of the leader.

Charismatic leadership Influence based on high levels of personal charisma within the leader. It sometimes results in unhealthy levels of loyalty and obedience by the followers.

Coding A case study method of translating evidence into categories that can be counted. This method was used in the parish case study.

Coercion Forcing people to follow one's own will. This is not considered a form of leadership.

Collaboration Working together to meet the needs and interests of multiple parties.

Community approach Name given to medium-sized parishes that develop a healthy sense of community.

Competence The human, technical, or cognitive skills needed to do something. It leads to the ability to try.

Confidence The belief in one's ability to do something. It leads to a willingness to try.

Core values The philosophical beliefs that define the culture and affect the behaviors of an organization.

Credibility The believability of a leader based on extent that he or she is trustworthy.

Delegation Designating an assignment to another person. This includes support and feedback from the leader to the designee.

Effectiveness Successful completion of critical results, sometimes described as "doing the right thing."

Efficiency The productive use of resources such as time, energy, and technology, sometimes described as "doing things right."

Emerging Models of Pastoral Leadership A national Catholic partnership to create new models of leadership for parishes.

Empirical findings Research based on scientific evidence and measurable data.

Empowering A servant leader behavior that builds the capacity of others to act, often involving a change in structures and systems.

Empowerment The sharing of power and development in others of the skills, abilities, or capacities for them to act on their own behalf.

External focus of the parish Attention given to areas of concern outside the parish, such as social justice issues in the community or in the world.

Family approach Name given to smaller-sized parishes that feel like a family.

Follower-centric leader behavior Actions of the leader based upon the needs and interests of the followers. This takes the focus away from the leader.

Followership The process of being influenced by a leader. This concept emphasizes the interaction between leader and follower.

Helping A voluntary, prosocial member behavior that assists another member of the organization. This was one of four organizational citizenship behaviors used in the case study.

High-performing parish A vibrant faith community in which people are growing in their faith and actively involved in all areas of ministry.

Initiating A voluntary, prosocial member behavior whereby the member acts without being asked or told to do so. This is an organizational citizenship behavior.

Inspiration Intrinsic motivation that emerges from within the spirit.

Integrity The integration of one's beliefs and values with one's actions and behaviors.

Keys to servant leadership Four direct and three indirect behavioral mechanisms that explain how the actions of the leader increase the likelihood that the follower will respond with servant-oriented behaviors.

Leadership A process of influencing a group of people to confront reality and move toward a shared vision or common goal.

Leadership behaviors The observable actions taken by a leader, depicting the leader's outward journey.

Leadership development More than simple training, a holistic approach to nurturing, coaching, and preparing potential candidates for leadership.

Leadership traits The personal characteristics that describe a leader, depicting the leader's inward journey.

Lead Like Jesus A church-based movement focused on exploring the leadership style of Jesus.

Management The administration or handling of the technical, financial, and operational matters of an organization. It can be equated with transactional leadership when involving the influence of others.

Managerial proficiency The knowledge, skills, and abilities to succeed in managerial duties such as budgeting, fundraising, operations, and technical matters.

Mission The ultimate purpose of an organization, explaining why the organization exists.

Mission statement A simple statement that reflects the purpose, business, and core values of an organization.

Normative advice Opinion based on one's values, beliefs, or judgments, not necessarily on scientific evidence.

Operational measures Numeric indicators of success associated with financial and demographic data.

Organizational citizenship behaviors (OCBs) Prosocial member behaviors that go above and beyond expectations in service to the organization, such as helping, initiating, participating, and self-developing.

Organizational culture The norms, values, and customs that explain the way decisions are made, people are treated, and things are done in an organization.

Organizational structure The assembly of policies, procedures, and systems that are constructed by the leaders of an organization.

Parish case study Name given to intensive study of leadership and membership behaviors in three high-performing parishes in the Diocese of Davenport.

Parish life evaluation Name given to subjective evaluation of all eighty-four parishes in the Diocese of Davenport conducted by twenty-four evaluators, including the bishop, vicar general, fifteen other diocesan staff, and seven members of the priests' personnel board.

Parish life evaluator survey Name given to the survey instrument used to determine what factors the twenty-four evaluators used in evaluating the eighty-four parishes of the Diocese of Davenport.

Parish life study Name given to two-year study of eighty-four parishes within the Diocese of Davenport, including a self-assessment by all parishes and the gathering of financial and demographic data.

Parish self-assessment Name given to the instrument utilized by all eighty-four parishes in the Diocese of Davenport to assess their activity in nine areas of ministry.

Participating A voluntary, prosocial member behavior whereby the member gets involved in the basic activities of the organization. This is an organizational citizenship behavior.

Pedestal leadership Leadership that looks down on others from a high and mighty position.

Positional power Formal leadership based primarily on one's organizational position.

Power The ability to act.

Prosocial behaviors Actions taken by leaders or members to build social capital and improve relationships within an organization.

Recognizing A servant leader behavior. It includes the process of identifying gifts and talents of followers as well as affirming and appreciating those gifts and talents.

Referent power A source of power based on the personal reputation, wisdom, or experience of the person. It is not based on positional sources of power.

Relationships The people side of leadership, including the development of social capital in an organization.

Self-developing A voluntary, prosocial member behavior whereby members take personal responsibility to improve their knowledge, skills, and abilities. This is an organizational citizenship behavior.

Sense of urgency The attitude created by leaders to focus on the need for change, to shift one's attention from low-priority activities to critical priorities of the organization.

Servant leader behaviors (SLBs) What the leader does to motivate and inspire members to serve the organization, including recognizing, empowering, and serving.

Servant leadership A process of influencing others to confront reality and move toward a shared vision, this approach places the interests of the people and the common good of the organization ahead of the personal interests of the leader.

Serving Actions that meet the needs and interests of others or the organization.

Shared vision A unifying picture of success for the future of the organization, based on common goals held by leaders, followers, and other stakeholders.

Social capital The net assets of the relationships in an organization, often measured by levels of trust, commitment, and cohesion.

Stewardship The care, attention, and gratitude afforded to God's gifts, blessings, and creation.

Strategic measures General indicators of success associated with the mission, vision, and goals of an organization.

Strategic planning The rational, intentional practice of evaluating an organization and its environment, setting goals, and establishing priorities for future action.

Strategic thinking The ongoing process of evaluating an organization and its environment, reflecting on changes, and making adjustments to the strategic plan.

Supportive leadership Leadership that offers support for members of the organization, such as affirmation, training, and resources.

Tasks The plans, projects, or activities to be completed by the leader and followers.

Teams approach Name given to larger-sized parishes that need to get smaller by utilizing teams, work groups, or commissions.

Transactional leadership Influence that motivates individuals to handle relational, operational, financial, and technical matters of an organization.

Transformational leadership Influence that transforms people from followers into leaders and transforms the strategy, structure, and culture of the organization to face external realities and adapt to environmental challenges.

Transformational servant leadership The integration of transformational leadership and servant leadership into a synergistic theory of leadership.

Triangulation The use of multiple methods, investigators, and sources of data. This gives empirical strength to case studies.

Trust The confidence or belief that one has for the leader or others in an organization. This has been described as both the grease and the glue of organizational life.

Vision An image, idea, or mental picture of the future that provides a sense of direction to an organization.

Visioning The process of imagining, planning, and involving others to create a sense of direction.

Vision statement A simple statement that reflects how the world would be different if the organization lived out its core values, met its strategic goals, and accomplished its mission.

BIBLIOGRAPHY

Abbot, Walter M., ed. *The Documents of Vatican II.* New York: America Press, 1966.

Allison, Michael, and Jude Kaye. *Strategic Planning for Nonprofit Organizations: A Practical Guide and Workbook.* New York: Support Center for Non-Profit Management, Wiley, 2005.

Autry, James A. *The Servant Leader: How to Build a Creative Team, Develop Great Morale, and Improve Bottom-Line Performance.* Roseville, CA: Prima, 2001.

Bandura, A. *Social Foundations of Thought and Action: A Social-Cognitive View.* Englewood Cliffs, NJ: Prentice-Hall, 1986.

Barna, G. *Today's Pastors: A Revealing Look at What Pastors Are Saying about Themselves, Their Peers and the Pressures They Face.* Ventura, CA: Regal Books, 1993.

Bass, Bernard M. *Leadership and Performance beyond Expectations.* New York: Free Press, 1985.

Bass, Bernard M., and R. E. Riggio. "The Transformational Model of Leadership." Chap. 1 in *Transformational Leadership,* 2nd ed., edited by B. M. Bass and R. E. Riggio, 3–7. Mahwah, NJ: Erlbaum, 2006.

Bateman, T. S., and Dennis W. Organ. "Job Satisfaction and the Good Soldier: The Relationship Between Affect and Employee 'Citizenship.'" *Academy of Management Journal* 26, no. 4 (1983): 587–95.

Benedict XVI. *God Is Love.* Washington, DC: United States Conference of Catholic Bishops, 2006.

———. "World Day of Peace Message: The Human Family, a Community of Peace." January 1, 2008.

Blake, Robert R., and Jane S. Mouton. *The Managerial Grid.* Houston: Gulf Publishing, 1964.

Blanchard, Ken, and Phil Hodges. *Lead Like Jesus: Lessons from the Greatest Role Model of All Time*. Nashville: Thomas Nelson, 2005.

Block, Peter. *Stewardship: Choosing Service over Self-Interest*. San Francisco: Berrett-Koehler, 1993.

Bolino, Mark C., William H. Turnley, and J. M. Bloodgood. "Citizenship Behavior and the Creation of Social Capital in Organizations." *Academy of Management Review* 27, no. 4 (2002): 505–22.

Bowditch, James L., and Anthony F. Buono. *A Primer on Organizational Behavior*. 6th ed. Hoboken, NJ: Wiley, 2005.

Boyatzis, Richard. E. *Transforming Qualitative Information: Thematic Analysis and Code Development*. Thousand Oaks, CA: Sage, 1998.

Brinckerhoff, Peter C. *Faith-Based Management: Leading Organizations That Are Based on More Than Just Mission*. San Francisco: Jossey-Bass, 1999.

———. *Financial Empowerment: More Money for More Mission*. New York: Wiley, 1996.

———. *Mission-Based Management*. Dillon, CO: Alpine Guild, 1994.

Briner, Bob, and Ray Pritchard. *Leadership Lessons of Jesus: Timeless Wisdom for Leaders in Today's World*. New York: Random House Value Publishing, 1998.

Bryson, John M. *Strategic Planning for Public and Nonprofit Organizations: A Guide to Strengthening and Sustaining Organizational Achievement*. 3rd ed. San Francisco: Jossey-Bass, 2004.

Burns, James MacGregor. *Leadership*. New York: Harper & Row, 1978.

———. *Transforming Leadership*. New York: Grove Press, 2003.

Catechism of the Catholic Church. 2nd ed. Washington, DC: United States Catholic Conference, 1997.

Churches United of the Quad City Area. *Shopper's Guide for Visiting Parishes*. Rock Island, IL: Churches United of the Quad City Area, 2005.

Cohen, Don, and Laurence Prusak. *In Good Company: How Social Capital Makes Organizations Work*. Boston: Harvard Business School Press, 2001.

Collier, Ken, and Matt Williams. *Biblical Leadership: Becoming a Different Kind of Leader*. Greenville, SC: Ambassador Emerald International, 2004.

Collins, Jim. *Good to Great: Why Some Companies Make the Leap…and Others Don't*. New York: HarperCollins, 2001.

Conference for Pastoral Planning and Council Development. *Pathways for the Church of the 21st Century: A National Study of Recent Diocesan Efforts at Parish Reorganization in the United States.* Mt. Laurel, NJ: Conference for Pastoral Planning and Council Development, 2003.

Covey, Stephen R. *Seven Habits of Highly Effective People.* Salt Lake City, UT: FranklinCovey, 1989.

Crow, Kenneth. "A Network of Congregations: Congregation Size in the Church of the Nazarene." Research paper from the Church of the Nazarene Research Center, October 5, 2004.

Cummings, Owen F. *Saintly Deacons.* New York and Mahwah, NJ: Paulist Press, 2005.

Daft, Richard L. *Essentials of Organizational Theory and Design.* Cincinnati, OH: Southwestern Thomson Learning, 2005.

Deal, Terence E., and Alan A. Kennedy. *Corporate Culture: The Rites and Rituals of Corporate Life.* Reading, MA: Addison-Wesley, 1982.

DeLambo, David. "In Search of Pastoral Excellence." *Church,* Summer 2007, 5–9.

Diocese of Davenport. *The Diocesan Church: Six Areas of Ministry.* Davenport, IA: Diocese of Davenport, 2000.

Ditewig, William T. *The Emerging Diaconate.* Mahwah, NJ: Paulist Press, 2007.

———. *101 Questions and Answers on Deacons.* Mahwah, NJ: Paulist Press, 2004.

Drucker, Peter F. "Sticking to Your Mission: The Importance of Saying No." *Leadership Journal.* Christianity Today International, 2000.

Dudley, Carl S. *Effective Small Churches in the Twenty-First Century.* Nashville: Abingdon Press, 2003.

Ebener, Dan R. "The Servant Parish: A Case Study of Servant Leadership and Organizational Citizenship Behaviors in High-Performing Catholic Parishes." Unpublished doctoral dissertation, College of Business, St. Ambrose University, 2007.

Ehrhart, Mark G. "Leadership and Procedural Justice Climate as Antecedents of Unit-Level Organizational Citizenship Behavior." *Personnel Psychology* 57 (2004): 61–94.

Finke, Roger. "The Quiet Transformation: Changes in Size and Leadership of Southern Baptist Churches." *Review of Religious Research* 36, no.1 (1994): 3.

Fisher, Roger, and William Ury of the Harvard Negotiation Project, with Bruce Patton. 2nd ed. *Getting to Yes: Negotiating Agreement without Giving In*. New York: Penguin Books, 1991.

Freire, Paulo. *Education for Critical Consciousness*. New York: Seabury, 1973.

————. *Pedagogy of the Oppressed*. New York: Herder & Herder, 1970.

French, John R. P., and Bertram Raven. "The Bases of Social Power." In *Studies in Social Power*, edited by Dorwin Cartwright. Ann Arbor: University of Michigan, Institute for Social Research, 1959.

Frick, Don M., and Larry C. Spears, eds. *On Becoming a Servant Leader: The Private Writings of Robert K. Greenleaf*. San Francisco: Wiley, 1996.

Ganin, Carole, ed. *Shaping Catholic Parishes: Pastoral Leaders in the Twenty-First Century*. Chicago: Loyola Press, 2008.

George, Bill. *Authentic Leadership: Rediscovering the Secrets to Creating Lasting Value*. San Francisco: Jossey-Bass, 2003.

Gerzon, Mark. *Leading through Conflict: How Successful Leaders Transform Differences into Opportunities*. Boston: Harvard Business School Press, 2006.

Gluck, F. W. "Can the Church Learn from Wal-Mart?" *America* 190, no. 17 (2004): 12–15.

Greenleaf, Robert K. "The Servant as Leader." *Journal of Religion and Applied Behavioral Sciences* 3 (1982): 7–10.

————. *Servant Leadership: A Journey into the Nature of Legitimate Power and Greatness*. New York: Paulist Press, 1977.

————. *Servant Leadership*. 25th anniversary edition. New York: Paulist Press, 2002.

————. *The Servant-Leader Within: A Transformative Path*, edited by Hamilton Beazley, Julie Beggs, and Larry C. Spears. Mahwah, NJ: Paulist Press, 2003.

Greiner, Larry E. "Evolution and Revolution as Organizations Grow." *Harvard Business Review* 50, no. 4 (July–August 1972).

————. "Evolution and Revolution as Organizations Grow." *Harvard Business Review*, (May–June 1998).

Hesse, Hermann. *Journey to the East*. London: P. Owen, 1956.

Hersey, Paul, and Kenneth H. Blanchard. "Situational Leadership." Chap. 8 in *Business Leadership: A Jossey-Bass Reader*. San Francisco: Jossey-Bass, 2003.

Hesselbein, Frances. *Hesselbein on Leadership*. San Francisco: Jossey-Bass, 2002.

Holland, Joe. *Modern Catholic Social Teaching: The Popes Confront the Industrial Age, 1740–1958*. Mahwah, NJ: Paulist Press, 2003.

Holland, Joseph, and Peter Henriot. *Social Analysis: Linking Faith and Justice*. Maryknoll, NY: Orbis, 1983.

Hougland, J. G., and J. R. Wood. "Participation in Local Churches: An Exploration of Its Impact on Satisfaction, Growth, and Social Action." *Journal for the Scientific Study of Religion* 21, no. 4 (1982): 338–52.

House, Robert J., and Terence R. Mitchell. "Path-Goal Theory of Leadership." *Journal of Contemporary Business*, Autumn 1974, 81–97.

Jenning, Ken, and John Stahl-Wert. *The Serving Leader: Five Powerful Actions that will Transform Your Team, Your Business and Your Community*. San Francisco: Berrett-Koehler, 2003.

Katz, Daniel, and Robert L. Kahn. *The Social Psychology of Organizations*. 2nd ed. New York: Wiley, 1978.

Katzenbach, Jon R., and Douglas K. Smith. "The Discipline of Teams." Chap. 1 in *Harvard Business Review on Teams That Succeed*. Boston: Harvard Business School Publishing, 1993.

———. *The Wisdom of Teams: Creating the High-Performing Organization*. New York: HarperCollins, 1999.

Keenan, T. "Church Health: Finding the Focal Point." *Leadership*, Summer 1997.

Keith, Kent M. *The Case for Servant Leadership*. Westfield, IN: Greenleaf Center for Servant Leadership, 2008.

———. *Do It Anyway: The Handbook for Finding Personal Meaning and Deep Happiness in a Crazy World*. Makawao, Maui, HI: Inner Ocean, 2003.

Kim, S-E. "Balancing Competing Accountability Requirements: Challenges in Performance Improvement of the Nonprofit Human Services Agency." *Public Performance & Management Review* 29, no. 2 (2005): 145–63.

King, Martin Luther, Jr. *I Have a Dream: Writings and Speeches that Changed the World*. New York: HarperCollins, 1992.

Kirkpatrick, Shelly A., and Edwin A. Locke. "Leadership: Do Traits Matter?" *Academy of Management Executive* 5, no. 2 (1991): 48–60.

Kotter, John P. *Leading Change.* Boston: Harvard Business School Press, 1996.

———. *A Sense of Urgency.* Boston: Harvard Business School Press, 2008.

———. "What Leaders Really Do." Chap. 2 in *Business Leadership: A Jossey-Bass Reader.* San Francisco: Jossey-Bass, 2003.

Kouzes, James M., and Barry Z. Posner. *Credibility: How Leaders Gain and Lose It, Why People Demand It.* San Francisco: Jossey-Bass, 2003.

———. *Encouraging the Heart: A Leader's Guide to Rewarding and Recognizing Others.* San Francisco: Jossey-Bass, 2003.

———. *The Encouraging the Heart Workbook.* San Francisco: Jossey-Bass, 2003.

———. *The Leadership Challenge: How to Keep Getting Extraordinary Things Done in Organizations.* 3rd ed. San Francisco: Jossey-Bass, 2002.

Lefton, Robert E., and Victor R. Buzzotta. *Leadership through People Skills: Using the Dimensional Model of Behavior to Help Managers.* New York: McGraw-Hill, 2004.

Lencioni, Patrick. *Five Dysfunctions of a Team.* San Francisco: Jossey-Bass, 2002.

Liden, Robert C., Sandy J. Wayne, Hao Zhao, and David Henderson. "Servant Leadership: Development of a Multidimensional Measure and Multi-Level Assessment." *Leadership Quarterly* 19 (2008): 161–77.

Lussier, Robert N., and Christopher F. Achua. *Leadership: Theory, Application, Skill Development.* 3rd ed. Mason, OH: Thomson Higher Education, 2007.

Manz, Charles C. *The Leadership Wisdom of Jesus: Practical Lessons for Today.* San Francisco: Berrett-Koehler, 1999.

Maxwell, John C. *The 21 Indispensable Qualities of a Leader.* Nashville: Thomas Nelson, 1999.

McBrien, Richard P. *Catholicism.* New York: HarperCollins, 1994.

McCallum, Shelly, and David O'Connell. "Social Capital and Leadership Development." *Leadership and Organization Development Journal* 30, no. 2 (2009): 152–66.

Merton, Thomas. "A Letter to a Young Activist," February 21, 1966. *Fellowship*, September/October 1997.

Miles, M. B., and A. M. Huberman. *Qualitative Data Analysis: An Expanded Sourcebook*. 2nd ed. Thousand Oaks, CA: Sage, 1994.

Mogilka, Mark, and Kate Wiskus. *Pastoring Multiple Parishes*. Chicago: Loyola Press, 2009.

Nahavandi, Afsenah. *The Art and Science of Leadership*. 4th ed. Upper Saddle River, NJ: Pearson, 2006.

Northouse, Peter G. *Leadership: Theory and Practice*. Thousand Oaks, CA: Sage, 2007.

Nouwen, Henri. *In the Name of Jesus: Reflections on Christian Leadership*. New York: Crossroad, 1989.

———. "Moving from Solitude to Community to Ministry." *Leadership* 16, no. 2 (1995): 62–80.

Organ, Dennis W. *Organizational Citizenship Behavior: The Good Soldier Syndrome*. Lexington, MA: Lexington Books, 1988.

Organ, Dennis W., Philip M. Podsakoff, and Scott B. MacKenzie. *Organizational Citizenship Behavior: Its Nature, Antecedents, and Consequences*. Thousand Oaks, CA: Sage, 2006.

Oswald, Roy M. *How to Minister Effectively in Family, Pastoral, Program, and Corporate Sized Churches*. Herndon, VA: Alban Institute, 2007.

Pierce, Jon L., and John W. Newstrom. *Leaders and the Leadership Process: Readings, Self-Assessments and Applications*. 4th ed. Boston: McGraw Hill, 2006.

Pinto, L. J., and Kenneth E. Crow. "The Effects of Size and Other Structural Attributes of Congregations within the Same Denomination." *Journal for the Scientific Study of Religion* 21 (1982): 304–16.

Podsakoff, Philip M., and Scott B. MacKenzie. "The Impact of Organizational Citizenship Behavior on Organizational Performance: A Review and Suggestions for Future Research." *Human Performance* 10, no. 2 (1997): 133–51.

Podsakoff, Philip M., Scott B. MacKenzie, J. B. Paine, and D. G. Bachrach. "Organizational Citizenship Behaviors: A Critical Review of the Theoretical and Empirical Literature and Suggestions for Future Research." *Journal of Management* 26, no. 3 (2000): 513–63.

Rost, Joseph. *Leadership for the Twenty-First Century*. New York: Praeger, 1991.

Sands, G. D. "A Study of the Difference between the Effectiveness of the Church of God Pastoral Leaders in Texas According to Their Situational Leadership Score." Unpublished doctoral dissertation, Southwest Baptist Theological Seminary, 2004. (Dissertation No. 01020308253349)

Sashkin, Marshall, and Molly G. Sashkin. *Leadership That Matters: The Critical Factors for Making a Difference in People's Lives and Organizations' Success*. San Francisco: Berrett-Koehler, 2003.

Schaller, Lyle R. *The Middle Size Church: Problems and Perspectives*. Nashville: Abington, 1985.

Schein, Edgar H. *Organizational Culture and Leadership*. 3rd ed. San Francisco: Jossey-Bass, 2002.

Schuth, Katarina. "Structuring a Viable Future for Parishes." *Church*, Spring 2009, 29–33.

Scott, W. Richard. *Organizations: Rational, Natural, and Open Systems*. 5th ed. Upper Saddle River, NJ: Prentice-Hall, 2003.

Short, Robert. "The Pope's Divisions." *Times Literary Supplement*, April 10, 2009, 23–24.

Sipe, James W., and Don M. Frick. *Seven Pillars of Servant Leadership: Practicing the Wisdom of Leading by Serving*. Mahwah, NJ: Paulist Press, 2009.

Spears, Larry C., and Michele Lawrence, eds. *Focus on Leadership: Servant-Leadership for the Twenty-First Century*. New York: Wiley, 2002.

Stewart, David W., and Prem N. Shamdasani. *Focus Groups: Theory and Practice*. Newbury Park, CA: Sage, Inc., 1990.

Stonebraker, Robert J. "Optimal Church Size: The Bigger the Better?" *Journal for the Scientific Study of Religion* 32, no. 3 (1993): 231.

Tertullian. "Apology." Second century. In *The Ante-Nicene Fathers*, edited by Alexander Roberts and James Donaldson. Vol. 3, *Latin Christianity: Its Founder, Tertullian*. Arranged by A. Cleveland Coxe. Grand Rapids: Eerdmans, 1976.

Thomas, Kenneth W. "Conflict and Negotiation Processes in Organizations." In *Handbook of Industrial and Organizational Psychology*. Vol. 3, edited by M. D. Dunnette and L. M. Hough, 651–717. Palo Alto, CA: Consulting Psychologist Press, 1992.

Tidwell, M. V. "A Social Identity Model of Prosocial Behaviors within Nonprofit Organizations." *Nonprofit Management & Leadership* 15, no. 4 (2005): 449–67.

Ulrich, Tom. *Strategies for Success: Parish Social Ministry*. Notre Dame, IN: Ave Maria Press, 2001.

United States Conference of Catholic Bishops. *Stewardship: A Disciple's Response*. Washington, DC: Catholic Conference of Bishops, 1992.

Weber, Max. *The Theory of Social and Economic Organizations*. New York: Free Press, 1947.

Weick, Karl E. *Sensemaking in Organizations*. Newbury Park, CA: Sage, 1995.

Weldon, Michael. *A Struggle for Holy Ground: Reconciliation and the Rite of Parish Closure*. Collegeville, MN: Liturgical Press, 2004.

Wilken, P. H. "Size of Organizations and Member Participation in Church Congregations." *Administrative Science Quarterly* 16, no. 2 (1971).

Wilkes, Paul. *Excellent Catholic Parishes: The Guide to Best Places and Practices*. Mahwah, NJ: Paulist Press, 2001.

Wilkes, C. Gene. *Jesus on Leadership: Discovering the Secrets of Servant Leadership from the Life of Christ*. Wheaton, IL: Tyndale, 1998.

Wooden, John R., and Steve J. Jamison. *Wooden on Leadership*. New York: McGraw-Hill, 2005.

Woodley, M. "Good Pastor, Lousy Leader." *Leadership* 20, no. 3 (1999): 35–39.

Yin, Robert K. *Case Study Research*. 3rd ed. Thousand Oaks, CA: Sage, 2003.

Yukl, Gary A., and W. S. Becker. "Effective Empowerment in Organizations." *Organizational Management Journal* 3, no. 3 (2006): 210–31.

Zaleznik, Abraham. "Managers and Leaders: Are They Different?" *Harvard Business Review*, January 2004.

Zech, Charles E., and Robert J. Miller. *Listening to the People of God: Closing, Rebuilding and Revitalizing Parishes*. Mahwah, NJ: Paulist Press, 2008.

INDEX

green
press
I N I T I A T I V E

Paulist Press is committed to preserving ancient forests and natural resources. We elected to print this title on 30% post consumer recycled paper, processed chlorine free. As a result, for this printing, we have saved:

8 Trees (40' tall and 6-8" diameter)
3 Million BTUs of Total Energy
778 Pounds of Greenhouse Gases
3,748 Gallons of Wastewater
228 Pounds of Solid Waste

Paulist Press made this paper choice because our printer, Thomson-Shore, Inc., is a member of Green Press Initiative, a nonprofit program dedicated to supporting authors, publishers, and suppliers in their efforts to reduce their use of fiber obtained from endangered forests.

For more information, visit www.greenpressinitiative.org

Environmental impact estimates were made using the Environmental Defense Paper Calculator. For more information visit: www.papercalculator.org.